AF505461

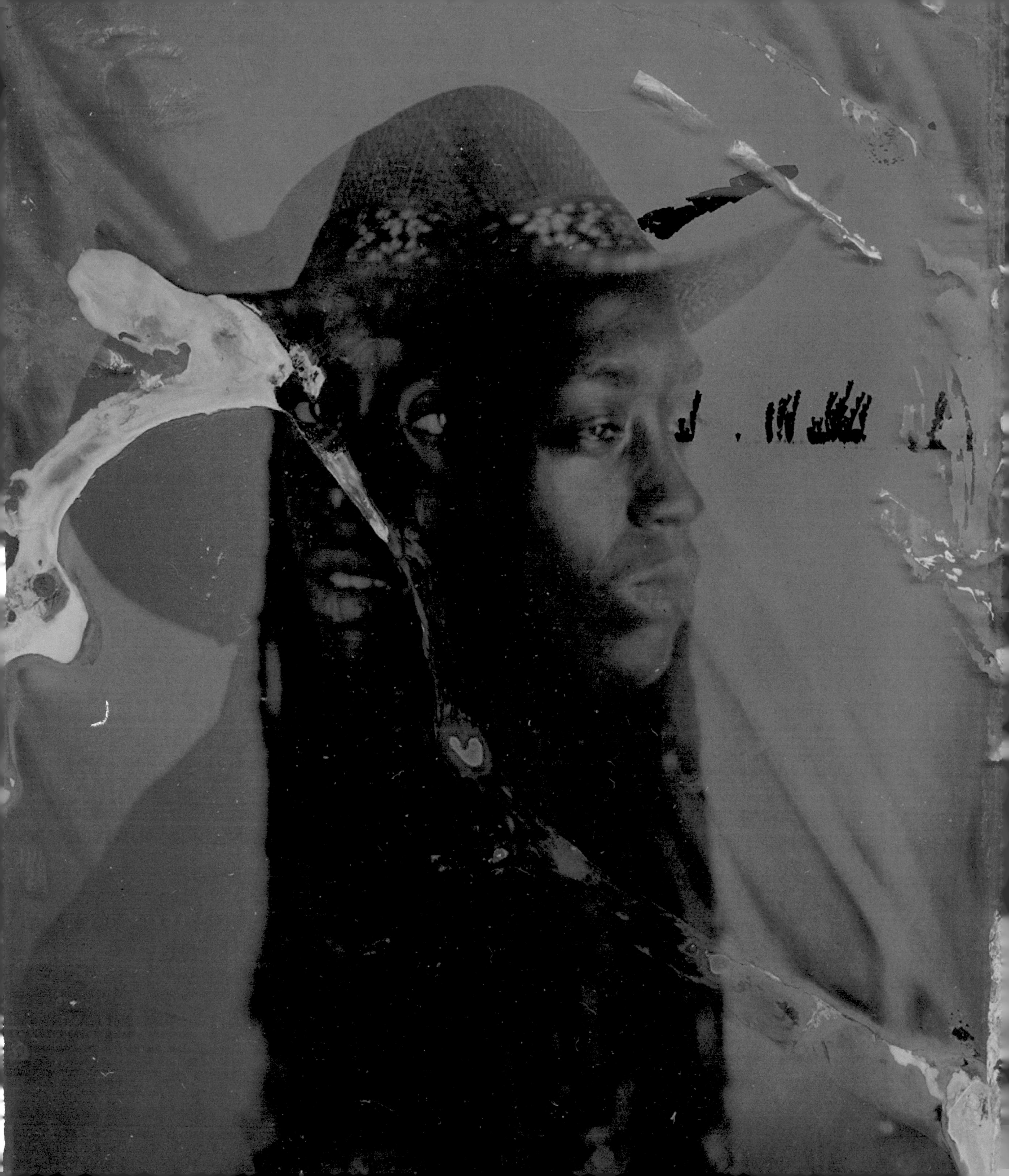

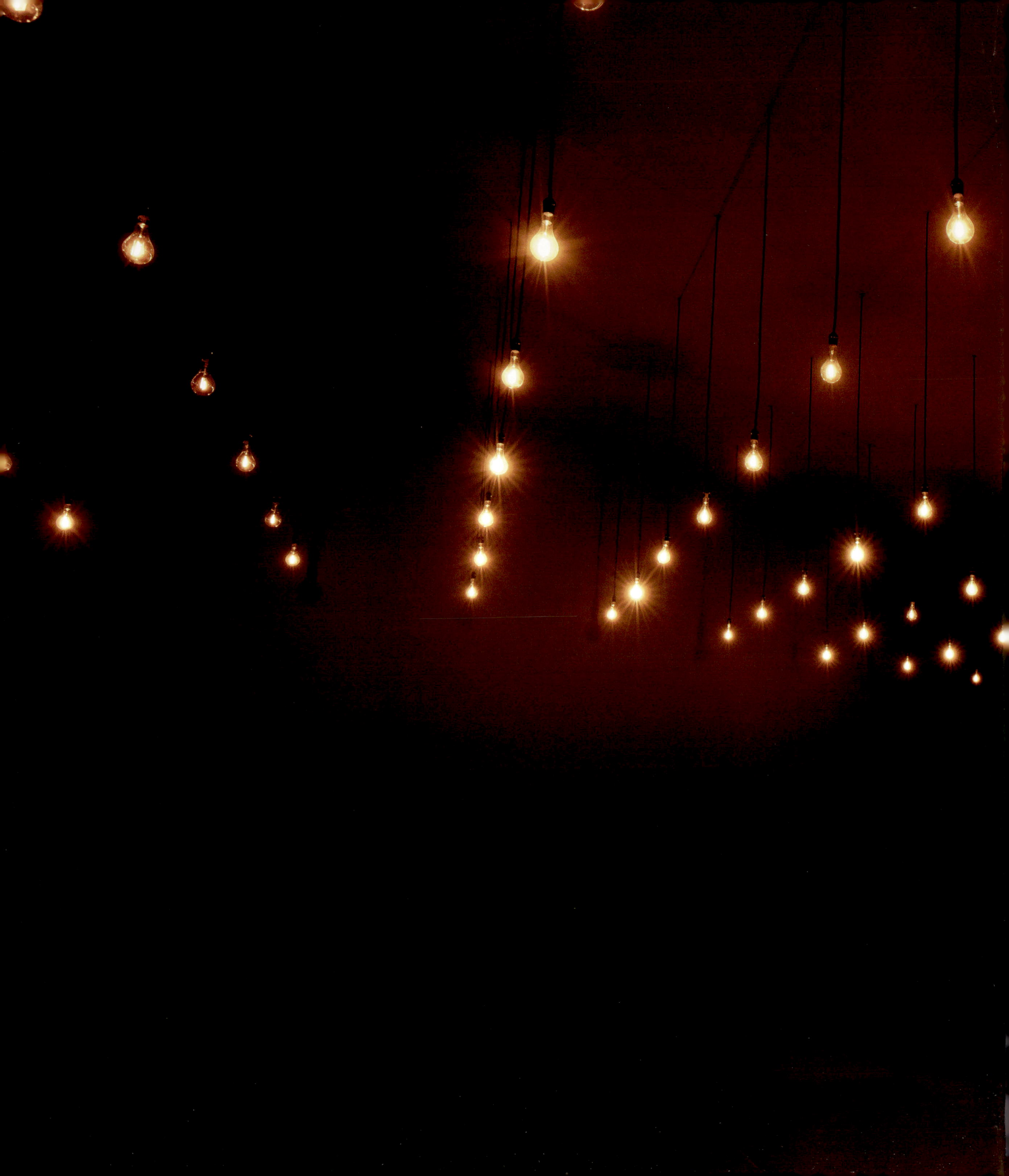

WHAT IS LEFT UNSPOKEN,
LOVE

Essays by
Michael Rooks
Sonia David
Noel Quiñones

Poem by
Pearl Cleage

High Museum of Art, Atlanta
DelMonico Books • D.A.P. New York

Contents

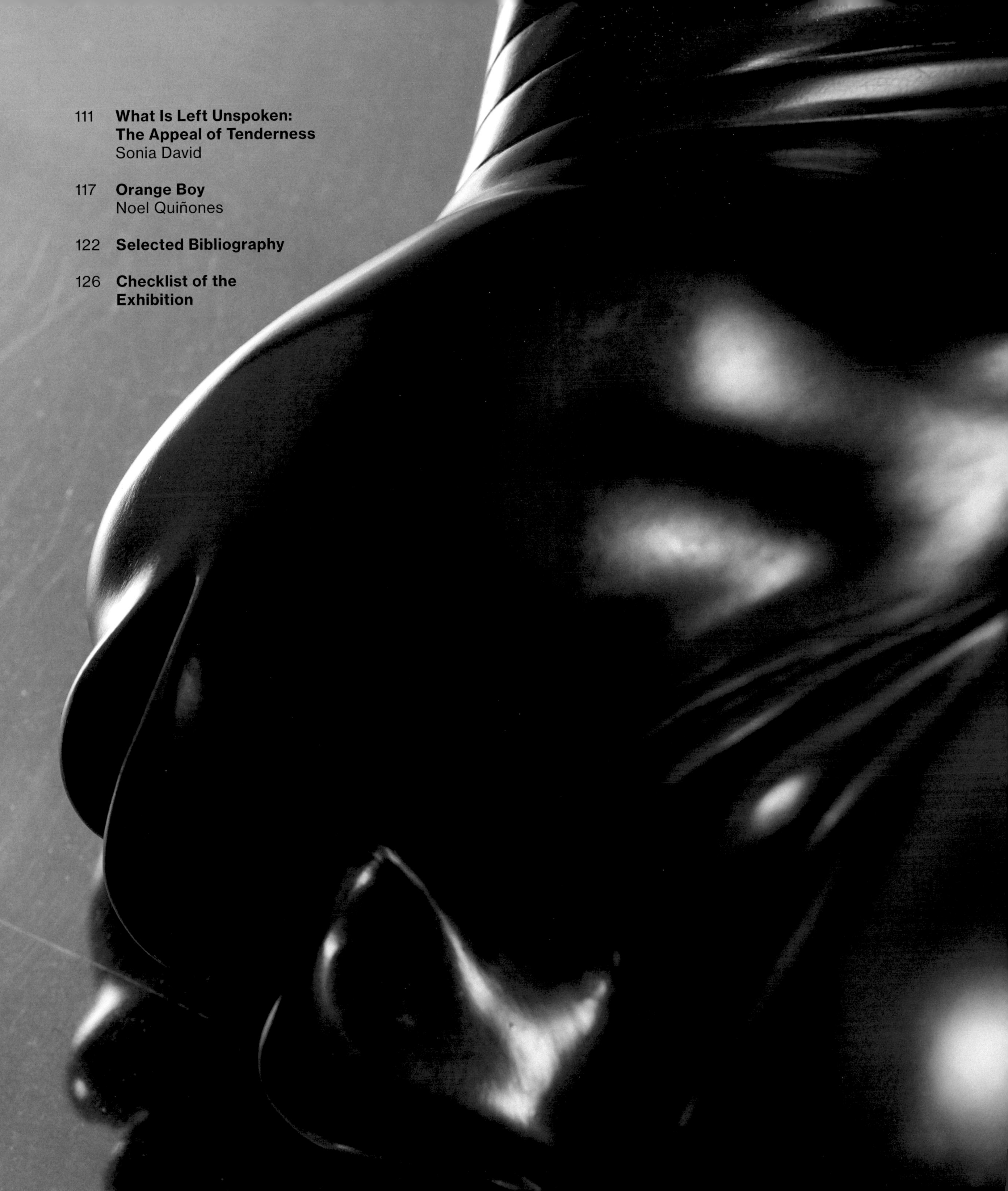

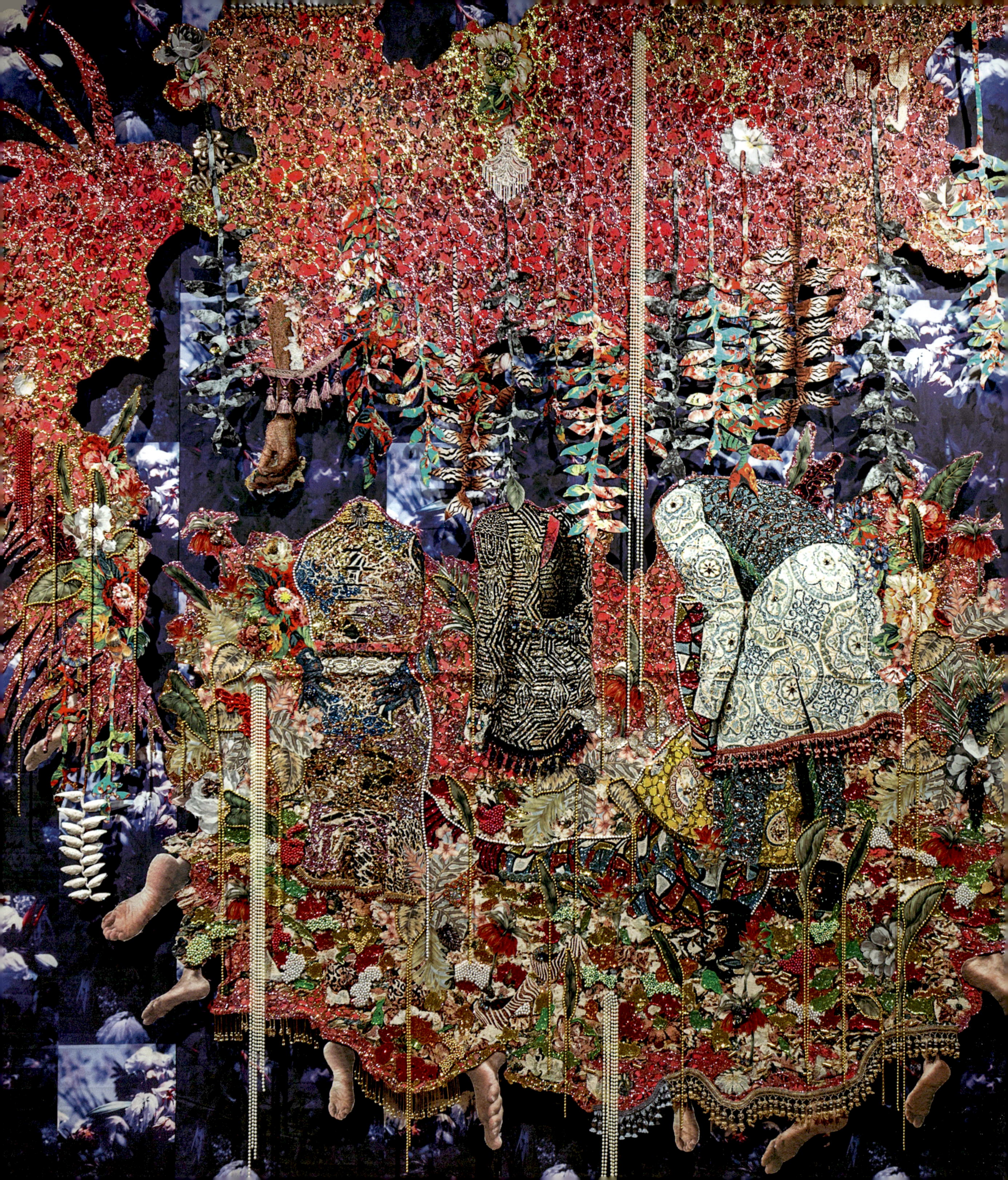

Director's Foreword

What Is Left Unspoken, Love is an exhibition of contemporary art across media from the early 1990s to the present. It is about the different ways the most important thing in life—love—is expressed yet is often difficult or even dangerous to verbalize. The exhibition has been organized during a time of social and political discord when diplomacy, reason, common sense, decency, and truth itself seem inoperable. In focusing on something so essential and so vast, the exhibition serves as a foundation for understanding forms love might take based on widely held beliefs and assumptions. Atlanta, the cradle of the civil rights movement and the birthplace of Dr. Martin Luther King Jr.'s Beloved Community, seems at this moment like the right place for this exhibition when the culmination of racialized hate crimes and White supremacist terrorism has demonstrated the depths of lovelessness from which some of the most malignant ideas have come to shape certain political and social realities in the United States today.

Although I like to think that those of us who work in museums are in the forever business, I am reminded every day that what we do is vitally important in the here and now. The moment of discovery in a museum between a person and a work of art can change that person's life and alter the direction it may take—subtly, imperceptibly at first, or perhaps all at once like an epiphany. In this way, an art encounter can be like falling in love—unplanned, unexpected, and mysterious—an exchange that occurs over many different frequencies at once, although it may seem at the time to have little or no personal value. A similar encounter, or exchange, with a work of art is what philosopher Alain Badiou called a "truth procedure," that is, a compelling event in which the formation of certain truths becomes an ongoing, inexhaustible process. Love is an essential truth procedure that, like art, allows us to find in a person or in a work of art something greater than ourselves alone—something eternal.

Artists, colleagues, and others who work in culture and the arts may recognize the quizzical statement, "you must love what you do." It may be more accurate to say that there is love in what we do and that it is the result of a process; it is proactive, or, as Badiou said about love, it is "less miraculous and more hard work." And on that subject, I would be remiss if I did not recognize Michael Rooks, our Wieland Family Curator of Modern and Contemporary Art, for his thoughtful conception and critical consideration of this daunting subject.

The Museum's work is a loving practice that requires effort, intention, and commitment. This is reflected in our exhibitions, collections, and educational and public programs. It is also inscribed in our institutional commitment to growth, inclusivity, collaboration, and connectivity. Viewed through this lens, it is a process that is thus self-reflexive while nonetheless related to the world outside our walls, empowering the sharing of artistic expression, itself a loving practice, with the communities we serve.

Rand Suffolk
Nancy and Holcombe T. Green, Jr., Director
High Museum of Art

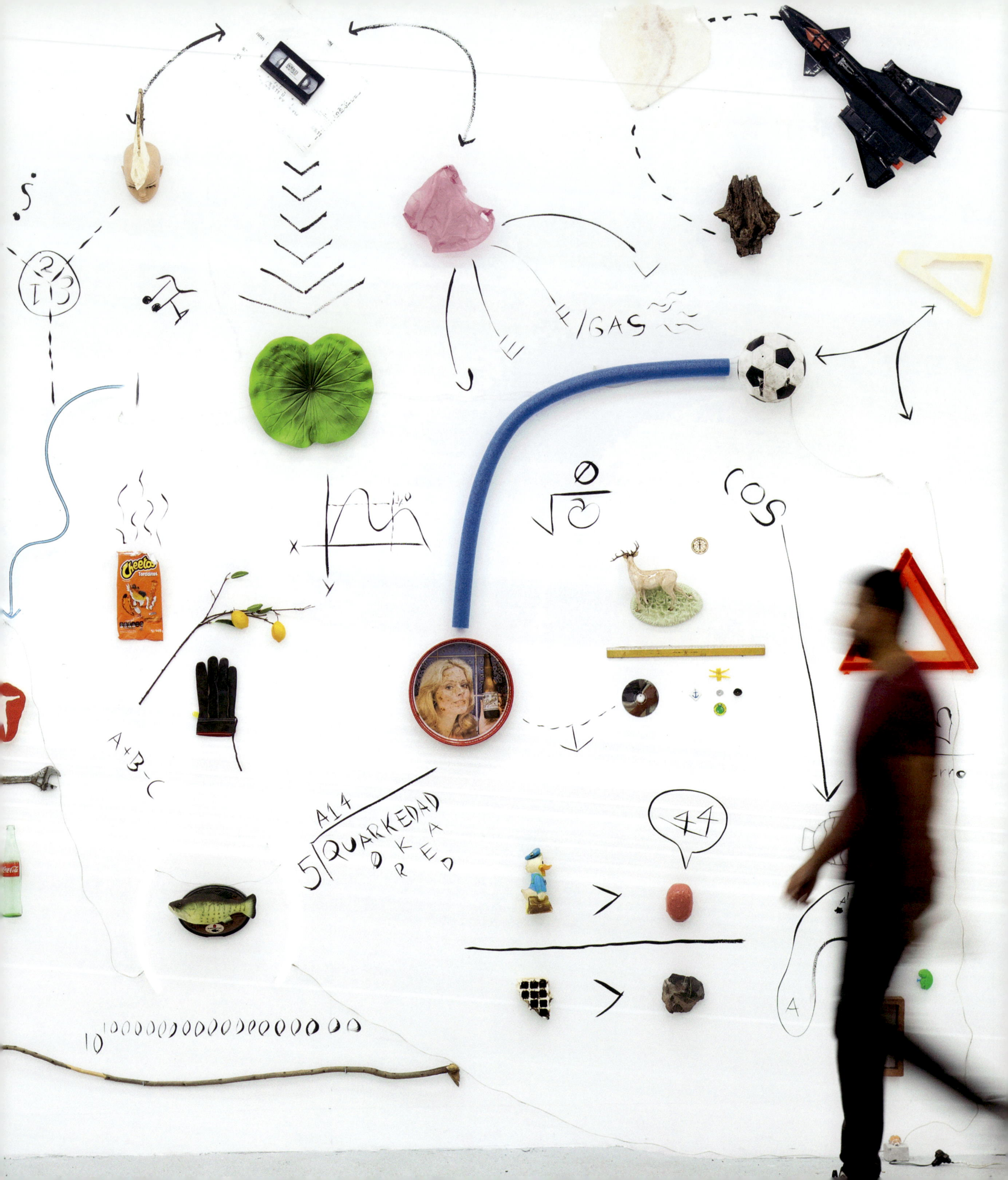

Curator's Acknowledgments

This exhibition was conceived in 2003 as a conceptual exercise in the wake of what might fairly be described as its antecedent, an exhibition at the Museum of Contemporary Art Chicago titled *War, What Is It Good For?* Of course, we all know the answer to that question. The "love" show began as an imaginary selection of artworks that spoke to, or about, our "better angels" after going through a particularly traumatic moment in time when the *War* show was on view. Nevertheless, fifteen years later, after proposing the idea, I was encouraged to develop it as an exhibition for consideration by the High Museum's director, Rand Suffolk, and Chief Curator Kevin Tucker. I owe them a debt of gratitude for allowing me to pursue this idea despite its ambitions and potential pitfalls, thus bringing full circle a stream of thought that began eighteen years ago.

The exhibition is organized into six thematic sections. Although themes may complement, overlap, contradict, and disaffirm one another, they provide categories that allow us to grapple with some of the most firmly rooted concepts of love, beginning with a philosophical proposition of the union of two people and their co-belonging in a shared destiny that we are calling "The Two." Inspired by philosopher Alain Badiou's "The Scene of the Two" in his book *In Praise of Love*, this theme considers the union of two as another order of awareness, a transformation in which one plus one is greater than two, wherein "the two" must form a relation to the world and not simply to each other's differences and subjectivities. Certainly, love is not a realm of awareness exclusive to adult relationships. For most people, love is first felt, grasped, absorbed, and adapted in the home. It is where one learns how to be loveable and, in turn, how to love. We call this section "The School of Love," with all credit due to the expression coined by bell hooks in *all about love*. This is followed by "The Practice of Love," comprising works that relate to the notion of a loving practice as something that comes from action, intention, and commitment inside and outside of the home.

Next, "Loving Community," named after Dr. Martin Luther King Jr.'s vision of society based on justice, equality, and brotherly love, considers a love ethic encompassing relationships among friends, comrades, and community. If love is difficult to express as suggested in the exhibition's title, it is given fluid expression in the language of poetry and the multivalency of meaning inherent in poetic language, which we consider in the next section, "The Poetics of Love." Finally, "Love Supreme"—inspired by the title of John Coltrane's 1964 album, which for Coltrane was an acknowledgment of the importance of faith in his musical artistry—considers relations between feelings of love and premonitions of the divine in nature and culture.

In the process of developing the exhibition, I have benefited from the generosity of colleagues and counterparts in museums and commercial galleries who have generously shared suggestions and advice, particularly Toby Kamps, now director of external projects at White Cube, with whom I developed an earlier iteration of this exhibition (never realized) when he was affiliated with the Contemporary Arts Museum Houston. I'm grateful for Toby's welcome encouragement and am grateful to the

OPPOSITE PAGE
Gabriel Rico (Mexican, born Lagos de Moreno, Mexico, 1980; active Guadalajara, Mexico), *VI Mural from the series Reducción objetiva orquestada* (detail), 2021, mixed media, acrylic paint, and neon, courtesy of the artist and Perrotin. © Gabriel Rico.

following colleagues for their generosity, friendship, and collegiality: Radcliffe Bailey; Simone Battisti at Gladstone Gallery and his former colleagues Isaac Alper, Maxwell Taylor-Milner, and Danielle Cardoso Shaeffer; Courtney Willis Blair at Mitchell-Innes & Nash; Liz Bower at Galerie Lelong; David Castillo; Karine Charbonneau, Guillaume Tremblay, Gabriel Rizzotti, and Stephan Schulz at the production studio Antimodular Research led by Rafael Lozano-Hemmer; Jeanne Chvosta at The Warehouse; Amy Brost, Carla Caputo, Stuart Comer, Erica Papernik, Jodi Hauptman, Sarah Primm, Thomas Lax, and Andy Wolf at the Museum of Modern Art; Cristopher Canizares at Hauser & Wirth; Lucas Cooper at Paula Cooper Gallery; Dean Daderko of the Contemporary Arts Museum Houston; Michael Darling formerly of the Museum of Contemporary Art Chicago; Kimberly Davis of LA Louver; Lauren Schell Dickens at San Jose Museum of Art; Kerstin Erdmann at Galerie OMR; Alexandra Ernst at the Rashid Johnson studio; Pujan Gandhi at the Minneapolis Institute of Arts; Jack Shainman, Alexandra Giniger, and Tamsen Greene at Jack Shainman Gallery; Photios Giovanis at Callicoon Fine Arts; Anna Maria Gonzalez Cuevas and Jason Murison at Petzel Gallery; Kimberly and Ben Gould; Amelia Hinojosa at kurimanzutto; Todd Hosfelt; Kerry Inman and Michael O'Brien at Inman Gallery; Nathalie Karg; Charlotte Ketabi-Lebard at Galerie Nathalie Obadia; Emily-Jane Kirwan at Marian Goodman Gallery; Peggy Leboeuf at Perrotin; Jeanne Greenberg Rohatyn, Zoe Fisher, Maxime Van Melkebeke, and Trang Tran at Salon 94 Design; Holly McHugh at the Felix Gonzalez-Torres Foundation; Monique Meloche and Allison Moore at Monique Meloche Gallery; René Morales at the Pérez Art Museum; Mary Mitsch and Bauby Tan at Marianne Boesky Gallery; Asma Naeem at the Baltimore Museum of Art; Cory Nomura at Matthew Marks Gallery; Wendy Olsoff at P•P•O•W; Natsu Oyobe at University of Michigan Museum of Art; Heather Pesanti formerly of The Contemporary Austin; Yan Qi and Rumi Xue at Three Shadows Photography Art Centre; Julie and Bennett Roberts at Roberts Projects; Steven Sacks at bitforms gallery; Jose Silva at the Michelle Stuart studio; Carol Thompson; Connie Rogers Tilton; Mathias Ussing Seeberg at the Louisiana Museum; David Spalding at Haines Gallery; Trevor Schoonmaker at the Nasher Museum; Margherita Tinagli at Galleria Continua; and Matt Watkins at Parafin.

The exhibition includes nearly seventy works of art from artists' studios, museums, and private collections in locations across the United States, Central America, Asia, and Europe. I am enormously grateful to all the artists, who are listed on another page of this publication, and to members of their studios, for their unwavering commitmentto the exhibition and for their enthusiastic support. Special thanks go to Keith Edmier, the only artist in this "love" show who also participated in the "war" show.

Although most works in the exhibition have been loaned directly by the artists, many private collectors have generously shared their treasured works, including Andrew Arnot and Michelle Jaffee, Charles Jing, Linda Garrison, Suzanne McFayden, Arthur Lewis and Hau Nguyen, Ron Pizzuti, Cindy and Howard Rachofsky, and Marianne and Goran Strokirk, to whom I give my heartfelt thanks. Likewise, I am grateful to the many museums who have loaned important works to the exhibition, including the Art Institute of Chicago, the Dallas Museum of Art, the Denver Art Museum, the Museum of Contemporary Art Chicago, the Museum of Modern Art, and the Pérez Art Museum Miami. The exhibition also includes works acquired recently for the High Museum through the extraordinary generosity of Andrea Galvani, John Auerbach, and Charles Roth, to whom I am forever grateful.

This catalogue is the result of the remarkable talents of the High's dedicated design and editorial staff, led by Angela Jaeger and including Laura Malone and Emma Simmons. I could not be more fortunate to include contributions by three brilliant writers who illuminate the exhibition's subject through memoir, prose, and poetry. French author Sonia David writes about the discovery of tenderness from the perspective of a postmenopausal woman, an experience of love at the close of one chapter in a woman's life and the opening of another in which desire is conditioned by friendship and care. Puerto Rican author Noel Quiñones writes about the sadness, joy, vulnerability, and empowerment following the physical and emotional turns of queer postadolescence, when, at the threshold of adulthood, the color orange became an equivalent for his emergent intersectionality. And author and poet Pearl Cleage has contributed a narrative poem that considers aspects of love across all of the exhibition's six thematic categories, speaking on the subject in the original language of love—poetry. The exhibition and this publication are profoundly enhanced by their contributions, for which I am most grateful.

I would like to extend my sincere thanks to Nancy and Holcombe T. Green, Jr., Director Rand Suffolk and directors Allison Chance, Brady Lum, Amy Simon, and Kevin Tucker, and former directors Kristie Swink Benson and Virginia Shearer. Among other colleagues at the High Museum, I am grateful for the collaboration, contributions, and support of Hannah Amuka, Eva Berlin, Caroline Corbitt, Erin Dougherty, Julia Forbes, Frances Francis, Gregory Harris, Robert Howells, Rachel Katz, Laurie Kind, Danielle Kiser, Leah-Lane Lowe, Faron Manuel, Kate McLeod, Justin McNeight, Larry Miller, Chelsea Morey, Skye Olson, Caroline Prinzivalli, Ivey Rucket, Tommy Sapp, Nancy Seda de Léon, and Awot Solomon, as well as former colleagues Paula Haymon, Catherine Huff, Sarah Kennel, Rainey Rawles, Tomasina Ray, and Jill Wickenheiser.

An exhibition on this scale necessarily entails extraordinary costs. We are proud to have received major funding for this exhibition from the National Endowment for the Arts and funding from the Taylor Family Fund. We give profound thanks to our Premier Exhibition Series Sponsor Delta Air Lines, Inc., and our Premier Exhibition Series Supporters ACT Foundation, Inc., Sarah and Jim Kennedy, Louise Sams and Jerome Grilhot, Dr. Joan H. Weens Estate, Harry Norman Realtors, and wish foundation. We are grateful for our Benefactor Exhibition Series Supporters Robin and Hilton Howell; our Ambassador Exhibition Series Supporters the Antinori Foundation, Corporate Environments, the Arthur R. and Ruth D. Lautz Charitable Foundation, and Elizabeth and Chris Willett; and our Contributing Exhibition Series Supporters Farideh and Al Azadi, Sandra and Dan Baldwin, Lucinda W. Bunnen, Marcia and John Donnell, Mrs. Peggy Foreman, Helen C. Griffith, Mrs. Fay S. Howell and the Howell Fund, Mr. and Mrs. Baxter Jones, Joel Knox and Joan Marmo, Dr. Joe B. Massey, Margot and Danny McCaul, The Ron and Lisa Brill Family Charitable Trust, Wade Rakes and Nicholas Miller, the Fred and Rita Richman Fund, funds In Memory of Elizabeth B. Stephens, USI Insurance Services, and Mrs. Harriet H. Warren. We're thankful also for the generous support for High Museum exhibitions provided by the Alfred and Adele Davis Exhibition Endowment Fund, Anne Cox Chambers Exhibition Fund, Barbara Stewart Exhibition Fund, Dorothy Smith Hopkins Exhibition Endowment Fund, Eleanor McDonald Storza Exhibition Endowment Fund, The Fay and Barrett Howell Exhibition Fund, Forward Arts Foundation Exhibition Endowment Fund, Helen S. Lanier Endowment Fund, Isobel Anne Fraser–Nancy Fraser Parker

Exhibition Endowment Fund, John H. and Wilhelmina D. Harland Exhibition Endowment Fund, Katherine Murphy Riley Special Exhibition Endowment Fund, Margaretta Taylor Exhibition Fund, and RJR Nabisco Exhibition Endowment Fund.

Finally, I am grateful for the friendship, advice, and discernment of my dear friends, authors James Swearingen and Joanne Cutting-Gray, whose encouragement and critical feedback have kept the project moving forward at times when it was stuck in a rut, for the brilliant editorial input and excellent advice of Sarah Eby-Ebersole, for the memory of my sister and brother from another mother Kimberly Ann Smith and Hironori Soma, and to my partner of thirty years, Jeffrey Cassens, who is living proof that love is real and forever.

Michael Rooks
Wieland Family Curator
of Modern and Contemporary Art

OPPOSITE PAGE
Alanna Fields (American, born Marlboro, Maryland, 1990; active New York, New York), *Our Love Was Deeply Purple* (detail), 2021, pigment prints mounted on museum board; encaustic on panel, courtesy of the artist.

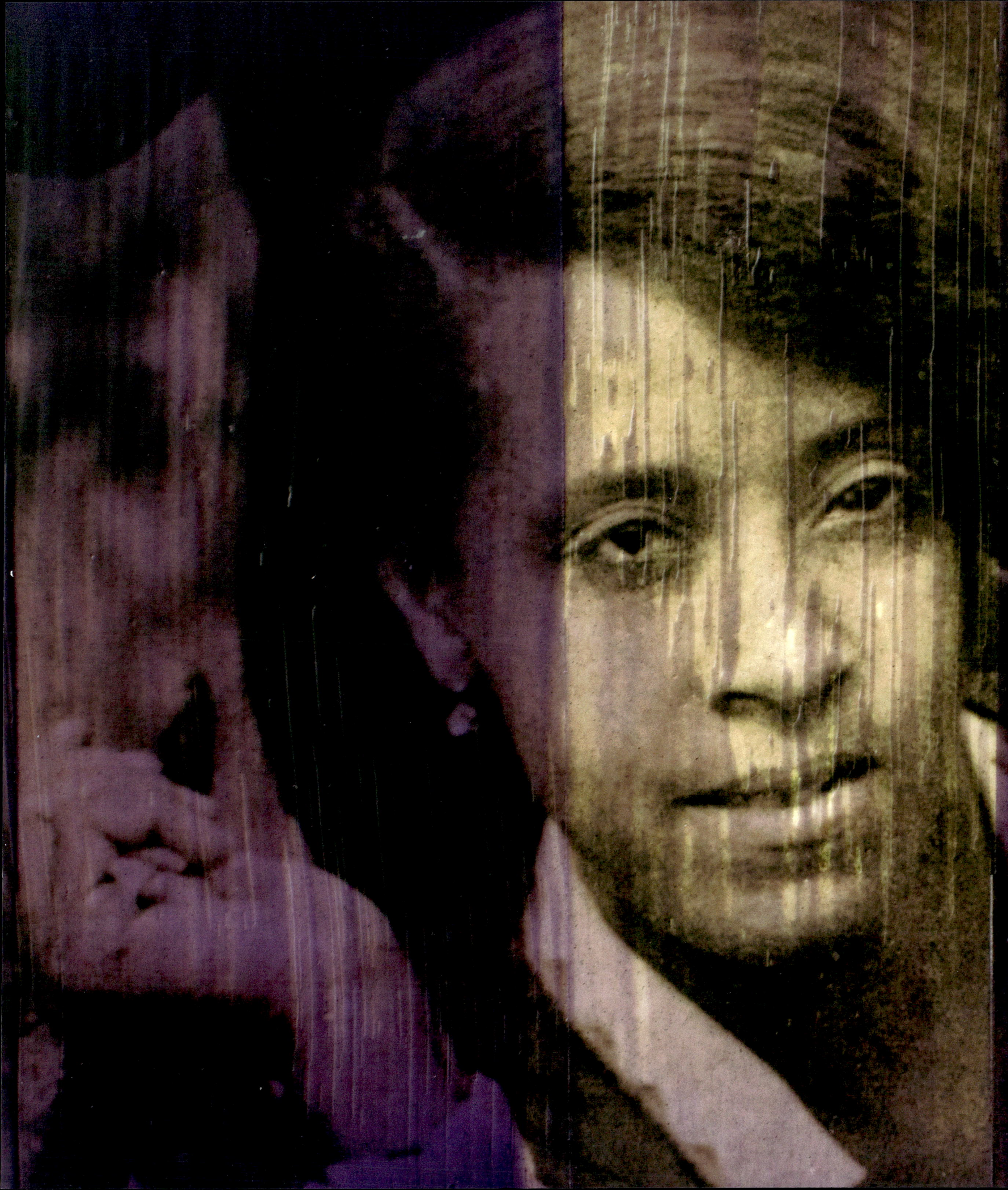

Artists in the Exhibition

Ghada Amer
Rina Banerjee
Thomas Barger
Patty Chang
Susanna Coffey
James Drake
Keith Edmier and Farrah Fawcett
Alanna Fields
Dara Friedman
Andrea Galvani
General Idea
Jeffrey Gibson
Felix Gonzalez-Torres
Kahlil Robert Irving
Tomashi Jackson
María de los Angeles Rodríguez Jiménez
Rashid Johnson
Gerald Lovell
Rafael Lozano-Hemmer
Kerry James Marshall
Felicita Felli Maynard
Wangechi Mutu
Ebony G. Patterson
Paul Pfeiffer
Magnus Plessen
Gabriel Rico
Dario Robleto
RongRong&inri
Michelle Stuart
Vivian Suter
Jana Vander-Lee
Carrie Mae Weems
Akram Zaatari

Lenders to the Exhibition

Andrew Arnot and Michelle Jaffee
The Art Institute of Chicago
John Auerbach
BANK Gallery, Shanghai, China
Dallas Museum of Art
David Castillo
Denver Art Museum
Estate of General Idea
Galerie Lelong & Co., New York
Linda Garrison
Gladstone Gallery, New York and Brussels
Hosfelt Gallery, San Francisco
Inman Gallery, Houston, Texas
Jack Shainman Gallery, New York
Charles Jing
kurimanzutto, Mexico City/New York
Arthur Lewis and Hau Nguyen
Suzanne McFayden
Mitchell-Innes & Nash, New York
Monique Meloche Gallery, Chicago
Museum of Contemporary Art Chicago
Museum of Modern Art, New York
Paula Cooper Gallery, New York
Pérez Art Museum Miami
Perrotin
Petzel Gallery, New York
Pizzuti Collection
P•P•O•W, New York
Private Collector, Miami, Florida
Cindy and Howard Rachofsky, The Rachofsky Collection
Charles Roth
Salon 94 Design
Marianne and Goran Strokirk
Tibor de Nagy Gallery, New York
Tilton Gallery, New York
Tina Kim Gallery, New York
White Cube

All Is Forgiven

And when you stop to ask me

How I can write about love

In the midst of so much blood

So much slavery

And smallpox

And internment camps

And labor camps

And breeding farms

And babies at the border

And genocide

And fratricide

And blood money in the bank

And lies with a life of their own—

"How can you write about love in wartime," you will say,

"When the penalty for everything is death,

"Or does this mean the war is over?

"Does this mean all is forgiven?"

And I will say, "do I know you?"

And you will say, "no, I'm just asking,

"How can you do it?"

And I will say:

How can I not do it?

How can I not stand in the rubble

Of everything we have ever known

Clutching my lover's hand

And vowing 'til death do us part,

Clinging to, singing to the power of love

While I call in the Spirits

Who are charged with looking out for women like me,

Especially in wartime when we are surrounded

By wild-eyed revolutionaries wrapped in rags

And broken-hearted shamans wrapped in wishes

Asking will the circle be unbroken

And daring us to answer yes.

I always answer yes.

How can I not do it?

Anybody can rhyme a rhyme in praise of springtime,

Raise a song of joy in swing time

When all you have to do is dance and make romance,

Cross your fingers and take a chance.

But in wartime, there are other considerations.

There is always blood and risk

And bravery and betrayal,

Just like in the movies,

Except John Wayne won't be there.

So you have to trust me on this one

And every one that comes hereafter

Since I am incapable of lying.

I gave it up for freedom and never looked back.

But you shake your head unconvinced,

As if you have a right to any opinion at all

Just because I was walking by and caught your eye.

"I'm just asking," you say, "does this mean all is forgiven?"

No more fears, I say? No more tears, I say?

It's only been 400 years, I say, but okay,

Let's pretend all is forgiven.

Now take off your clothes and shave your head

While I sit on the edge of this big brass bed

And count your teeth and slice your toes

And turn out the light so we can see if it glows

Like a transparent fish in an underground cave

Floating in the darkness where only the brave glide by

In boats that stink of dead fish and black mold,

Looking for a story they can hold onto,

A story about you:

A see-through fish, blinded by the light

Swimming circles in a lake at the bottom of the world.

Yeah, that looks like you.

Fish face, fish tail, fish lips and eyes and gills,

Never saw the sun,

Never gonna see it.

Never been the moon,

Never gonna be it.

Born in a cave, die in a cave;

Must be a lot like being enslaved

Except for the chains.

And the water.

But now you say you'll forget the things I said

If I forget the things you said,

And you'll forgive the things I did

If I forgive the things you did.

No harm, no foul, and an even swap ain't no swindle

If I can just rekindle that long-lost flame with a love poem,

With a thousand love poems

Released into the air like Marquez's golden butterflies

To swarm around the heads of guilty lovers

As I pray me down to sleep,

Because love is always, at the deepest heart of it, a prayer,

From the very start of it, a prayer,

To the part of it where you stand in the rubble

Of everything you've ever known

And still promise 'til death do you part and mean it.

Always a prayer.

So consider this an omen and an amen,

A testimony in tongues and fire,

An idea past its prime

But just coming into its own,

A poem with a price on its head

Rounding third and headed for home.

Because if that's the way it is, so be it.

We hidin' in plain sight right now

'Cause that's the way we see it,

And a nod is as good as a wink to a blind horse.

So mark the cards

And fix the fight;

Give me my money,

And we'll call it a night.

And I'll forget the things you said

If you forget the things I said,

And I'll forgive the things you did

If you forgive the things I am about to do.

No harm, no foul, and everybody knows

An even swap ain't no swindle, until it is,

And then you have to sleep with one eye open,

But you can't decide which one,

So you lie there, blinking, winking and confused

Until you expire of exhaustion and amnesia and irrelevance.

And it doesn't even matter,

Because it's always wartime somewhere.

But still, in this moment, night is falling,

And the guns have stopped,

If not for long at least for now,

And we turn to each other as if in a beautiful dream.

There is a moon,

And I whisper in my lover's ear:

"Say the poem where you cannot live without me,

"Where my lips are sweet as cherry wine and soft.

"Say the one where you try to make me laugh

"And I do and you realize you cannot live without me,

"Especially when I laugh." And he smiles.

"They are the same poem," he says.

"Aren't they all the same poem," I say.

"Oh yes," he says,

"And they're for you."

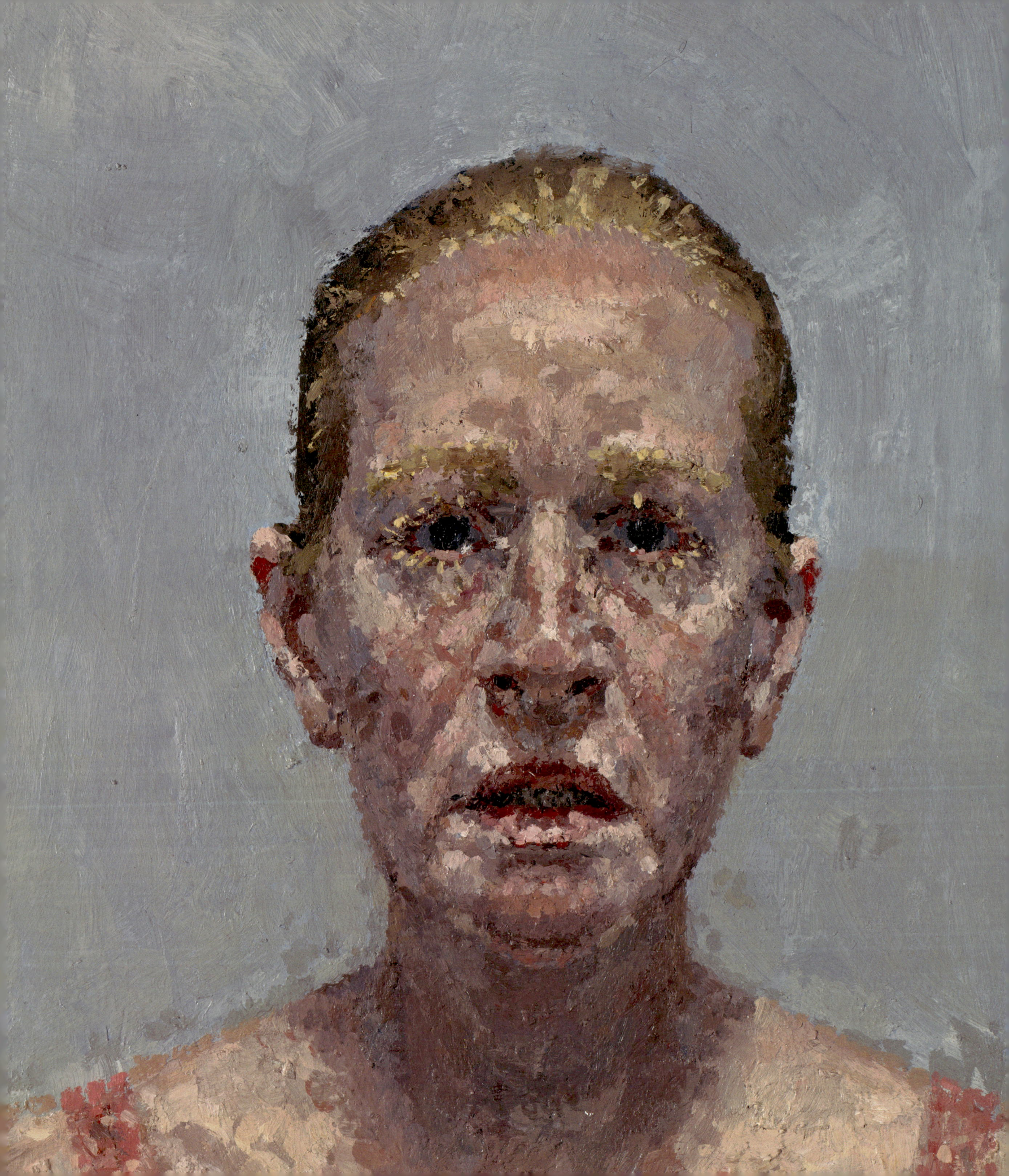

What Is Left Unspoken

One of the moral diseases we communicate to one another in society comes from huddling together in the pale light of an insufficient answer to a question we are afraid to ask.

—Thomas Merton[1]

When in love, one becomes a bird: one stretches one's neck and hears a song not meant to be pronounced. One is speechless. But they are more and more numerous those who won't risk their lives for that moment. [. . .] We can understand them: love in all its forms is the most important matter we will ever face, but also the most dangerous, the most unpredictable, the most maddening. But it is also the only salvation that I know of.

—Etel Adnan[2]

Whatever is unnamed, undepicted in images, whatever is omitted from biography, censored in collections of letters, whatever is misnamed as something else, made difficult-to-come-by, whatever is buried in the memory by the collapse of meaning under an inadequate or lying language—this will become, not merely unspoken, but unspeakable.

—Adrienne Rich[3]

Like art, *love* is one of those monosyllabic words that means so much but is often reduced to a mere accomplice to sexual pleasure and self-interest. Although love has been the subject of critical commentary from time immemorial, it remains elusive. Is it an emotion, a virtue, an affection, an obsession? It seems love is, as poet and painter Etel Adnan wrote, "not to be described, it is to be lived."[4] It is hard to wrap one's head around love because of its enormity. Its dimensions have been described for millennia in discourse and dialogue from the philosophical to the spiritual, between the ontological and the eschatological. Its scope ranges from the most intimate of relationships between two people, through the ties that bind family and friends, to social movements that promote the worth and well-being of community. At its most epic, it embraces the family of humankind and the natural world and even extends to the universe. Its power is not only the strength of its passion but also its endurance and ability to transcend time. The Hebrew King Solomon, who reigned during the tenth century BCE and was renowned for his wisdom, asserted that love is stronger than death.

Figure 1.
Joanna Beall Westermann (American, 1935–1997), Handwritten letter with envelope, April 25, 1971, the David and Alfred Smart Museum of Art, the University of Chicago; the H. C. Westermann Study Collection, gift of Joanna Beall. Photo © 2022 courtesy of the David and Alfred Smart Museum of Art, the University of Chicago.

Of course, any art exhibition about love can offer only a very limited set of propositions based on the assumption that love, despite its ineffability, is still a subject worthy of consideration. We live in the thrall of late-stage global capitalism in which love is often reduced to an indifferent sharing of heart-shaped emojis. However, instead of diminishing its value and shirking our responsibility to it, why not take up the subject head-on? As poet and playwright Pearl Cleage says in her poem for this catalogue, "How can I write about love [. . .] How can I not do it?" In the face of the cynicism, hatred, bigotry, and mistrust that seem to have become more powerful and prevalent than ever, why not ask such questions: Is love intrinsic, or is it a habit? What is the relationship of love to truth, freedom, and justice? Is love possible without mystery? Can love be scientifically proven? Why is it so hard to say, "I love you"?

This exhibition approaches the subject of love through a series of similar questions that are both abstract and practical, for although love is somehow linked to the grand scale of human destiny, we live it in the quotidian of our daily lives. The goal is not only to consider examples of how love is commonly understood but also to explore how its various forms might open pathways to a greater awareness of the many ways that love manifests itself and to the responsibilities love calls us to assume. The exhibition's title refers to the many situations in which love is unacknowledged or unresolved and to the regret that may follow when people cannot bring themselves to give voice to the words "I love you." The apprehension or inability to say those words seems an expression of the romantic notion that love transcends language, as in the expression "words cannot describe." This idiom was reified by the late artist H. C. Westermann in one of his famous love letters to his wife Joanna Beall Westermann, which began with, "Dearest Sweety" followed by line after line of scribble. She responded in kind with her own scribbled love letter to her husband (fig. 1). Nevertheless, philosophers Alain Badiou and Giorgio Agamben argue that declaring love is an essential part of properly sharing it. Agamben suggests love's "meaning coincides with the act of its utterance," and Badiou writes that "the declaration [of love] is inscribed in the structure of the event itself."[5] If its enunciation is a critical component of love, how is it possible to develop a loving relationship with another if love remains unspoken or is only expressed axiomatically?

A fundamental assumption about love is that it cannot survive in the absence of truth, which is another one-syllable word of prodigious proportions and no less central a subject in philosophy. Badiou calls love a "truth procedure," a process in which an event leads to action and struggles specific to the situation and its participants.[6] Theologian and social activist Thomas Merton wrote that "to love others well we must first love the truth."[7]

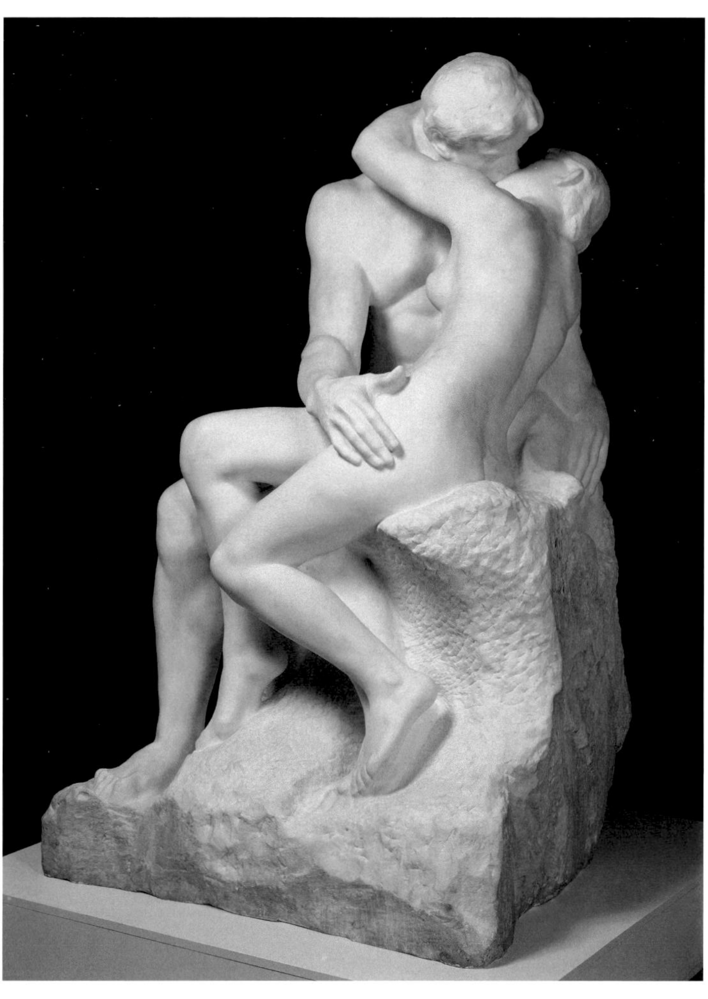

The Two

If love is a process of discovery and its declaration is the event that marks the "transition from chance to destiny," then speech between two people is essential to the formation of this truth.[8] The spoken voice is an intrinsic part of Houston-based Dario Robleto's sculpture *Time Measures Nothing But This Love* (plate 61). For more than a decade, Robleto has focused his research on the history of audio recording and upon themes of longing, loss, spirituality, memory, and love. Art historian and Harvard professor of humanities Jennifer Roberts describes Robleto's project as the "validation of emotional knowledge, particularly through the promotion and testing of empathy as the fundamental function of art."[9] *Time Measures Nothing But This Love* includes two sets of glass containers displayed on stepped shelves on either side of a satin-lined valise resembling that of a traveling salesman. Hand blown into a lemniscate shape, the containers resemble the infinity symbol and are graduated from large to small, top to bottom, giving the valise a coffin-like appearance. They contain plant matter associated with love, passion, and friendship, such as rose hips, as well as once-playable audiotape, now stretched and pulled into attenuated magnetic-coated threads. The tape once preserved the voices of "the world's oldest married couple," along with the recording of a clock marking time recorded in the nineteenth century. Robleto reanimated both recordings and then disfigured them through physical stretching to symbolize the figurative extension of time. The artist's sculpture evokes the notion of love as everlasting and eternal through a process involving both the restoration and inhumation of a bygone love.

Romantic stories of love are often tragic, sometimes violent, and may include themes such as enslavement, madness, sacrifice, and the losing of oneself in the other. In this tradition, love is a process led by desire. Diane Ackerman describes this illusion of falling in love through a portentous encounter in *A Natural History of Love* as a magical moment of combustion in which two lovers meet in a blind passion that leads ultimately to their destruction.[10] Their union becomes a "heroic act against the world," as in the story of the adulterous lovers Paolo and Francesca.[11] Unlike Paolo and Francesca, who were the inspiration for Rodin's *The Kiss* (fig. 2), the kissing couples featured in Dara Friedman's *Romance* are unafraid to share their affections in public (plate 20). Shot by the artist during walks in Rome with her daughter, the film's nonnarrative structure includes no prelude to or cessation of the young couples' intimacy. Instead, it centers on the kiss as a form of communication in a complex system of human relations. The couples' "sweet toil of romance" transcends the libidinal to become a silent negotiation of their differences and secrets through touch and the releasing of their bodies to one another.[12] At first the film's silence establishes a safe distance between the subjects and the viewer. However, viewers become enmeshed in the film through a sort of furtive triangulation, seeming to be acknowledged at times by the lovers on the screen, who themselves imply the possibility of a kiss or a desire for intimacy.

The romantic trope of love that spontaneously ignites in an encounter between two people despite the vagaries and vicissitudes of everyday life is the MacGuffin of Akram Zaatari's *Tomorrow Everything Will Be Alright* (plate 69). This short film begins with a typewritten conversation between former lovers, initiated when an unexpected greeting instantly appears like a text message above the line indicator of an old-fashioned typewriter. A short period of flirtatious patter between the correspondents culminates in a plan to reunite after more than a decade apart: a meeting at sunset at the place of their first encounter. Although the film's explicit reference to Eric Rohmer's 1986 film *Le Rayon Vert* seems to cast it as a classic fairy-tale love story, the allusion serves as a point of departure for a weightier consideration of how feelings both real and imagined, expressed and suppressed or repressed, complicate the relationship between two people.[13] Even as it employs the usual tropes of intimacy and romance, the work transmits a sense of disconnection through an obfuscation of words that skirt around the protagonists' desire and longing. Rather than a renewed surge of passion, the brief and impromptu illusion of romantic love carries an air of reminiscence. The several ellipses used during their typewritten correspondence seem to serve as ciphers for unspoken nostalgic sentiments for something lost—wistful feelings suggested at the outset of Rohmer's film in a line from Rimbaud: "Ah! Que le temps vienne / Où les coeurs s'éprennent" ("Ah, let the time come / where hearts fall in love").[14]

To take a step beyond the traditional view that love causes two to become one is to imagine a union in which the whole is greater than the sum of "the two." In this union, love thrives rather than self-destructs in the creative tension between alterity and mutuality in a couple, liberating each individual from the constructs and strictures of selfhood and identity. Such was the case when Keith Edmier and the late actor and artist Farrah Fawcett collaborated on equal footing to produce a body of work titled *Recasting Pygmalion*. As a boy, Edmier had admired Fawcett (among millions of his generation) and in 1999 proposed the collaboration in a letter to Fawcett's publicist. Their efforts explore the problematic relationship between muse and maker, celebrity and fan, inspiration and collaboration, and representation and truth (fig. 3).[15] "Recasting" in the series title refers both to sculptural processes and to the film industry, in which both Edmier and Fawcett had professional ties. Of course, "Pygmalion" alludes to Ovid's *Metamorphoses* and to George Bernard Shaw's theatrical revision of it, suggesting themes of transformation, illusion, and inspiration. In *Keith Edmier and Farrah Fawcett, 2000* (plate 18),

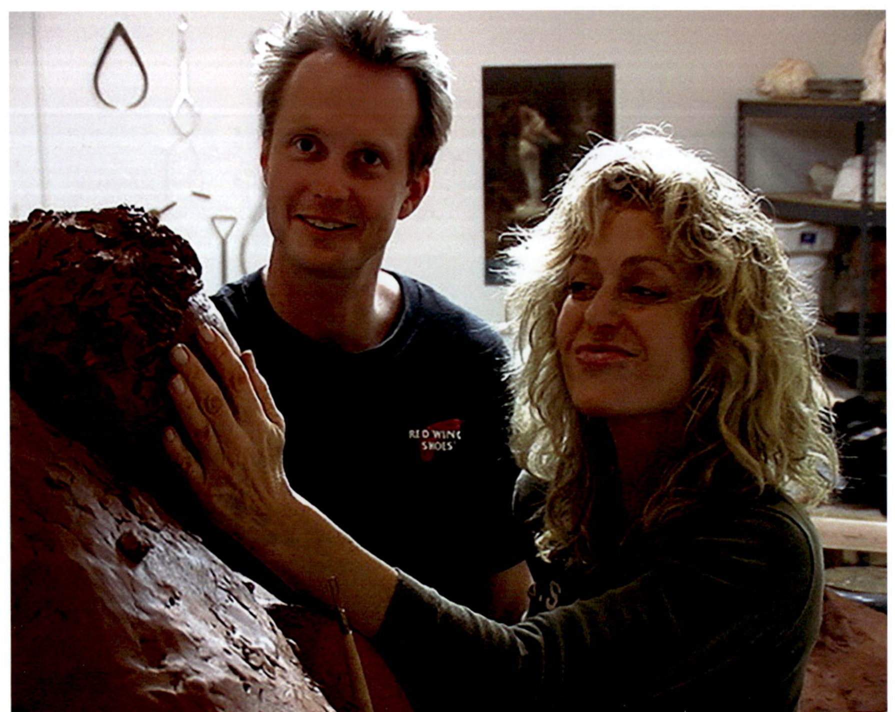

Figure 3.
Keith Edmier and Farrah Fawcett in the studio, ca. 2000. Photo courtesy of Keith Edmier and Petzel Gallery, New York.

Figure 4.
RongRong&inri (active Beijing, China; RongRong, born Zhangzhou, Fujian Province, China, 1968; inri, born Kanagawa Prefecture, Japan, 1973), *Tsumari Story No. 11-4*, 2014, gelatin silver print. Photo courtesy of the artists and Three Shadows +3 Gallery.

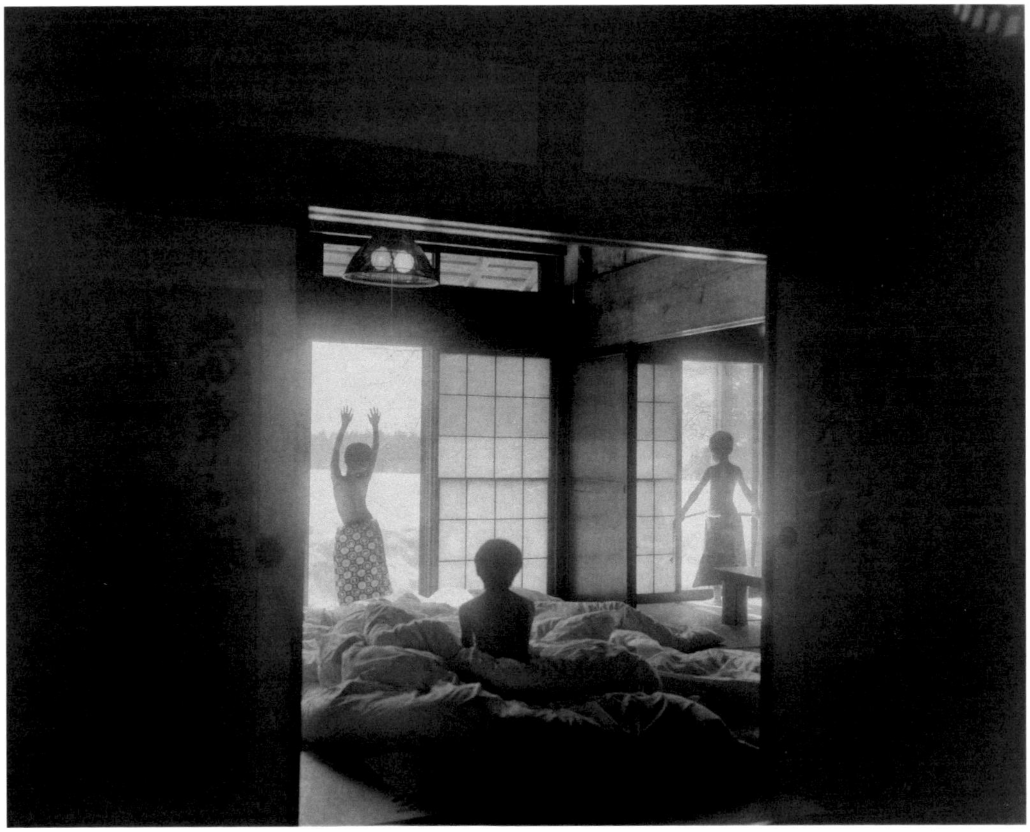

life-size nude figures of each artist, sculpted by the other, are representations of ideals, like Pygmalion's Galatea. In her contribution, Fawcett heightened Edmier's youthful vitality and handsome features, while Edmier portrayed Fawcett as she had appeared during his early adolescence in the role of Jill Munroe in the television series *Charlie's Angels*. Their chosen materials, bronze and marble, promote the concept of the figures as idols, conjuring the gods, goddesses, warriors, and nobles of ancient Greece and Rome. The figures appear as intermediaries between the present and the past, with their nudity evoking classical antiquity even as subtle details such as hairstyle and body shape snap them back into the here and now. In the process of their collaboration, Edmier and Fawcett established a close friendship that Edmier described as a "kind of marriage," suggesting that despite their divergent histories and backgrounds, they found common ground in the language of art and art history.

The marriage of Chinese artist RongRong and Japanese artist inri was the inspiration for a collaboration titled *In Fujisan, Japan* (plate 62). The iconic site of Mt. Fuji, on "the other shore of sensation," in the words of inri, was one of several locations where the artists staged performances to commemorate and document their union as a newlywed couple. They performed in the nude, representing timelessness, vulnerability, and the surrendering of secrets to each other (fig. 4). In sixteen images, shot in front of the mountain on Lake Yamanaka during the bitter cold of winter, the couple braved the danger of hypothermia and the precariousness of a partially frozen lake. At the time, neither could speak the other's language. Their joint performance was another iteration of the ritual of exchanging vows, wordless pronouncements that rescued and expressed aspects of their love for each other that may have been lost in translation. The work, part performance, part documentation, offers itself as a form of love's declaration at the horizons of the somatic and the spiritual, the temporal and the timeless.

The ephemeral and the eternal are crosscurrents in *"Untitled" (Perfect Lovers)* (plate 25) by Felix Gonzalez-Torres, a Cuban-born artist who became one of the most radical, transgressive, and venerated artists of his generation before succumbing to AIDS-related complications in 1996. Gonzalez-Torres employed minimalist and conceptualist strategies to produce politically relevant yet deeply personal and poetic artworks concerned with themes of the personal and the public, mortality and impermanence, and corporeality and consciousness. His work also seems resonant with the possibility of a mediating spirit between body and soul, and it often takes on themes of love and its conveyance between lovers. In *"Untitled" (Perfect Lovers)*, two identical alkaline-battery-operated wall clocks are set to the same time and placed on a wall so that their black rims touch. The work's parenthetical title evokes the union of two people whose lives are parallel and aligned romantically and biologically—the second hands suggesting the beating of their hearts. The work implies the timeless bond of love and the possibility of renewal, as the clocks are eventually reset when their batteries expire and they fall out of sync, losing pace with one another, as do life partners physically and perhaps also emotionally. Although the motif of the clock first appeared in his work as early as 1986, *"Untitled" (Perfect Lovers)* is the first instance in a morphology of two abutting rings or circles in Gonzalez-Torres's oeuvre that recurs until the end of his life and is one of two occurrences of the clock form in this family of works.[16] The two enclosed forms touch, approximating a kiss, suggesting a parable in which love relates to the totality of the other in and against time. At the same time, the work resists the illusion of romantic love because the clocks can never remain perfectly coordinated "despite the desire of the subjects to fuse into one, to constitute a perfectly doubled subjectivity."[17]

The space-time continuum of eternity and infinity is evoked in Andrea Galvani's *The End (Action #5)* (plate 21), a work that consists of a concrete pedestal supporting a gold MacBook Air, which plays looped footage of the sun seemingly arrested just above the horizon. The film was shot from the cockpit of a military aircraft flying at supersonic speed in the opposite direction of the Earth's rotation. Because the camera moves toward the horizon faster than the speed of sound, the sun never sets but remains suspended at the threshold of day and night even as the ocean below rushes past. The steady state of the sun attests to its centricity in our solar system, but the arrested motion of the Earth is the result of the aircraft's continuous race against the sun, a sleight of hand implying that our attempts at truth, represented by a fusion of horizons at which time stands still, are always contingent and require the questioning of certainty and of human finitude. In the context of the exhibition, it might also suggest that a steadfast love requires continual engagement to sustain it and that the notion of axiomatically timeless love is an illusion. By hypothetically stopping time just before sunset, Galvani's action qua performance also suggests infinity and immortality at the idiomatic "ends of the earth," suspending for a moment the inevitability of death. *The End* attempts to reconcile the perception of passing time with theories that describe the timelessness of the universe while alluding to the unfailing nature of love, epitomized in French novelist Honore de Balzac's line: "True love is eternal, infinite, and always like itself."

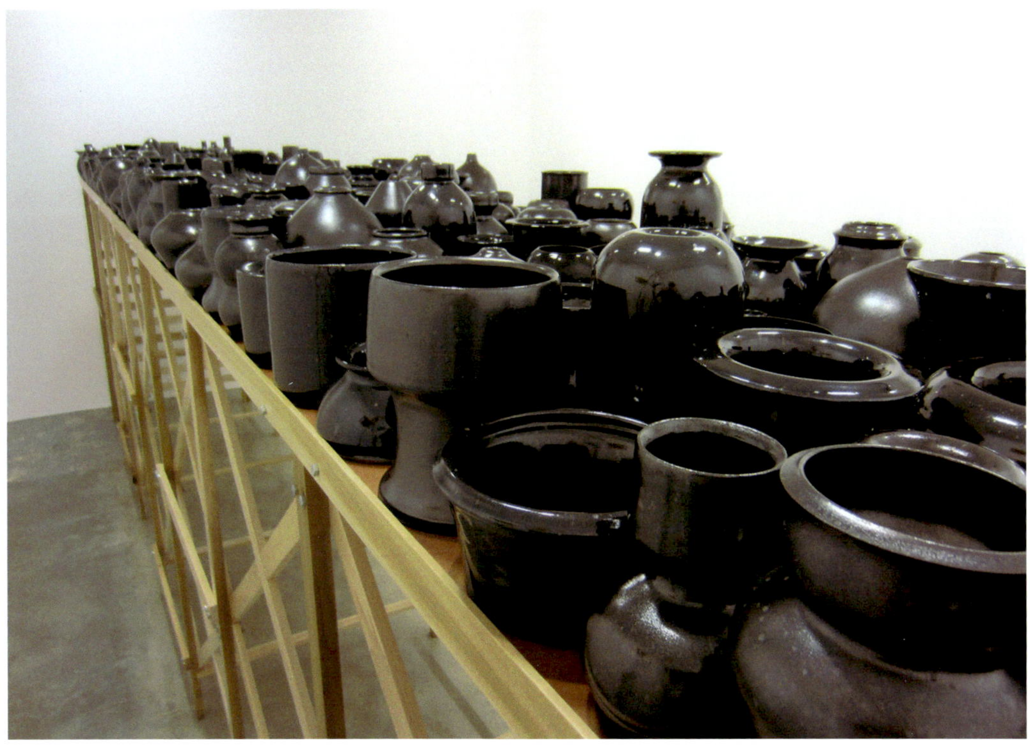

School of Love

For most people, the home is the traditional locus of family, where, as bell hooks explained, we learn that we are loveable and, in turn, how to love through care, affirmation, trust, commitment, and respect between family members.[18] In Kahlil Robert Irving's *My Grandmother's Cupboard (Artifact)* (plate 26), love is nourished in the space of the kitchen, the heart of the home. His installation contains hundreds of handmade ceramic objects, each unique and associated with ordinary serving ware, huddled together or arranged in stacks and rows in a traditional cabinet. Irving's handmade collection of black-glazed ceramics signifies Black togetherness, which provided love and strength to Irving's grandmother Ernestine Irving and her generation as they endured the crucible of racial injustice during the era of segregation. More generally, it pays homage to Irving's Black cultural ancestry. In his thesis, he describes conjuring ancestry through the labor of crafting objects from the fleshy substance of clay: "I press my fingers in the process, into the reality of how Black people came to this country carrying parts of their ancestry" (fig. 5).[19] Irving's groupings of black vessels represent Black bodies in space, suggesting social gatherings that are at once "confrontational and celebratory."[20]

The kitchen is also the site for Carrie Mae Weems's iconic portfolio *The Kitchen Table Series* (plate 68), a landmark work of postmodern feminism. Twenty photographs and fourteen text panels comprise its poetic narrative told from a woman's perspective from within the kitchen, a place of sociability and creativity and of domestic labor traditionally consigned to women. It tells of the narrator's relationship with her lover, of her career and her politics, and of her role as a mother. In this self-performance, the artist presents her endeavors to nurture self-love and

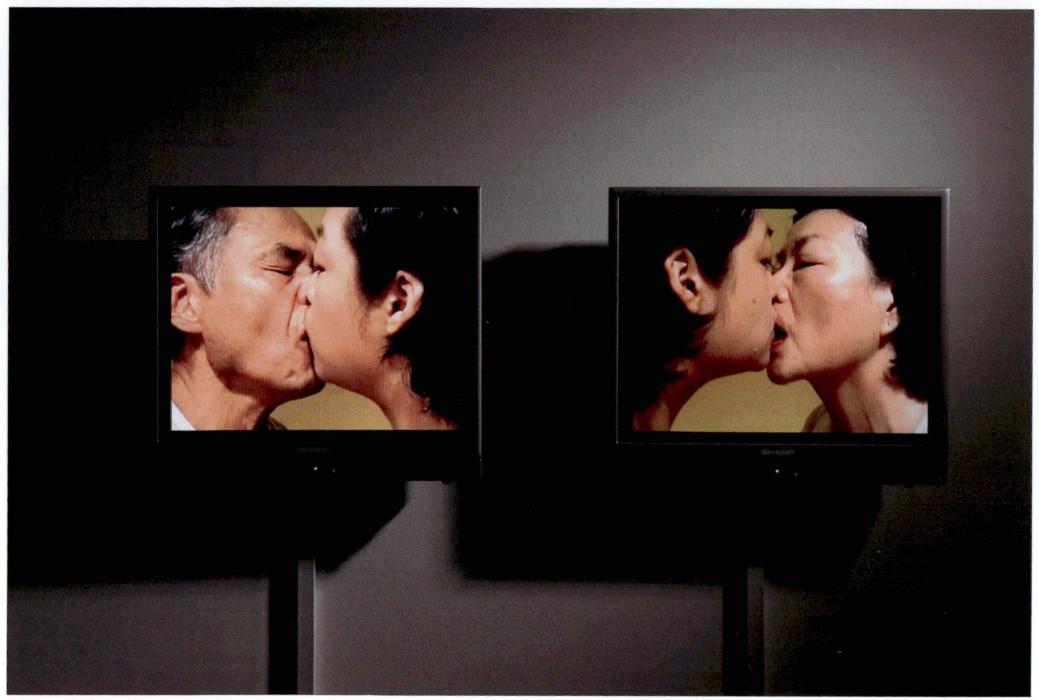

Figure 6.
Patty Chang (American, born San Leandro, California, 1972; active Los Angeles, California), *In Love*, 2001, two-channel video, running time: 3 minutes, 38 seconds. © Patty Chang. Photo courtesy of the artist.

self-respect within a romantic relationship encumbered by traditional roles and gender politics. Together, the texts and images describe thoughts and actions related to self-care, friendship, and the struggle for agency as a Black woman in the world. *The Kitchen Table Series* allows a glimpse into a woman's private cares, concerns, desires, and disappointments. Her inner-most thoughts recall the practice of self-care Pearl Cleage calls "The Constant Eye" in her memoir *Things I Should Have Told My Daughter*: "the eye that makes me feel I could possibly be embarrassed when no one is here but me."[21]

Patty Chang's *Que Sera Sera/Invocations* (plate 7) explores the navigation of uncomfortable or painful emotions and the impulse to minimize such feelings as an Asian American. This two-channel video nominally bridges more than a decade separating it from two earlier videos by the artist featuring her parents titled *In Love* (2001) and *On Love* (2003) (fig. 6). On one screen, the artist is shown in her father's bedroom, where he lies dying. Before him, she cradles and rocks her newborn son while quietly singing "Que Sera, Sera" ("Whatever Will Be, Will Be"). The song's lyrics, sung simultaneously by a child to her parent and by a parent to her child, allude to cycles of life and death and hint at the prospects of adulthood and its anxiety-provoking encumbrances influenced by personal choice and by destiny. On the other screen, a close-up of her mother's hand is shown scrolling on an iPad while she reads phrases that evoke memories of her husband's final days in which feelings of pain, anxiety, embarrassment, and discomfort are mitigated by expressions of love, tenderness, compassion, and respect. Chang has said that she "always dealt with certain anxieties" in her work—"undercurrents of ugly, or 'minor,' feelings," to use terms coined by cultural theorist Sianne Ngai and poet Cathy Park Hong respectively to refer to the Asian American experience of disenfranchisement and the disentitlement of one's own feelings.[22] Chang's work explores the possibility of reconciling the dispossession of one's culture with the desire for self-affirmation by making visible "those things we usually keep below surface."[23]

Thomas Barger's *Love Me, Protect Me Chair* (plate 6) reflects on the endurance of love between parents or life partners and their children, even when unavoidable emotional distress strains familial relationships. Barger was raised in rural Illinois in a religious family whose conservative social values came into conflict with his sexual identity after he came out to his parents as gay. Even in the face of his parents' difficulty accepting his revelation, Barger reflects on the love they had shown him. The sculpture is based on the simple, functional furniture of the artist's upbringing. Its soft suppleness lends the work an anthropomorphic quality, while the joining of two chairs speaks to the contingencies inherent in filial love. The "love me" part on the left side of his sculpture refers to the artist's stay-at-home mother, who provided nurturing love for him, a kind of love about which author Diane Ackerman says there is "nothing more absolute or unquestioning."[24] The "protect me" part on the right refers to Barger's father, who worked hard to provide for the family as a farmer—a love between father and child Ackerman describes as conditional and therefore distanced.[25] The chairs are joined in the center, simultaneously uniting and confining the family members as they reach a mutual understanding about their shared obligations to one another.

The traditional model of the biological family typically excludes the variety of relationships that may be characterized as familial among members of the LGBTQIA+ community. Confronting this paucity of historical accounts, artist Felicita Felli Maynard, who is genderqueer and Afro-Latinx, has created a fictional photo archive of queer family roots. Begun in 2017, their project used the antique wet-plate collodion process to stage an imagined history of queer and trans Black people. Their *Ole Dandy* series (plates 38–49) is centered on the lives of Jean Loren Feliz and Angelo Lwazi Owenzayo, fictive male impersonators/drag kings who lived during the late nineteenth century. Their personas were modeled after real-life drag king Florence Hines, who performed in the 1890s. The artist considers both Feliz and Owenzayo to be the queer ancestors they did not have before finding their voice in the Black queer community. Through narratives of loving, longing, and loss, Maynard celebrates the ancestry of their community and, in the process, constructs a heritage lodged within the possibility of a historical past (fig. 7).

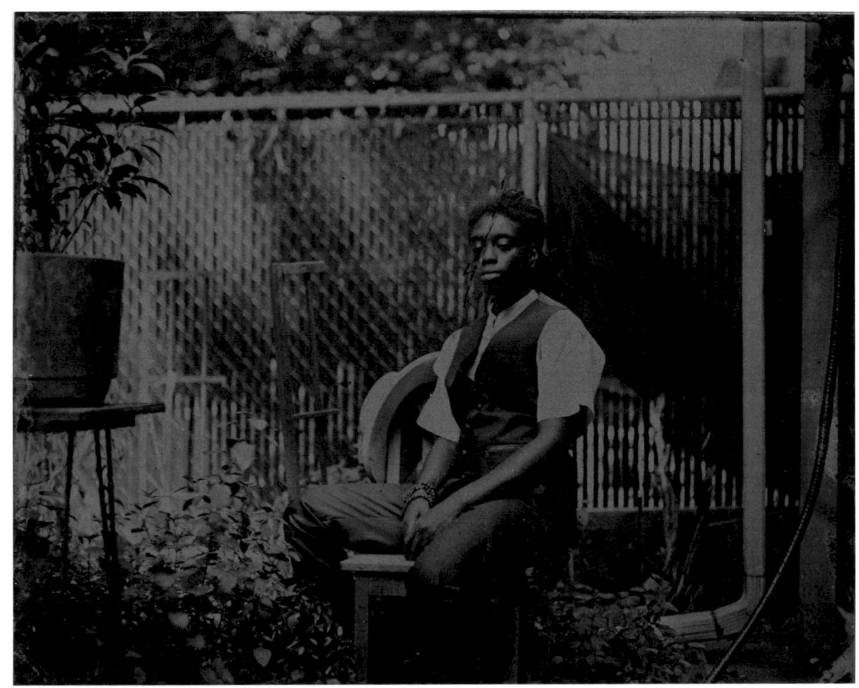

Figure 7.
Felicita Felli Maynard (American, born Brooklyn, New York, 1989; active New Orleans, Louisiana), *Jean in the Garden* from the series *Ole Dandy, the Tribute*, 2019, tintype, courtesy of the artist. © Felicita Felli Maynard. Photo courtesy of the artist.

The Practice of Love

The maxim that to have love, one must give it away is a paradox. How do you give what you don't have, and how can you keep what you have given away? Equally paradoxical is the commonly held belief that before one can love another, one must love oneself. Cultivating self-sacrificing love within oneself is perhaps the highest level of subjective experience according to Danish philosopher Søren Kierkegaard. However, the practice of self-denial and unconditional benevolence toward the other stands in contrast to the commandment to "love your neighbor as you love yourself."[26] In this line of ethical thought, cultivating a positive sense of self enables one to love others selflessly, opening the door to receiving love from others in return. Such love, as opposed to a narcissistic obsession with the self, implies a kind of discipline: it takes less effort to cultivate one's own empirical style and to forge an identity separate from others than it takes to practice the self-reflection and contemplation required to free oneself from a life of self-absorption and focus on sharing love with others.

Susanna Coffey's reflexive practice of self-portraiture has been a primary focus of her work for three decades. Painting mostly from observation and making decisions according to the changing conditions of light and atmosphere, Coffey follows the play of light and shadow as it falls across her head and face as if beholding the features of a landscape. In part because she maintains this objective distance from her subject matter (her self-image), her portraits (plates 8–15) impart a profound impression of clarity. They intimate a state of mindfulness that is integral to her practice and the discipline it requires, as well as what Buddhist monk and activist Thich Nhat Hanh would describe as "noble silence," a theme echoed in Coffey's painting *Video et Tacio* ("I see and remain silent"; plate 14).[27] Although bathed in the light of the external world, Coffey's portraits also seem to be figuratively illuminated from within by an internal state of tranquility, bestowing them with a sense of physical and psychical equipoise. This balance gives Coffey's self-portraits a sense of the self that is independent of selfhood, suggesting a disassociation of mind and body. Her *self* portraits suggest the reflexive practice of self-love described by bell hooks as "the work that love demands [. . .] a place of critical awakening and pain [. . .] a participatory emotion" in which tension between the self and selflessness becomes a generative force.[28]

The practice of self-reflection is quite literal in Wangechi Mutu's *Sisters* (plate 50), which consists of two bronze heads lying on their sides upon a mirrored tabletop. Each face is unique, but both heads are crowned with intricate braids that declare their shared African ancestry. Placed facing toward each other, they peer into their own reflections. Their adjacency suggests Black kinship as a source of power and knowledge. Their closed eyes and recumbent positions indicate the possibility of a shared dream, or a state of becoming yet to be achieved—a possibility intimated by their dual reflections, which simultaneously imply the interior and the exterior. The double redoubling of self through the reflections in the mirror suggests a profound meditation on sisterhood among women of the African diaspora.

Like truth, freedom is believed to be an essential condition for love to thrive. Truth and freedom comprise the fabric of Dr. Martin Luther King Jr.'s "inescapable network of mutuality tied in a single garment of destiny."[29] Thomas Merton wrote that freedom is not fully free until "it is brought into the right relation with the freedom of another," and the same could be said of equality and justice.[30] This idea echoes a central theme in Jeffrey Gibson's work, which relates themes of freedom and social justice to liberation movements associated with Indigenous rights and the LGBTQIA+ community. Of Cherokee heritage and a citizen of the Mississippi Band of Choctaw Indians, Gibson chooses materials such as glass beads and metal jingles that reflect traditional powwow regalia while also drawing on the aesthetics of queer culture. His work often includes popular song lyrics related to issues of social justice and freedom to raise political and collective awareness of social movements, past and present. The title of Gibson's *The Love You Give Is the Love You Get* (plate 24) refers to John Lennon's misquotation in a 1980 *Playboy* interview of Paul McCartney's lyric, "The love you take is equal to the love you make." Lennon's version was made into a clothing patch that Gibson owns in his personal collection of ephemera related to social movements. The motto, embellished on the side of an Everlast brand punching bag, suggests that love is a form of conditioning that requires practice and discipline and is contingent upon reciprocity, necessarily casting uncertainty upon the notion of "unconditional love."

Inspired by the ritual practices and customs of the Lucumí and Yoruba in her native Cuba, María de los Angeles Rodríguez Jiménez has focused on "questions pertaining to the body as a temporal vessel" and to the spiritual as it is observed and represented in material culture. In her own practice, Jiménez both acknowledges and questions the beliefs of Catholicism and her Afro-Cuban ancestors. *Caridad (Charity)* (plate 31) is a sculptural installation composed of fleshy satin stretched over a frame of industrial fencing materials. It is the outcome of a performance by the artist while completing her postgraduate work at Yale in 2018 (fig. 8 and plate 32). In video documentation of that performance, she kneels on a concrete floor

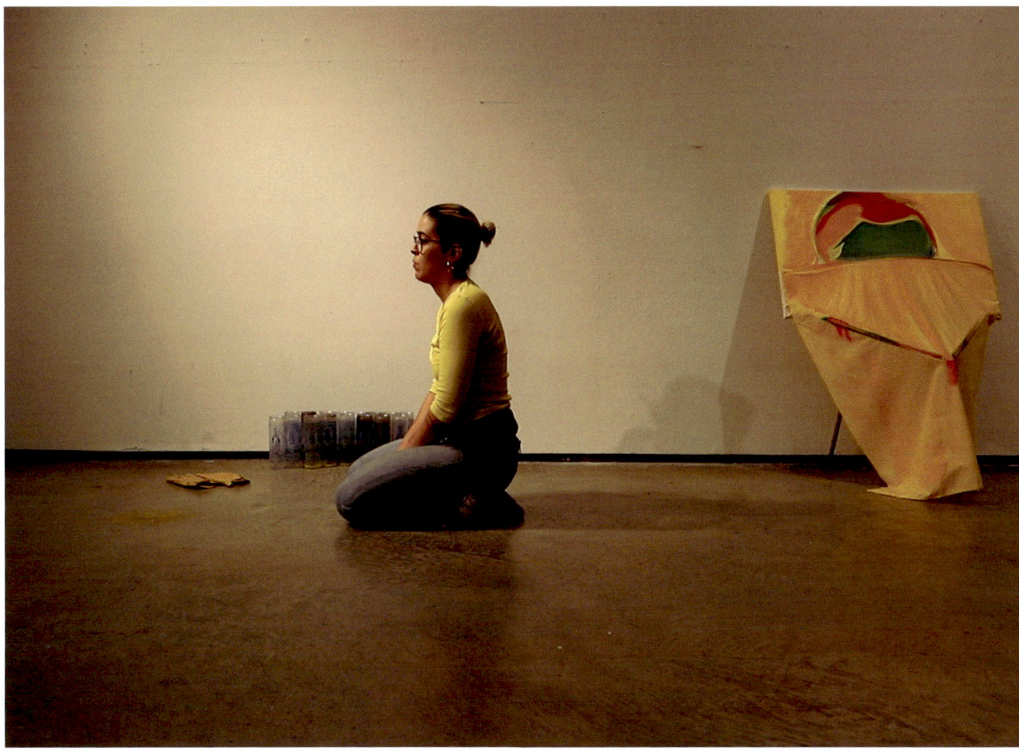

Figure 8.
María de los Angeles Rodríguez Jiménez (Cuban, born Holguín, Cuba, 1992; active Miami, Florida), *Glass, Yale University, December 14, 2018* (detail), 2018, single-channel video, running time: 3 minutes, 34 seconds, courtesy of the artist and David Castillo.

as if in prayer or supplication. With nothing but her hands, she violently shatters a collection of glass votive jars depicting "Nuestra Señora de la Caridad del Cobre" (Our Lady of Charity), the patron saint of Cuba and a quintessential symbol of Cuban identity representing hope and salvation. Some of the residual shards of glass Jiménez subsequently incorporated into *Caridad* form a heavy sag near the center of the work that evokes a pregnant belly. Jiménez's allusion to the syncretic spiritual practices of Cuba imparts the work with a feeling of the sacred, as if its swollen form represents the promise of a virgin birth, while the shards of glass beneath it call into question the efficacy of either spiritual or socially engaged practice, or such Christian theological virtues as charity.

Ebony G. Patterson's *. . . they stood in a time of unknowing . . . for those who bear/ bare witness* (plate 52) addresses the absence of such virtues as charity in postcolonial societies shaped by economic globalization in which groups of people are rendered invisible through race-based class and social divisions. Her tapestry features a garden setting in which a group of figures crowds around a partially concealed body. While some figures are clearly visible, others are presented as silhouettes, suggesting their absence. Their spectral quality suggests spirits bearing witness to the discovery before them. Patterson's work commemorates the lives of the invisible in society, including those who have fallen victim to political violence and hate crimes. She bestows dignity upon the dead and honors their lives through a visual elegy of resplendent decorative materials she describes as a "neo-baroque" lavishing of color, texture, and materials. As a place where ephemeral loveliness is cultivated and nourished, then fades away in a cycle of life, death, and regeneration, a garden can offer beauty, dignity, spirituality, and release for the community of the dead and their kinfolk—the living made invisible in society. The artist has described gardens as "an amalgamation or collection of ecologies that are living together, but the[ir] sustainability depends on what plants are put next to each other and how well they thrive together, what things may eat each other or not. In many ways, I am kind of thinking about how a postcolonial space kind of mirrors a garden in that way."[31] Patterson's *. . . they stood in a time of unknowing . . .* invokes the practice of bearing witness and empowering the love of community to reclaim space, visibility, and agency for the disenfranchised.

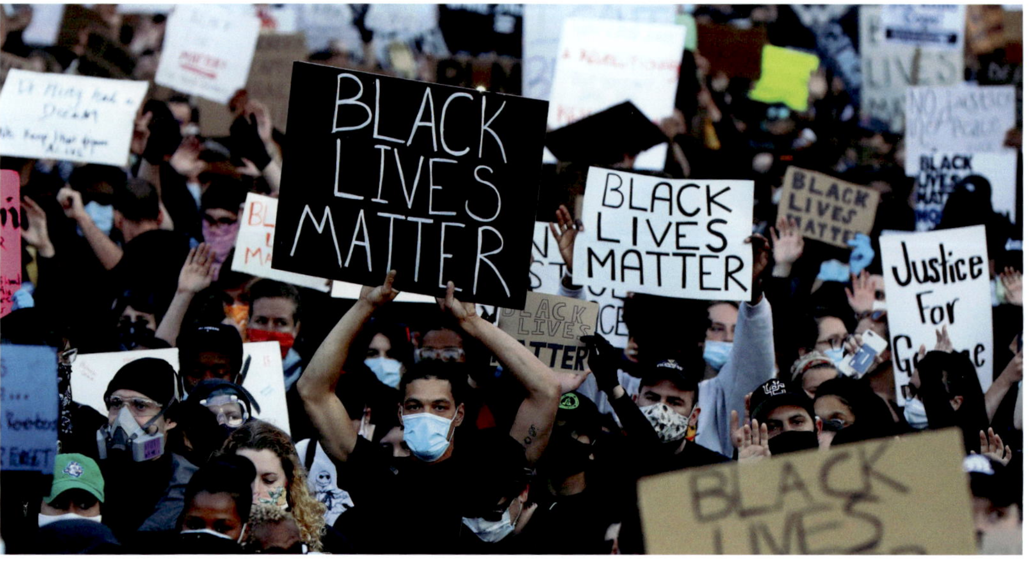

Figure 9.
Demonstrators protest in response to the recent death of George Floyd on May 31, 2020, in Boston, Massachusetts. Photo by Maddie Meyer/Getty Images.

Loving Community

It is common to refer to community in terms of friendship. For some, the bonds between friends and community are stronger than the bonds of family. In *The Nicomachean Ethics*, Aristotle posits that all kinds of love exist in community. Although he draws distinctions between love that exists by "a kind of agreement" and love that is "kindred and comradely," both are influenced by feelings of goodwill.[32] In the absence of goodwill, collectivity gives rise to authoritarianism, religious fundamentalism, and forms of organized prejudice that adulterate love, using it to polarize people based on their differences and redirecting feelings of love from collective altruism to tribal veneration dominated by figures of central authority. However, when something held in common is shared through networks defined by mutuality and loving practice, the exercise might be described as a politics of love. In loving communities, people live in a web of relationships and responsibilities to themselves, their family, others in their community, and ultimately to some notion of truth that guides them in their collective action on behalf of the "noble" and the "good." When Alicia Garza, Patrisse Cullors, and Opal Tometi cofounded Black Lives Matter in 2013 after the acquittal of George Zimmerman in the killing of Trayvon Martin, it became the most influential and far-reaching social movement of a generation "fueled by love: a love for Black life, Black joy, and a vision for the world in which we collectively love on Black communities."[33] Before, during, and since the nationwide protests in the summer of 2020 (fig. 9), a vast network of local, community-based BLM chapters organized to apply this loving practice through collective action, calling for the dismantling of systemic racism and for conversations about justice and injustice, freedom and incarceration, and equality and inequality centered on Black lives.

Rashid Johnson's *The Hikers* (plate 33) opens with a montage that features a compressed frame, frenetic pacing, and double exposures, representing a world in which Black mobility and expression are limited and prescribed by racist structures that reinforce the subjection of Black bodies in the public sphere. The film's prelude features two dancers from the Martha Graham Dance Company who wear masks based on Johnson's *Anxious Men* series (fig. 10) and whose movements and gestures coincide with fast-paced rhythmic drumming.[34] The narrative arc of the film, accom-

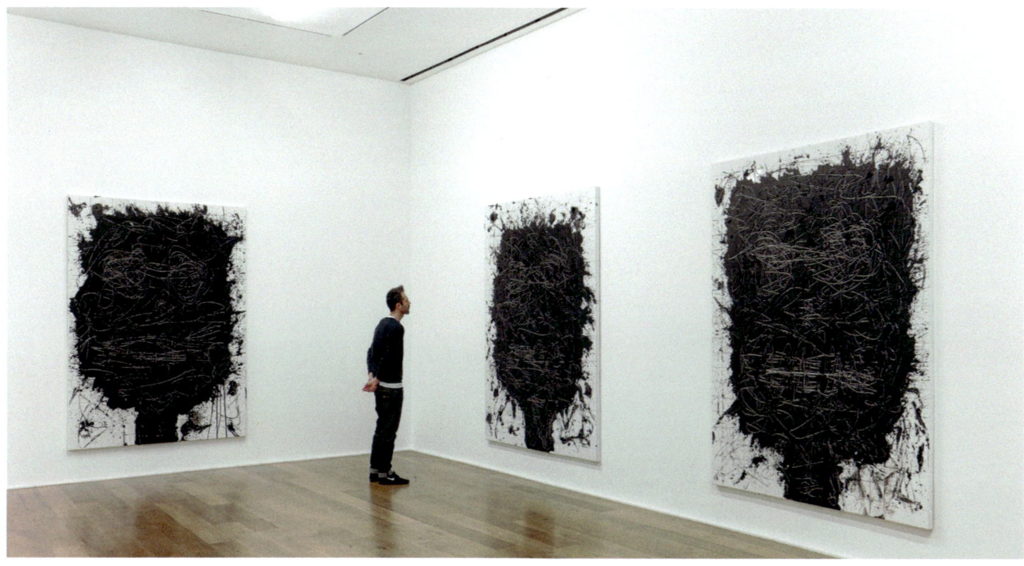

Figure 10.
Installation view of *Rashid Johnson: Smile* at Hauser & Wirth, London, 2015. Photo by Alex Delfanne.

panied by a piano étude, begins as two men wearing disguises approach one another on a wilderness trail, one ascending and the other descending. From a distance, they engage in a tense, silent colloquy of movements.[35] Ranging from expressions of apprehension, defensiveness, and wariness to balletic flourishes, their movements convey bluster and grace, awkwardness and physical agility. When they meet face to face, they remove their masks and perform a pas de deux in which their tension, representing the threat and danger of anti-Black racism, melts away in relief as they take comfort in their mutual Blackness. Johnson says this moment in the film represents instances when "people of color recognize the existence of one another. Oftentimes, when people see each other in such circumstances, there's this kind of joy, almost love."[36] The encounter of Johnson's hikers recalls Dr. Martin Luther King Jr.'s explanation of the parable of the Good Samaritan on the road from Jerusalem to Jericho, recounted in *Strength to Love*. The story, King wrote, illustrates that "love is mankind's most potent weapon for personal and social transformation. [. . .] In the final analysis I must not ignore the wounded man on life's Jericho Road, because he is a part of me and I am a part of him. His agony diminishes me, and his salvation enlarges me."[37]

Tomashi Jackson's research-based work of the past several years (see plates 27–30) has been inspired by the signing of the 1965 Voting Rights Act, a landmark piece of legislation prohibiting racial discrimination in the American electoral system that inexorably continues to be challenged. Jackson juxtaposes vintage images of individuals who fought against racial injustice with images and text from the recent past to cast light upon ongoing attempts to undermine the voting rights of all Americans of color. Jackson's work is built up in layers using transparencies on top of opaque, painted images and text, suggesting a compression of time in which progress and setbacks, truth and distortion, history and revisionism are relative and in flux. Several prominent Georgians, including the Reverend Ralph David Abernathy, Dr. Martin Luther King Jr., John Lewis, and Stacey Abrams, are featured in this body of work tracing the decades-long arc of the struggle for equality. These figures represent the community that fought through the years to uphold the rights of Black Americans as certain individuals in power assiduously sought to undo them. Jackson's project honors and commemorates the collective action of King's Beloved Community in the face of extreme prejudice, intimidation, and physical violence while drawing parallels with the present-day struggle for racial justice and questions pertaining to the efficacy of a politics of love.

The present is haunted by the past in Kerry James Marshall's iconic *Souvenir* series (fig. 11). In *Souvenir I* (plate 37), the fallen heroes of Martin Luther King Jr.'s Freedom Movement are memorialized and immortalized. The painting includes a commemorative banner featuring images of King, John F. Kennedy, and Robert F. Kennedy. Produced in the months following King's assassination, the banner was commonly found in the homes and businesses of Black Americans. Along the top of the painting, in the form of angelic spirits painted in pale hues of white, pink, and blue, are images of civil rights activist Medgar Evers; Malcolm X; Black Panther activists Fred Hampton and Mark Clark; Freedom Riders Andrew Goodman, James Chaney, and Michael Schwerner; and the four children murdered in the 16th Street Baptist Church bombing, Addie Mae Collins, Carol Denise McNair, Carole Rosamond Robertson, and Cynthia Dionne Wesley. Its brightly lit, domestic interior depicts a

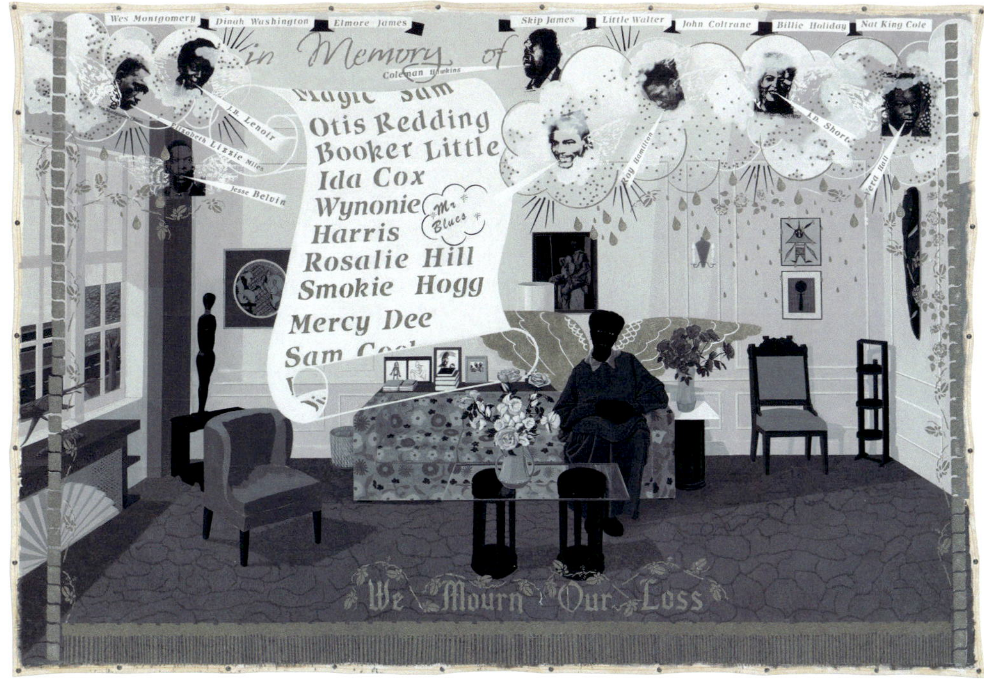

Figure 11.
Kerry James Marshall (American, born Birmingham, Alabama, 1955; active Chicago, Illinois), *Souvenir IV*, 1998, acrylic, glitter, and screenprint on paper on tarpaulin, with metal grommets, Whitney Museum of American Art, New York, purchase with funds from the Painting and Sculpture Committee. © Kerry James Marshall, courtesy of Jack Shainman Gallery, New York.

middle-class Black home representing both a graceful and welcoming living room and a portal to a timeless dimension. A clear, diffused light brings every corner of the room into focus, including a knick-knack cabinet in the left corner, neatly folded draperies against the windows, and a flower arrangement in the center of a marble-top table. In its compression of past and present, the painting creates a space in which the remembrance of the struggle for equality gives way to a reflection on the present-day realities of continued racial injustice. The painting's central figure stands as matron of the household, the embodiment of an enlightened witness and a messenger of the divine. She peers out directly as if to welcome one into the picture or to ask, "Where do you position yourself within this history, within this struggle?"

Because the effort and commitment required to achieve good for community is analogous to the essential work that love requires, that effort takes on the characteristics of a loving practice described by bell hooks in *all about love*: care, commitment, trust, responsibility, respect, and knowledge.[38] The love ethic that these qualities describe is the basis for Alanna Fields's research into vintage vernacular photography documenting Black queer expression from the 1920s to the 1980s. In *Our Love Was Deeply Purple* (plate 19) from the series *Constellations*, Fields presents incisive passages from stories suggested by images that were originally shared only among a trusted community of friends. Through a process of fragmentation, repetition, and the veiling of details with translucent color, she presents and reimagines the lives of people she never met to create a history of community. She focuses on the subtle shifts and gestures that conceal and reveal the queerness of her subjects, underscoring the private quality of images originally intended for the queer eye to which certain gestures and glances are obvious and familiar. *Our Love Was Deeply Purple* alludes to Alice Walker's *The Color Purple*. For Fields, "This work points to and identifies queer women and queer love as the personification of the color

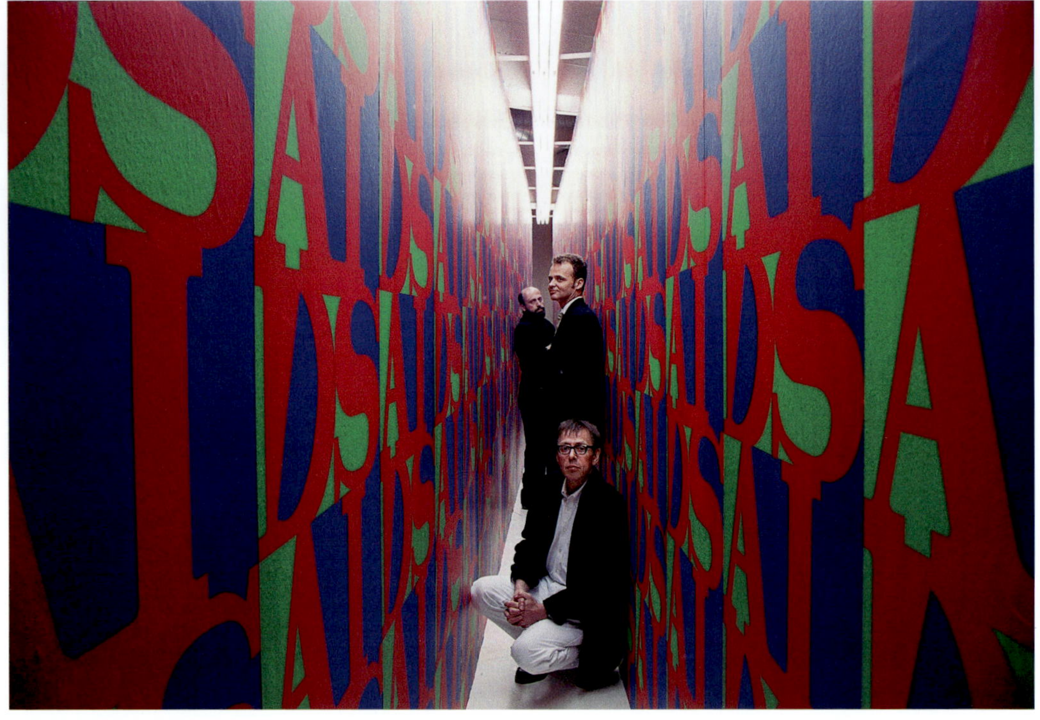

purple, ever-present but historically unseen [. . .]. I'm thinking about the refusal to acknowledge amorous love between women as being in opposition to god, spirit, higher power. [. . .] As the violet wax washes over the frames, it accentuates and illuminates rather than hides, forcing us to see deeply into each frame's depiction of love, protection, and intimacy between black queer women."[39]

Gerald Lovell is a Georgia-based artist whose subjects include members of his community of friends and family. The realism of Lovell's work (see plates 34–35) results both from its basis in photographs he has taken and from the ease of his subjects who are enjoying downtime together in relaxed social environments. The bond of trust they share with each other and with the artist has enabled them to let down their guard and project a sense of affection for one another devoid of any affectation or self-interest. They are pictured in the moment, enjoying one another's companionship. The artist's cohort, perhaps more keenly than earlier generations, feels the pressures of financial insecurity, social and political strife, and environmental uncertainty. In a world where the deck seems stacked against them, they coalesce around each other in peace, camaraderie, and friendship made palpably real by Lovell's technique, which uses impasto to suggest the soft, vulnerable substance of the flesh and blood that binds them together.

General Idea, formed in 1969 by AA Bronson, Felix Partz, and Jorge Zontal, was among the first voices to explore and inhabit media critique and queer theory. Most of General Idea's work from 1987 through the early 1990s addressed the AIDS crisis, which ultimately claimed the lives of Partz and Zontal (fig. 12). Bronson described the impact of community in the early 1990s when Partz and Zontal were dying:

On a personal level, I was forced to acknowledge my love, a love that would have been shameful a few years before. And I think this was true of gay men in general. Because of AIDS, they learned how to love or learned how to be more open about their loving. Before that, it was all about sex and being hot. Suddenly people were dying, and this awareness of who and how you loved came to the surface. I remember the feeling of love permeating the AIDS ward the first time I went into St. Vincent's. There were a lot of people hanging out there, helping. The nurses were really understaffed, and they had no money in that ward. So, all the people in the neighborhood were helping out. It was unlike anything I'd ever experienced before. And when we moved back to Toronto, in late 1993, it was the first time in my life that I was able to fully receive love.[40]

In 1987, General Idea produced a design that conflated Robert Indiana's famous "Love" image with the acronym AIDS. In an allusion to the poetry of William S. Burroughs, they called this new form an "image virus"—something that, once introduced into the public sphere, replicates itself through cultural transmission. Described by General Idea as a logo for an advertising campaign, the image brought attention to feelings of love between gay men at the height of the AIDS pandemic and generated ambiguity in society's relationship with HIV/AIDS. In *Great AIDS (Cadmium Orange Light)* and *Great AIDS (Pyrrole Orange)* (plates 22–23) created by the collective in 1990 and executed posthumously by Bronson in 2019, the AIDS logo is twice mirrored and inverted, suggesting forms of viral mutation as well as the logo's potentially transgressive illegibility and subliminality.

The Poetics of Love

Love dwells at home in poetry and art. Since ancient times, it has been expressed, invoked, evoked, and put to the test in love poetry, love songs, love letters, and slow dances. Diane Ackerman traces the history of the love poem from Ancient Egypt and Sumeria to the biblical Song of Solomon to contemporary love poetry and in themes such as the transformational power of love and the idealization of the beloved.[41] The connection between poetry and art extends as far back as Horace's "Ars Poetica."[42] It is famously illustrated in *Hypnerotomachia Poliphili*, the fifteenth-century romance on the theme of courtly love, and has been a persistent feature of conceptual and text-based contemporary art since the 1960s. For many of the artists in the exhibition, language is an integral part of their practice (fig. 13), evoking in a poetic way the roots, associations, and evocations of words, from Rina Banerjee's dreamy titles to James Drake's poetry written specifically for *Tongue-Cut Sparrows* (see plates 16–17) and Ghada Amer's specific use of Arabic language in *The Words I Love the Most* (plate 1). Love letters—often, and at best, a subset of poetic endeavors—were a recurring subject for Felix Gonzalez-Torres between 1988 and 1992. In 1988, he sent a letter to his lover, Ross Laycock, that includes a drawing that evokes the work *"Untitled" (Perfect Lovers)* (fig. 14; plate 25):

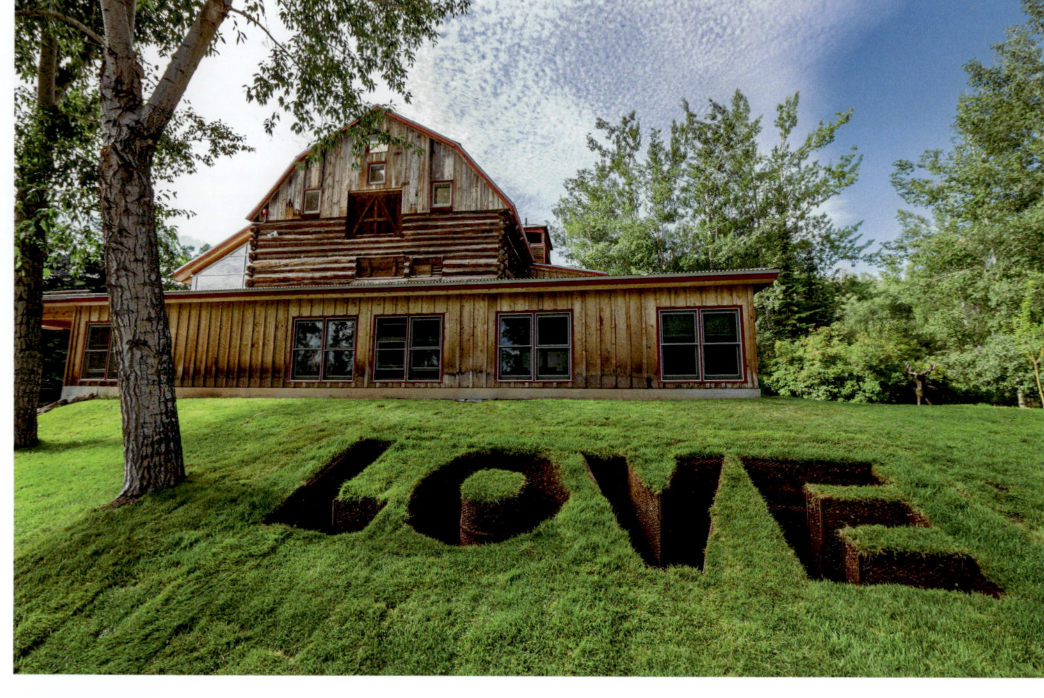

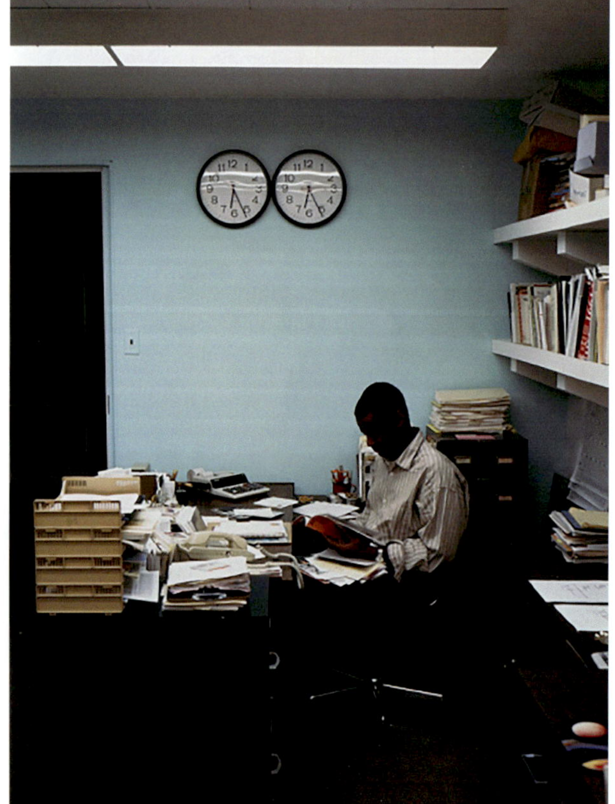

Don't be afraid of the clocks, they are our
time, time has been so generous to us.
We imprinted time with the sweet taste of
victory. We conquered fate by meeting at
a certain TIME in a certain space. We are
a product of the time, therefore, we give
back credit were [*sic*] it is due:
time.
We are synchronized now, and forever.
I love you.[43]

In poetry and in visual art, the heart is a universal metaphor for
love. The use of the heart to represent love originated in the poetry
and music of the Middle Ages. In art, early depictions outside of
anatomical studies cleaved more closely to the pinecone-shaped
organ than to the emblematic stylized heart shape. This adherence
to depicting the biological heart is founded in medieval physiology,
which locates the heart as the root of all functions powered by the
spirit.[44] In his recent body of work based on the pioneering endeavors of nineteenth-century physiologists who invented the field of
cardiology, Dario Robleto argues that the biological organ is a
subject rich with symbolic and poetic significance. In the 1850s, the
German physiologist Karl Vierordt made pulse-wave recordings that
captured the rhythm of the pulse and heartbeat in various physical
states of disease. Produced nearly a half century before the invention of electro-
cardiology, the recordings used a single human hair as a stylus upon a surface
coated with soot from a candle. This process translated the ephemeral and almost
imperceptible movements of the pulse (and later, the heartbeat) into abstract, wave-

form images. This medical-visual breakthrough—imaging the once invisible interior movements of the ephemeral heart—would initiate the era of the physiological study of emotional states. Robleto's *Love, Before There Was Love* (plate 60) features two brass-plated stainless-steel casts taken from the actual rendering of scientist Paul Lorain's 1870 recordings, depicting their graphic trace of the pulse in three dimensions. The work embodies the behavior of the human heart while its owner was falling in love, recovering and preserving for posterity the event of love as it was physically experienced almost two hundred years ago.

Love poetry was co-opted as a means of communication between loved ones inside and outside of the penal system in James Drake's *Tongue-Cut Sparrows (Inside and Out)* (plate 16). Drake's video and related drawing (plate 17) are part of a project the artist conceived while observing the silent communication between incarcerated men and their partners on the outside in El Paso, Texas. To get around the bureaucracy of in-person visits, the prisoners' loved ones gathered every day outside the El Paso jail and communicated using a sign language they had invented with their hands and arms (plate 17). Drake worked with three of the women, Gabriella, Angie, and Liz, to include lines of poetry in their daily unspoken conversations, offering them Shakespearean sonnets and poems by Jorge Borges, Federico Lorca, Benjamin Sáenz, Cormac McCarthy, and Antonio Machado. He documented their conversations in a video, from which he also produced a series of charcoal drawings depicting the signs used to convey their silent love messages. As curator and art historian Rob Storr observed in his text for the fifty-second Venice Biennale (2007), lyricism in Drake's project "infiltrated a brutal penal system and intimacy crossed frontiers, penetrated walls, and passed behind bars."[45]

The language of love is also the subject of Ghada Amer's *The Words I Love the Most* (plate 1), a hollow sphere made of a bronze latticework formed by one hundred interlinking Arabic expressions related to the word *love*. Understanding that words expressed in calligraphy are themselves a subject of art in Arabic culture, Amer transformed the words into objects whose interconnectedness suggests the fluidity and poetics of language. Paradoxically, they are spelled backwards from the perspective of the viewer and can only be read from inside the sculpture or by using a mirror. As such, the words resist easy comprehension, inviting the viewer to find meaning beyond their literal references. This work recalls the theories that love is privileged over more ordinary forms of communication and that its expression through language is impossible.[46] Even as it speaks to the poetic nature of love and offers a myriad of ways to express it, this sculpture also critiques contemporary Arabic culture and takes on derogatory Islamophobic stereotypes. In the years since the artist spent her childhood in Egypt, the Arab world has become more socially and religiously conservative, intensifying the allusion made by the indecipherability of the words to the cultural taboo placed on desire.

In ancient poetry, love and desire are often embodied by mythological deities. Wangechi Mutu based her sculpture *Water Woman* (plate 51) on one such divine being, a half human, half sea creature called *nguva* in East African mythology. Akin to the mermaids, selkies, and sirens of Western mythology and folklore, the nguva is described in African myth as a dangerous temptress. However, Mutu depicts her as the protagonist of a postcolonial love story. In *Water Woman*, the nguva's contemplative, reflective, and melancholic bearing, as if she is encumbered by a world-weariness, belie her notoriety as a seductress. Having retrieved the nguva from the realm of East African myth, Mutu seems to have burdened her with a knowledge of real-world events, such as the history of the transatlantic slave trade, the colonization of Africa, and the shadows these histories have cast upon the present.

Rina Banerjee's *Take me, take me, take me . . . to the Palace of love* (plate 2) forms a poetic nexus for the intersection of ephemeral and eternal love. Made of red cellophane and found objects, the work is a radically scaled-down simulation of India's famous "monument to love," the Taj Mahal, built by the seventeenth-century Mughal emperor Shah Jahan as a tomb for his wife Mumtaz Mahal. In choosing red, Banerjee challenges the Victorian-era use of white to symbolize innocence, purity, sacrifice, and virtue. Although red alternately signifies danger and sexual passion in Western cultures—the codification of a Victorian notion of the danger of pleasure—it has religious connotations in Latin American cultures and symbolizes good fortune and happiness in China. In India, red is associated with purity, and in Hindu religion and culture, it is used on auspicious occasions such as marriage or childbirth and suggests innocence and purity, as well as sensuality. For her red, diaphanous version of the temple to temporal and eternal love, Banerjee dispenses with the colonial-era social mores still imposed in the present day and relishes in the resplendent mate-riality of red-tinted cellophane, which might elicit any manner of emotion, including but not limited to passion, piety, euphoria, or love. Within the center of the palace are suspended a combination of objects including an antique, Anglo-Indian Bombay black wood armchair with a seat of red-colored moss crowned with a latticework moss dome. Arranged inside the space of the chair is an accumulation of red-colored spheres that echo the shape of an antique globe on the floor. The sensory nature of Banerjee's choice of materials is evocative, akin to imagistic poetry, manifesting in the senses something incorporeal, like the presence of a sentient being with an abundant capacity for feeling. The weightlessness of the suspended objects suggests both the mindfulness of contemplation and the exhilaration of ecstasy, the limitations of corporeality and the boundlessness of the spirit. For visitors to the "palace of love," the seemingly self-perpetuating biomorphic form of the red spheres becomes an iconic object of veneration and meditation. In the context of Jahan's monument to his dead wife, Banerjee's palace evokes the final line of Victorian-era poet and women's rights activist Elizabeth Barrett Browning's archetypal love poem, Sonnet 43, "How Do I Love Thee?": "I shall but love thee better after death."[47]

In Michelle Stuart's *In the Beginning: Time and Dark Matter* (plate 63), eighty-eight photographs presented in a grid portray images of astronomical bodies alongside images of aquatic animals, correlating the mysteries of the universe with the watery expanse of the oceans. These images from the artist's archive of analog and digital photography are presented together with a physical collection of shells and fossils, illustrating the relativity of time and offering radical shifts in scale from the finite measure of earthly matter to the limitless expanse of the cosmos. Stuart's uncon-ventional juxtaposition of photography and paleontological remains proposes a new visual language for reflecting upon such weighty subjects as the origin and compo-sition of the universe and its impact on earthbound phenomena such as tidal forces and the creatures that experience them. In the process, she preserves and privileges the mysteries and contingencies inherent in poetic expression.

Love Supreme[48]

Dr. Martin Luther King Jr. called love's place in the sacred "the love of God operating in the human heart."[49] Supreme love, or *agape*, describes one's love for God and the love that God in return manifests in the natural world and in the order of the universe.[50] In his "mystical ecology," Thomas Merton posited that with God's presence in nature, "all meaning is absorbed in one central tonic note, unheard, unuttered." In his renunciation of materiality and in the silence of his hermitage, Merton sought to find true love in nature.[51] He wrote about the fulfillment experienced when one's internal life is brought into harmony with nature through God as a "sacred tone" in which all meaning and reality is gathered into an experience of divine love. In his search for equilibrium with the natural world, Merton described the mystical dimensions of faith expressed in nature as an "ontology of nothingness" in which "love is the epiphany of God in our poverty" experienced outside of the isolation imposed by the empirical self.[52] In the eighteenth century, philosophers such as Edmund Burke and Immanuel Kant put forward theories of the sublime, expressing humankind's smallness in relation to nature in seminal texts. They sought to describe a quality of unbound, unlimited grandeur in the natural world and a presentiment that humankind and nature have a common creative force that is vast and unspeakable.

Living in Guatemala for more than thirty years, Argentinian-born artist Vivian Suter has taken a more literal approach to being in nature through her painting practice. In fact, she invites nature to participate in the creative process. Suter lives and works in Panajachel, a town located in the volcanic basin of Lake Atitlán in southwestern Guatemala. Her home and studio are situated in the rainforest on what was once a coffee plantation, now a verdant garden. There she often paints outside using trees as props and including organic substances and elements such as mud, rainwater, mold, and fish glue among her materials. At times, heavy rain might interrupt her work, altering paintings with water, mud, and algae. Other times, she may bury her canvases in the earth, allowing the soil and the life it supports to make their own contributions. Her collaboration with nature does not end when a work is finished but continues through its presentation (see plate 64). She often displays her paintings in her garden, subjecting them to the elements. It is a collaborative accord with nature that embodies a kind of love that Merton described as "perfect in proportion to its freedom. It is free in proportion to its purity."[53]

Similarly, Magnus Plessen's work is mediated by a "belief that the world is shaped by forces which are so often not represented or representable in text and image."[54] While Robleto connects the emotional with the physical inside the microcosm of the human heart in *Love, Before There Was Love* (plate 60), Plessen is much more expansive, associating love with atomic elements that comprise all matter and that trace back to the origins of the universe. In his series *Hoffnung, Liebe, Helium (Hope, Love, Helium)* (see plates 54–58), Plessen approaches love as something that resists objectification, and thus possession, and is subject to limitless permutation. His paintings appear to be in a state of continual development as his depictions of the human body and plant matter shift in and out of focus, captured in states of becoming—states that suggest the formation of chemical compounds through the association of atoms, or the process of dissociation in chemistry whereby molecules irreversibly split into new forms. The ever-changing biological structures of visible living organisms are drawn into analogy with the practically invisible atomic and quantum worlds in which physical laws do not apply. By focusing on "multi-morphological situations rather than multi-morphological objects," Plessen brings concepts such as hope and love into relation with the mystery of being.[55] His work insinuates that the figurative idiom of love as a result of "stardust" in one's eyes actually expresses the elemental composition of humankind.

Mexican artist Gabriel Rico's murals are imaginary propositions that suggest a process for understanding, or a beginning to understanding, the deep mystery of the origin of being. They imagine the possibility of a higher-level consciousness beyond the limitations of the physical and material. In *VI Mural from the series Reducción objetiva orquestada* (plate 59), Rico arranges objects on a wall and connects them with drawings that intimate mathematical equations and formulae, suggesting they are related on a plane that is beyond our understanding. In his "orchestrated reduction of objects," Rico imagines an infinity of variables, tested and measured in fantastical experiments that represent a quasi-epistemology in which the assumed value of objects, both machine made and natural, is open to infinite interpretation.

Inspired by her upbringing in the Dutch Calvinist Church, as well as her travels in the American Southwest and her study of Diné (Navajo) weaving traditions, Jana Vander-Lee employs abstraction in her fiber practice to express the dimensions of love radiating from a spiritual life in which "we earn our stripes by reaching out, energized by core values of wisdom and love, being/existing in truth." In commenting on her tapestry titled *Truthfully* (plate 65), she describes the benevolent power of love to empower self-care and transcendent wisdom.[56] *Enlightened Ones* (plate 67) suggests the power of enduring love in the pursuit of wisdom or truth. Through her study and practice of various fiber arts traditions, Vander-Lee has kept them alive and has continued the work of women pioneers such as Anni Albers, Claire Zeisler, and Lenore Tawney to champion fiber art as a valid mode of artistic expression in the United States, bridging the divide between art and craft. Vander-Lee summons forms of abstraction across cultures, from early European modernism and Indigenous American sources, to convey the power of the human spirit. Her woven compositions are reflections on abstract ideas such as the theological virtues of faith, hope, and charity, inspired by the faith of her Christian upbringing and the spirituality of native peoples, and on varieties of love from the sacrificial to the altruistic to the nurturing and devotional.

Paul Pfeiffer's *John 3:16* (plate 53) is a hybrid sculpture/video that plays on a screen that is slightly larger than that of a large mobile phone or a small tablet and extends three feet from the wall seven feet high.[57] At the center of the screen is a continuous loop of a spinning basketball suspended in air, shown against the blurred image of fans in an arena. Players' hands hover around the rotating ball as if engaged in an act of divination. Pfeiffer is known for using televised sports footage to reflect upon Debord's "The Society of the Spectacle," which contends that in today's culture, experiences such as sporting events and religion that are presumed to unify people actually serve to estrange them.[58] *John 3:16* was made at a time when it was not uncommon to spot spectators engaging in what they considered to be evangelism by holding aloft placards containing this scriptural citation for the benefit of television cameras (fig. 15). The reference is to a biblical passage explaining that God's love for humanity made redemption possible through Jesus's crucifixion. However, Pfeiffer

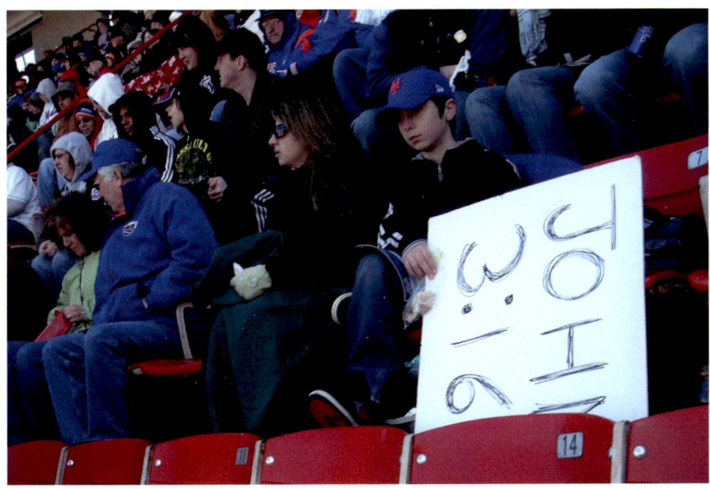

Figure 15.
John 3:16 proselytizer.
Photo: Skyco via Flickr.

questions whether such deeper meaning can be conveyed in a context where "love can be juxtaposed with almost any image or product to make a compelling visual statement because what you are really looking at, really affected by, is nothing more than the spectacle."[59]

In Rafael Lozano-Hemmer's multisensory *Pulse Room* (fig. 16; plate 36), one hundred incandescent light bulbs are hung from the ceiling in an even grid and flicker in rhythm with the heartbeats of past visitors to the exhibition. Visitors are invited to register their pulse on a sensor in the room. Each person's biometric data is transmitted to a nearby light bulb, causing its visible wire filament to glow and flicker in a rhythm unique to that participant's pulse. As successive visitors participate, the record of prior heartbeats is pushed farther and farther across the grid, projecting an image of collective humanity that is at once anonymous and communal. This visualization of a random gathering of heartbeats in a public space conjures Thomas Merton's famous epiphany on March 18, 1958, in Louisville, Kentucky, at the intersection of 4th and Walnut streets: all the people bustling about the inter-section were strangers to him, but he was struck by a realization that he loved them all "as if I suddenly saw the secret beauty of their hearts, the depth of their hearts [. . .] these billion points of light coming together in the face and blaze of a sun that would make all the darkness and cruelty of life vanish completely."[60] However, media scholar Kriss Ravetto-Biagioli argues that Lozano-Hemmer "does not claim to liberate the consumer-citizen from social controls in some endless free-floating modulation, but reminds us instead of the visible and invisible architectures that are already in place around us."[61] In addition to bringing people into relation with one another, Lozano-Hemmer's work also connects them to ubiquitous forms of information technology that conspire with networks around which identities are formed, societies are structured, and people are controlled.

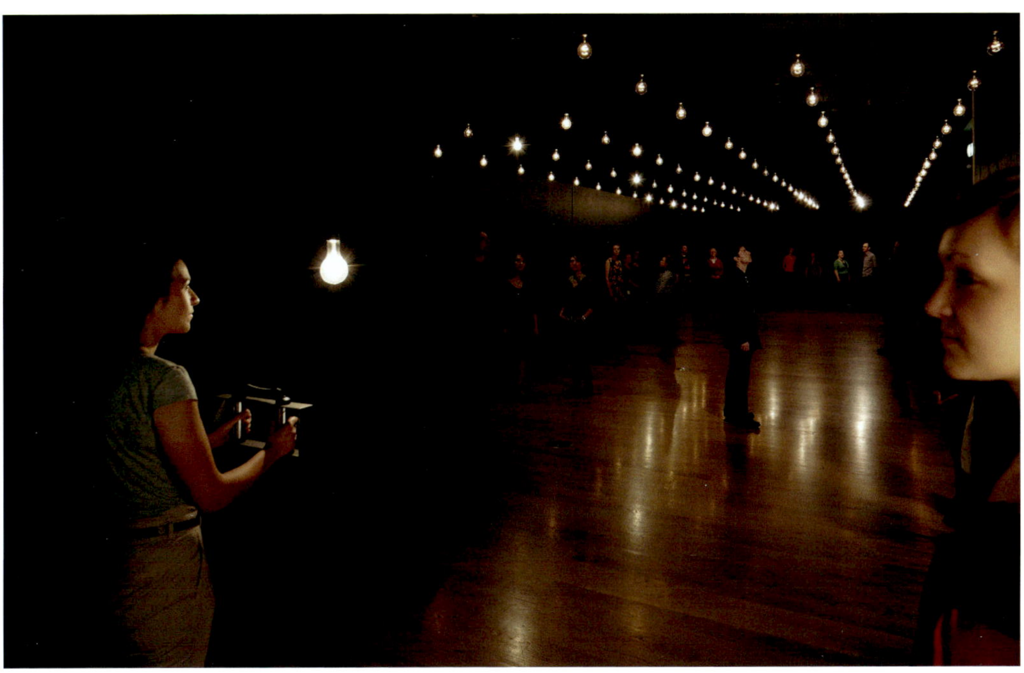

Figure 16.
Rafael Lozano-Hemmer (Mexican, born Mexico City, Mexico, 1967; active Montréal, Canada), *Pulse Room*, 2006, installed at Manchester Art Gallery, Manchester, United Kingdom, in 2010. © 2022 Artists Rights Society (ARS), New York/VEGAP, Madrid. Photo by Peter Mallet/courtesy of Recherche Antimodular/Antimodular Research.

Conclusion

The German word *Entwicklungsmöglichkeit* describes the possibility or capacity of something such as an idea to be developed. The implication is that its potential to unfold is not based in logic or history but is poetic in nature. The subject of love has an inexhaustible capacity for development in every arena of human endeavor, especially in the field of art, as demonstrated in the history of poetry alone. In the dearth of persuasive synonyms that capture the full meaning of love, *art* perhaps comes nearest. Like love, art can be described by Badiou's concept of a "truth procedure," in which an investigative process leads to certain truths that are described through new or invented languages. Both art and love are included in the philosopher's fields of activity in which truth unfolds through practice and struggle.

In this exhibition, acknowledgment of philosophical discourse is unavoidable—Badiou's narrative of love as an "existential project" is but one example. However, it sets the stage for the encounter of two people, which is an essential point of departure for the exhibition. Popular notions of romantic love are poles apart from the deeper consideration of love's mysterious ineffability, but both have guided the shape of the exhibition as it considers the scope of love, from its most intimate expression, through its role in the mobilizing of community and grassroots activism to effect social and political change, to the sense that at its most profound it extends beyond understanding.

Perhaps the most powerful contemporary expression of love is its practice in community. Bracketing this portion of *What Is Left Unspoken* are watershed periods of collective trauma that brought communities together on an unprecedented scale: the onset of the AIDS pandemic in the early 1980s and the persistent anti-Black violence that gave rise to the Black Lives Matter movement in 2013. Consequently, a significant portion of the exhibition points to the idea of a selfless, loving practice directed by community toward a common good and based on a belief in "a good deed producing only a good result."[62] As demonstrated by the Act Up and Black Lives Matter movements, the work of loving practice has historically been empowered by grassroots social movements, albeit often at the price of individual sacrifice. In her essay "The Cost for Love We Are Not Willing to Pay," Etel Adnan writes that love is a dangerous force precisely because it is powered by truth, and truth, when spoken to power, can lead to ostracization, imprisonment, even death for those who speak it:[63] Mahatma Mohandas Gandhi, imprisoned thirteen times before he was assassinated; Martin Luther King Jr., jailed twenty-nine times before he was assassinated; Nelson Mandela, who stood trial four times before being incarcerated for twenty-seven years; Marielle Franco, who was murdered for her work against gender violence and police brutality in Brazil. King's essay in *Strength to Love* based on the Christian parable of the Good Samaritan illustrates his belief in love as a universal, self-sacrificing and charitable practice. His retelling of the parable asserts that "the ultimate measure of a man is not where he stands in moments of comfort and convenience, but where he stands at times of challenge and controversy."[64]

Shouldering individual responsibility to forge a society that fosters love was the persuasive defense of Yegor Zhukov, a Russian university student accused of extremism for which he was arrested and tried in 2019. In the summary of his defense, Zhukov stated, "Love is impossible in the absence of trust. Real trust is formed of common action. Common action is a rarity in our country where few people feel responsible. [. . .] Where can trust come from in a country like this—and where can love grow?"[65] In the tumultuous 1960s, Merton asserted, "We are living under a tyranny of untruth which confirms itself in power [. . .]. Our submission to plausible and useful lies involves us in greater and more obvious contradictions, and to hide these from ourselves we need greater and even less plausible lies."[66] Written nearly sixty years ago, this statement rings true in today's quickening and incessant evacuation of reality in which fundamental disagreements regarding truth and fact are magnified by social media and filtered to suit individual and tribal prejudices and predispositions. The rise of White supremacy and its equivocations about freedom and oppression, justice and terrorism during the past several years is a metastasizing of the tyranny Merton wrote about. In her book *all about love*, cultural critic and writer bell hooks singles out the lie as a form of lovelessness essential to the patriarchal beliefs that underlie the perpetuation of hate. She writes, "Condoning lying is an essential component of patriarchal thinking [. . .]. To embrace patriarchy [one] must actively surrender the longing to love."[67]

The exigencies of the multileveled geopolitical struggles in which we find ourselves today demand just such a politics of love. We are called to merge a wide-awake awareness of the present with a consciousness of the past to forge a politics of love that is born in the nurturing care of one's family, practiced in the sharing of one's life with a significant other, enriched by the camaraderie of friends, expressed in community and through art and faith, and reflected in nature. In its cross-generational sampling of the ways artists have approached the subject of love in their work, this exhibition suggests that it is not in the correspondence of these layers but rather in their concurrence where the expression of love is universally experienced.

Notes

1. Thomas Merton, *No Man Is an Island* (New York: Harcourt, Brace and Company, 1955), xiii.

2. Etel Adnan, "The Cost for Love We Are Not Willing to Pay," in *100 Notes, 100 Thoughts: Documenta Series No. 006* (Stuttgart, Germany: Hatje Cantz, 2012), 4.

3. Adrienne Rich, "It Is the Lesbian in Us," in *On Lies, Secrets, and Silence: Selected Prose, 1966–1978* (New York: W. W. Norton and Company, 1979), 199.

4. Adnan, "The Cost for Love," 8.

5. Giorgio Agamben, *What Is an Apparatus?*, trans. David Kishik and Stefan Pedatella (Stanford, CA: Stanford University Press, 2009), 28–29; Alain Badiou, *In Praise of Love*, trans. Peter Bush (New York: The New Press, 2012), 40.

6. Badiou, *In Praise of Love*, 38.

7. Merton, *No Man Is An Island*, 6.

8. Badiou writes that love is a subject born from the conscious union of two people, the whole of which is greater than "the two" themselves, who must together form a relation to the world and not simply to each other's differences and subjectivities. Badiou, *In Praise of Love*, 43.

9. Jennifer L. Roberts, "Biography of a Wave," in *Dario Robleto: Unknown and Solitary Seas; Dreams and Emotions of the 19th Century* (Cambridge, MA: Radcliffe Institute for Advanced Studies, Harvard University, 2019), 11.

10. Diane Ackerman, *A Natural History of Love* (New York: Random House, 1995), 95–99.

11. Badiou, *In Praise of Love*, 30; as quoted in the story of the adulterous lovers Paolo and Francesca, from Canto V of Dante's *Inferno*, whose fiery passion consumes them for eternity in hell.

12. Ackerman, *A Natural History of Love*, 249.

13. Rohmer's film borrows its title from the 1882 novel by Jules Verne.

14. Arthur Rimbaud, "Chanson de la plus haute tour" ("Song of the Highest Tower"), 1872.

15. For Edmier, the risk involved in merging images and associations from the personal and public domains in his work is a "way to reveal emotional truths." Edmier paraphrased by Lynn Zelevansky in *Keith Edmier and Farrah Fawcett: Recasting Pygmalion* (New York: Rizzoli, 2002), 18.

16. There are subtle but important differences in these two works sharing the title *"Untitled" (Perfect Lovers)*. The first version, dated 1987–1990, was produced as an edition of three with one artist proof. This editioned work is exhibited with identical black wall clocks, fourteen inches in diameter. The second version, dated 1991, is unique and is exhibited with identical white wall clocks, thirteen and one-half inches in diameter, installed on an optional, blue-painted wall.

17. Adair Rounthwaite, "Split Witness: Metaphorical Extensions of Life in the Art of Felix Gonzalez-Torres," *Representations* 109, no. 1 (Winter 2010): 41.

18. In *all about love*, hooks refers to Judith Viorst's book *Necessary Losses* (New York: Simon and Schuster, 1986) in her discussion about the dynamics of parental relationships as they relate to varieties of familial love. bell hooks, *all about love: new visions* (New York: William Morrow and Company, 2000), 15.

19. Kahlil Robert Irving, "Black Matter" (MFA thesis, Sam Fox School of Design and Visual Arts of Washington University, 2017), 21.

20. Irving, "Black Matter," 14.

21. Pearl Cleage, *Things I Should Have Told My Daughter: Lies, Lessons, and Love Affairs* (New York: Atria Books, 2014), 262.

22. Patty Chang in an interview with Janelle Zara, "Patty Chang's Affecting Videos and Photographs Find Emotion in Breast Milk, Death, and More," *ARTnews*, October 23, 2020, https://www.artnews.com/art-news/artists/patty-chang-milk-debt-profile-1234574889. See Sianne Ngai, *Ugly Feelings* (Cambridge, MA: Harvard University Press, 2005), and Cathy Park Hong, *Minor Feelings: An Asian American Reckoning* (New York: One World, 2020).

23. Patty Chang in Osman Can Yerebakan, "'Humor Makes People Aware and Uncomfortable': Veteran Performance Artist Patty Chang Is Back with Her Most Anxiety-Provoking Work Yet," *Artnet News*, March 25, 2021, https://news.artnet.com/art-world/patty-chang-milk-debt-1953685.

24. Ackerman, *A Natural History of Love*, 160.

25. Ackerman, *A Natural History of Love*.

26. For Kierkegaard, God is the "middle term" in *The Nicomachean Ethics* in which Aristotle argues for the virtue of loving the friend or neighbor as oneself. See John Lippitt, *Kierkegaard and the Problem of Self-Love* (New York: Cambridge University Press, 2013).

27. *Video et Tacio* was the motto of Queen Elizabeth I. For Thich Nhat Hanh's definition of a "noble silence" as a conscious, "thunderous" mindfulness, see Thich Nhat Hanh, *Silence: The Power of Quiet in a World Full of Noise* (New York: Harper One, 2015). See also, "Remove the Dressing," *Thich Nhat Hanh Dharma Talks* (blog), April 10, 2018, https://tnhaudio.org/2018/04/10/remove-the-dressing/.

28. hooks, *all about love*, 165.

29. Dr. Martin Luther King Jr., "Letter from Birmingham Jail," June 12, 1963.

30. Merton, *No Man Is an Island*, 25.

31. Ebony G. Patterson quoted in Heike Dempster, "Ebony G. Patterson '...while the dew is still on the roses...,'" *ArtPulse*, accessed June 26, 2021, http://artpulsemagazine.com/ebony-g-patterson-.

32. David Konstan, trans., *Aspasius, Anonymous, Michael of Ephesus: On Aristotle's Nicomachean Ethics 8 and 9* (Ithaca, NY: Cornell University Press, 2001), 39.

33. Black Lives Matter Global Network Foundation, "Black Lives Matter 2020 Impact Report," https://blacklivesmatter.com/wp-content/uploads/2021/02/blm-2020-impact-report.pdf, 31.

34. Johnson introduced the theme of *Anxious Men* to the public in his 2015 Drawing Center exhibition to impart the Black experience of alienation and peril. Using Melvin Van Peebles's song "Love, That's America" as its soundtrack, the exhibition contrasts images of anti-Black violence and oppression with idiomatic expressions of patriotic love.

35. Movements for *The Hikers* were created by Martha Graham Dance Company members Lloyd Knight and Leslie Andrea Williams and choreographed by Claudia Shreier.

36. Rashid Johnson in an interview with Julie Belcove, "Artist Rashid Johnson Took a Hike in Aspen, Then Shot a New Film about the Black Experience," *Robb Report*, June 29, 2019, https://robbreport.com/shelter/art-collectibles/artist-rashid-johnson-the-hikers-2855719/.

37. Dr. Martin Luther King Jr., *Strength to Love* (Minneapolis: Fortress Press, 1981), 38.

38. hooks, *all about love*, 94.

39. Alanna Fields, from the artist's statement in an email to the author on October 12, 2021.

40. AA Bronson, in an interview with Jérôme Sans, "AA Bronson," *Purple Magazine*, The Love Issue #34, accessed June 8, 2021, https://purple.fr/magazine/the-love-issue-34/aa-bronson-3/.

41. Ackerman, *A Natural History of Love*, 13.

42. The phrase *"ut pictura poesis"* ("as in painting, so in poetry," or "poetry resembles painting") occurs most prominently in Horace's "Ars Poetica" ("The Art of Poetry").

43. Correspondence between Felix Gonzalez-Torres and Ross Laycock, 1988.

44. Giorgio Agamben, *Stanzas: Word and Phantasm in Western Culture* (Minneapolis: University of Minnesota Press, 1993), 85.

45. Robert Storr, ed., *Think with the Senses, Feel with the Mind: Art in the Present Tense; La Biennale di Venezia 52* (New York: Rizzoli, 2007), 86.

46. See Roland Barthes, *A Lover's Discourse: Fragments* (New York: Hill and Wang, 1993).

47. Elizabeth Barrett Browning, "Sonnet 43: How Do I Love Thee? Let Me Count the Ways," in *Sonnets from the Portuguese* (London: Caradoc Press, 1906; Project Gutenberg, 2015), https://www.gutenberg.org/cache/epub/2002/pg2002-images.html.

48 Love is the bedrock of the world's largest religions, so any overview of the history of thought related to the divine as expressed in nature, particularly in the context of this exhibition, must be embarrassingly brief.

49 King, *Strength to Love*, 52.

50 "A Love Supreme" is the title of John Coltrane's 1964 album, which he described as a "spiritual awakening." It was recorded during a time of mass conversion of African Americans to Islam compelled by racial injustice in the United States and the failure of White Christians to embrace a love ethic based on truth and freedom, which Martin Luther King Jr. addressed in his "Letter from Birmingham Jail."

51 Thomas Merton, "Day of a Stranger," in Lawrence S. Cunningham, ed., *Thomas Merton: Spiritual Master; The Essential Writings* (New York: Paulist Press, 1992), 222. For an interesting discussion of Merton's references to the Latin word *consonantia*, or harmony, in "Day of a Stranger," see Donald Grayston, "*Consonantia* in Thomas Merton: Harmony Personal, Social and Cosmic," *The Merton Annual* 28 (2015): 97–111.

52 Thomas Merton, "As Man to Man," *Cistercian Studies* IV (1969): 93.

53 Merton, *No Man Is an Island*, 133.

54 Magnus Plessen, from email exchanges with Daniel Marzona, November 2012 and August 2014, https://www.danielmarzona.com/wp-content/uploads/magnus_plessen-1914_essay.pdf.

55 Magnus Plessen as shared with the author in a phone call on March 19, 2021.

56 Jana Vander-Lee in an undated artist's statement provided by Inman Gallery, Houston, Texas, October 7, 2021.

57 *John 3:16* refers to the biblical passage: "For God so loved the world, that he gave his only Son, that whoever believes in him should not perish but have eternal life."

58 See Guy Debord, *The Society of the Spectacle*, trans. Fredy Perlman (Detroit: Black and Red, 1970).

59 Paul Pfeiffer in an interview with Jennifer Gonzalez, *Bomb Magazine*, April 1, 2003, https://bombmagazine.org/articles/paul-pfeiffer/.

60 Thomas Merton, *Conjectures of a Guilty Bystander* (New York: Doubleday, 1966), 156–157.

61 Kriss Ravetto-Biagioli, "Shadowed by Images: Rafael Lozano-Hemmer and the Art of Surveillance," *Representations* 111, no. 1 (Summer 2010): 136.

62 Gandhi, quoted in Merton, *Conjectures of a Guilty Bystander*, 117.

63 Adnan, "The Cost for Love."

64 King, *Strength to Love*, 35.

65 Masha Gessen, "A Powerful Statement of Resistance from a College Student on Trial in Moscow," *The New Yorker*, December 7, 2019, https://www.newyorker.com/news/our-columnists/a-powerful-statement-of-resistance-from-a-college-student-on-trial-in-moscow.

66 Merton, *Conjectures of a Guilty Bystander*, 62.

67 hooks, *all about love*, 39.

Plates

PLATE 1
Ghada Amer
American, born Cairo, Egypt, 1963; active New York, New York
The Words I Love the Most, 2012
Bronze with black patina
Courtesy of the artist and Tina Kim Gallery, New York

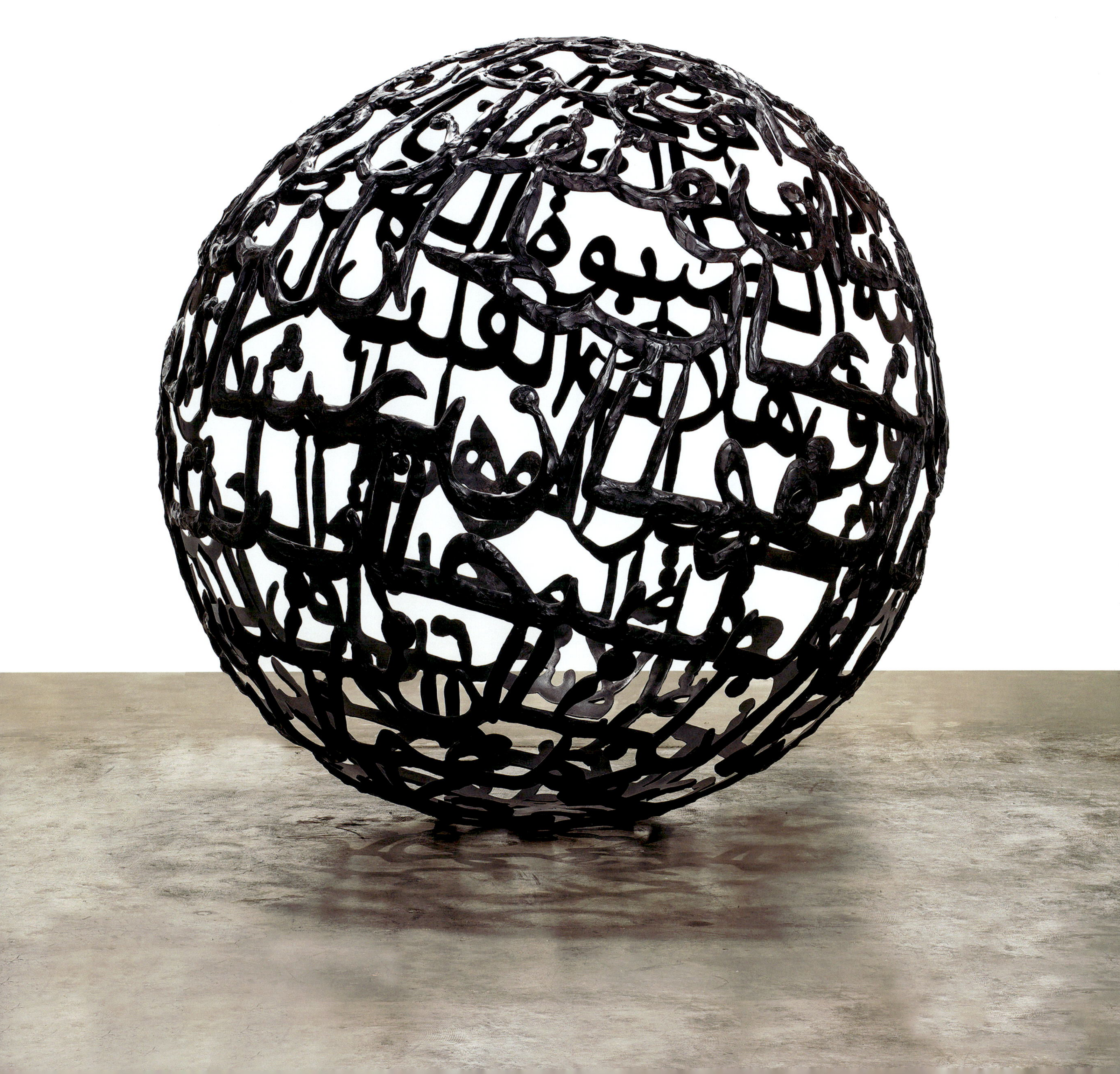

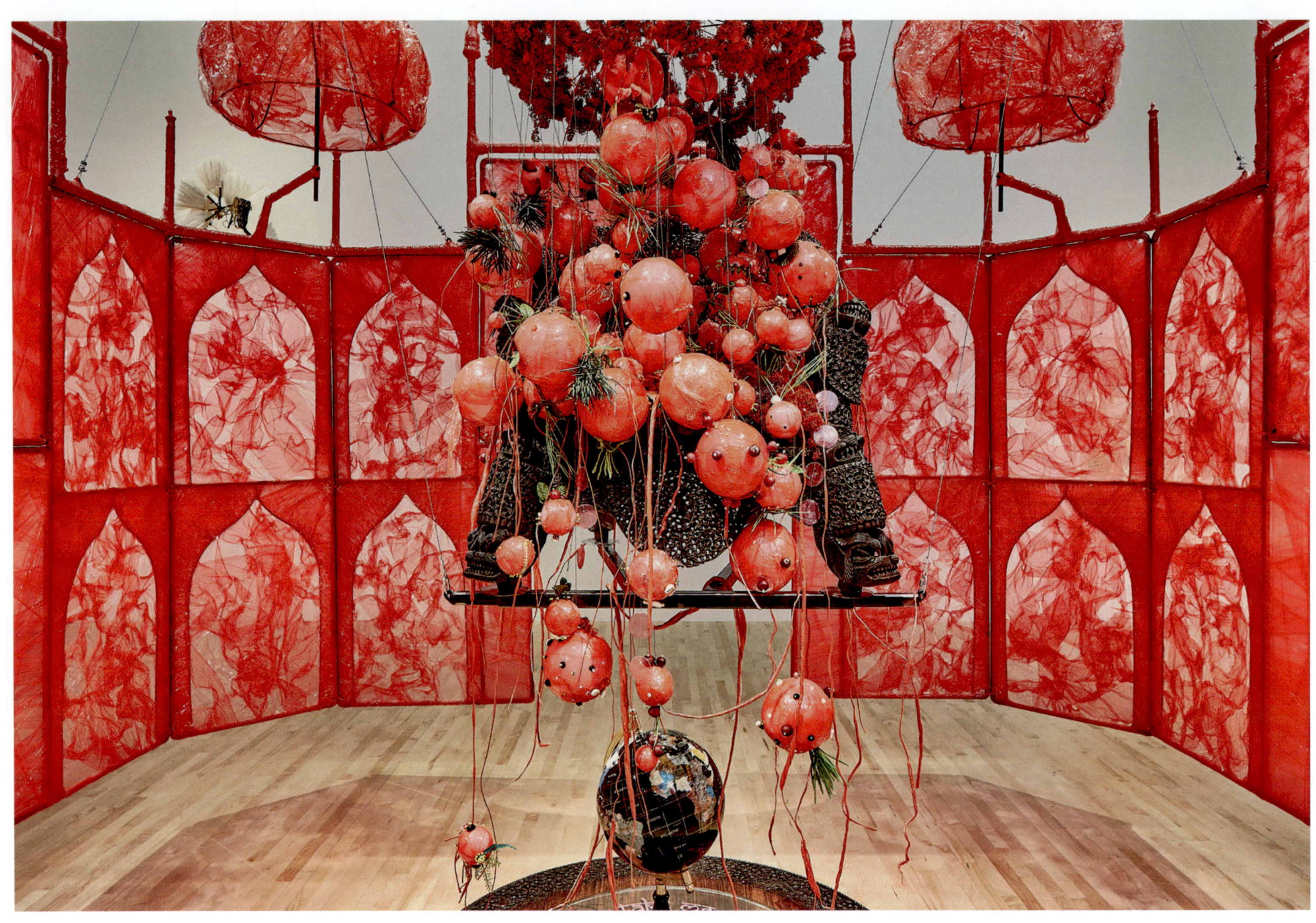

PLATE 2
Rina Banerjee
Indian, born Kolkata, India, 1963;
active New York, New York
Take me, take me, take me . . .
to the Palace of love, 2005
Plastic, antique Anglo-Indian Bombay black
wood chair, steel and copper framework, floral
picks, foam balls, cowrie shells, quilting pins,
red-colored moss, antique stone globe, glass,
synthetic fabric, shells, and fake birds
Courtesy of the artist

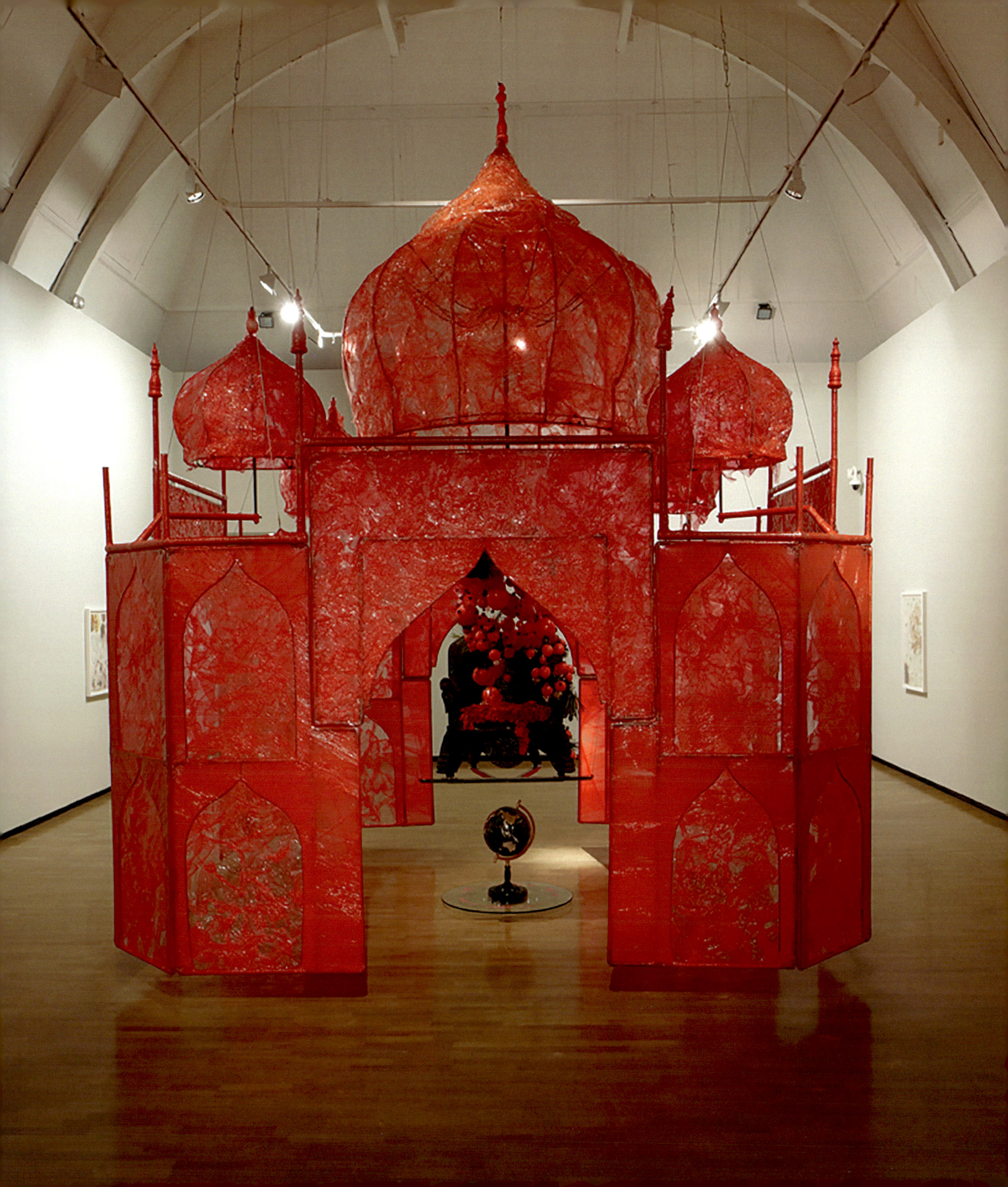

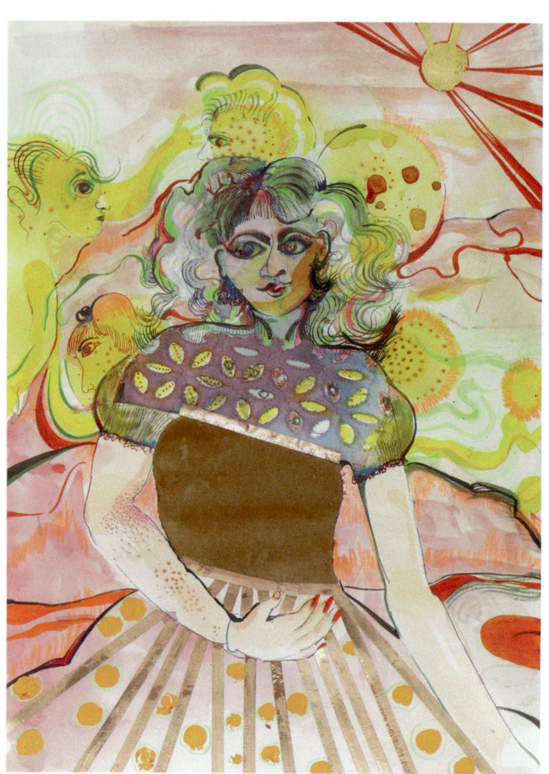 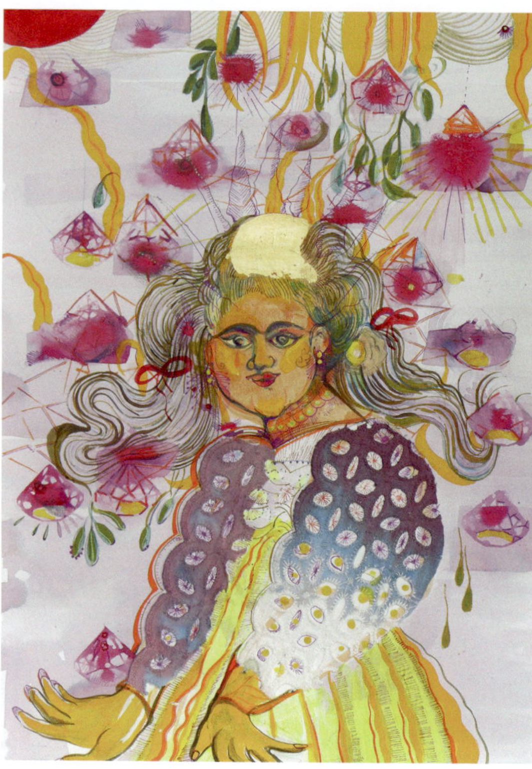 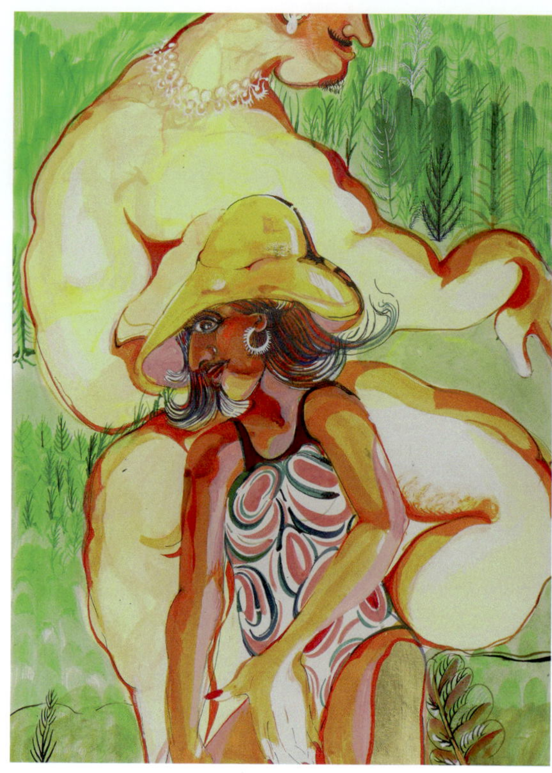

PLATE 3
Rina Banerjee
Indian, born Kolkata, India, 1963;
active New York, New York
*Garish and Golden while tied up pretty and never perfect she woke to walk
to do this and that. She never frittered or felt frozen. She broke all spells of
sluggishness, dressed brightly into sunny movement without his paternal
patronizing folded.*, 2021
Copper tape, gold leaf, cotton velvet, cotton eyelet fabric, acrylic, ink,
pencil, and dye on paper
Courtesy of the artist and Hosfelt Gallery, San Francisco

PLATE 4
Rina Banerjee
Indian, born Kolkata, India, 1963;
active New York, New York
*Her hair was there while lost in one place. Not to stare if her sunny dome
could be roped to be opened. Buttered in benevolence, seated dead center
her a balding beacon, her mind a temple, crossing all paths, all forsaken,
never stolen and always bolder.*, 2021
Ink and acrylic on paper
Courtesy of the artist and Hosfelt Gallery, San Francisco

PLATE 5
Rina Banerjee
Indian, born Kolkata, India, 1963;
active New York, New York
*Muscle and music made her cupid shy while he was quiet and stylist,
whisked her body, captured she traversed to guard false against
masculinities fated to be very stupid.*, 2020
Ink and acrylic on paper
Courtesy of the artist and Hosfelt Gallery, San Francisco

50

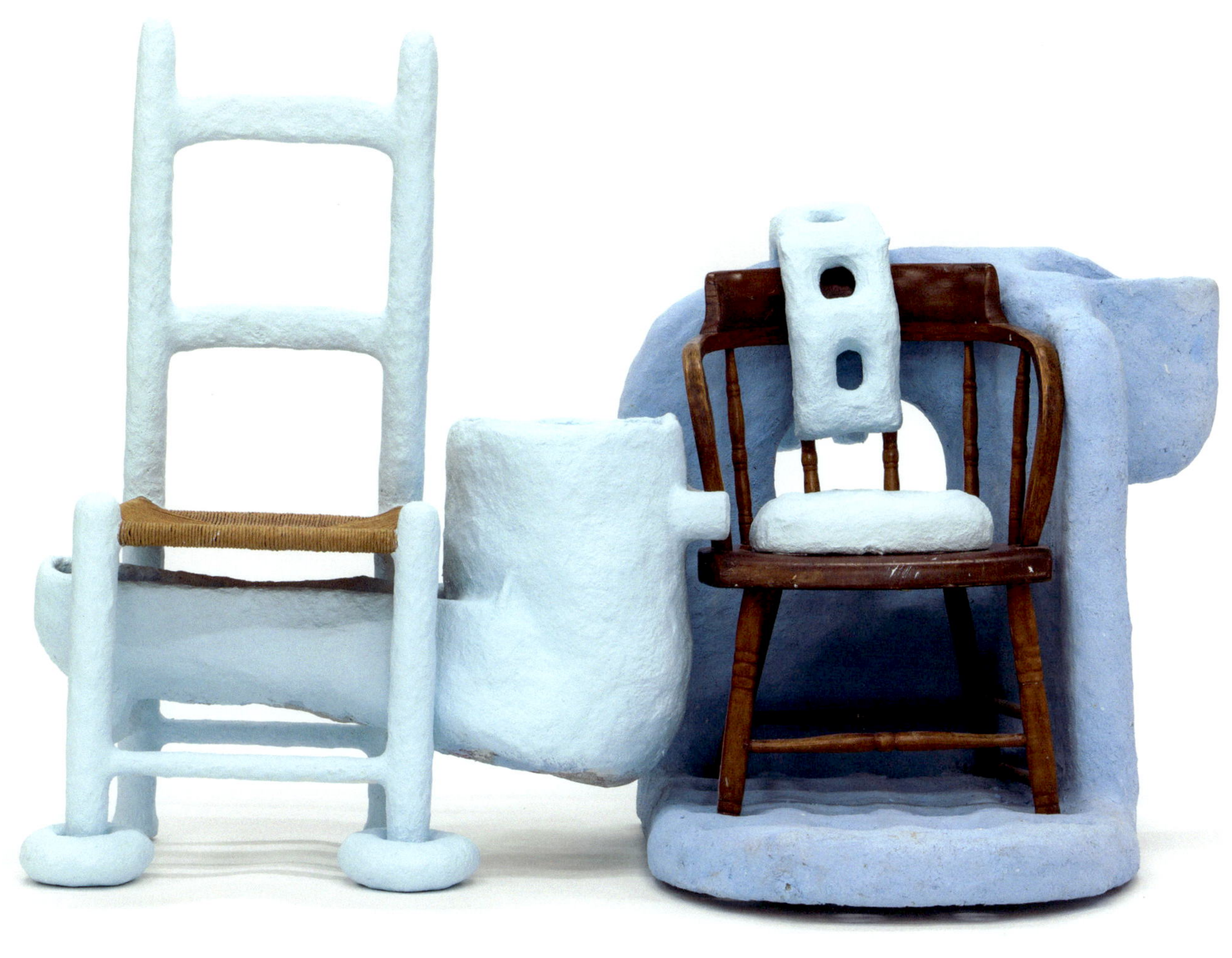

PLATE 6
Thomas Barger
American, born Mattoon, Illinois, 1992; active Brooklyn, New York
Love Me, Protect Me Chair, 2018
Paper pulp, plywood, two wooden chairs, polyurethane, and paint
Courtesy of the artist and Salon 94 Design

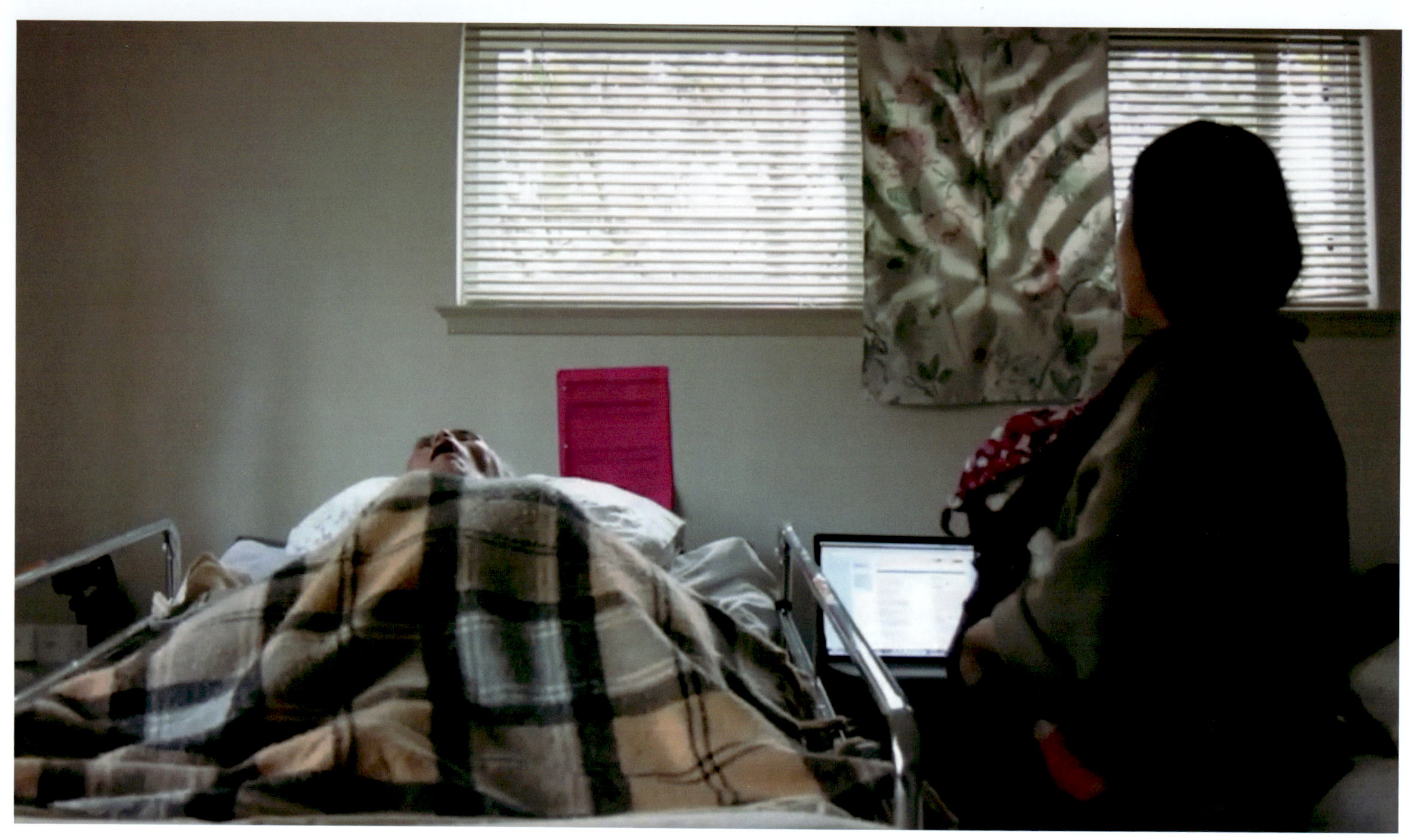

PLATE 7
Patty Chang
American, born San Leandro, California, 1972;
active Los Angeles, California
Que Sera Sera/Invocations, 2013
Two-channel video
Running time: 3 minutes, 45 seconds
Courtesy of the artist and BANK Gallery, Shanghai, China

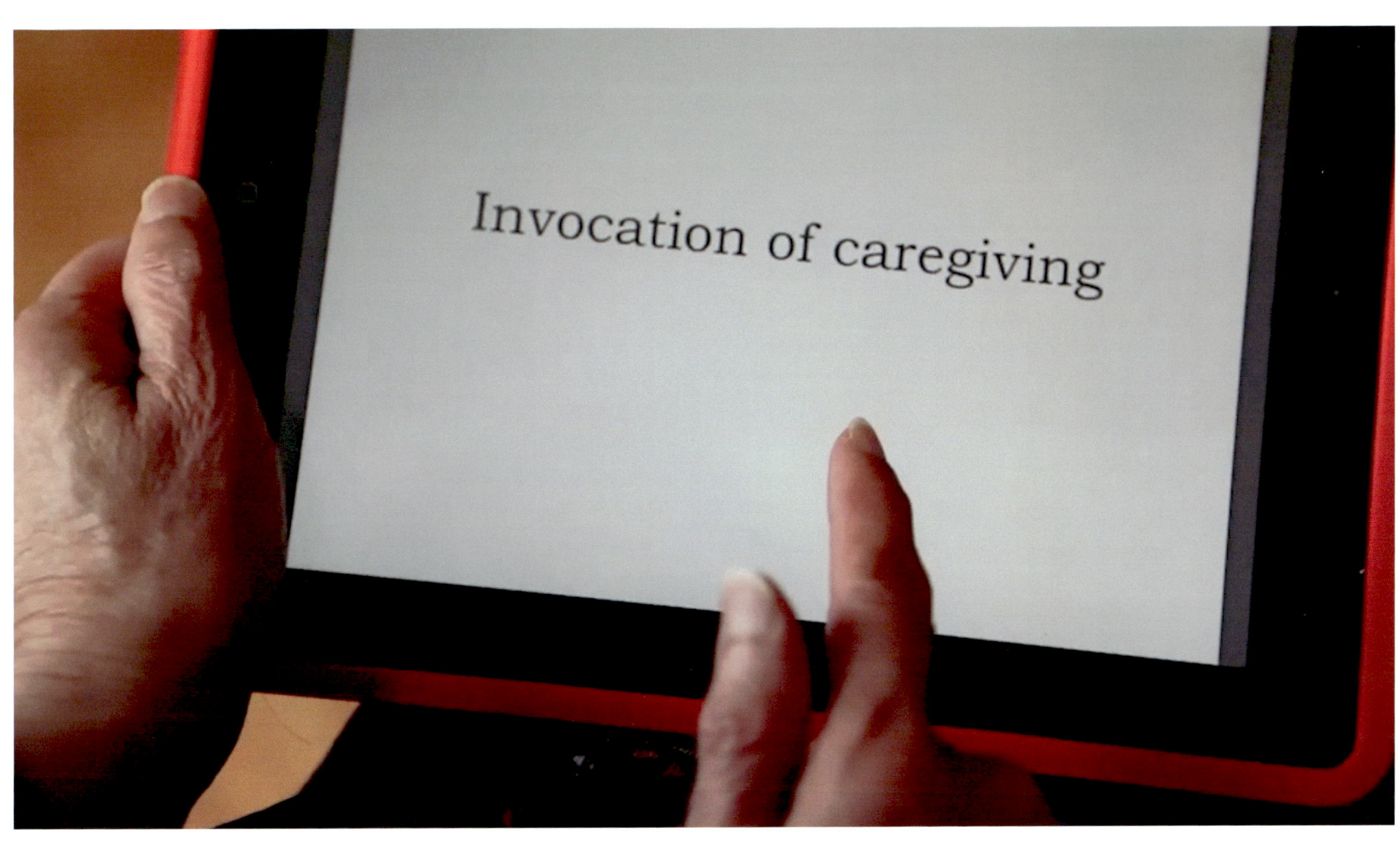
Invocation of caregiving

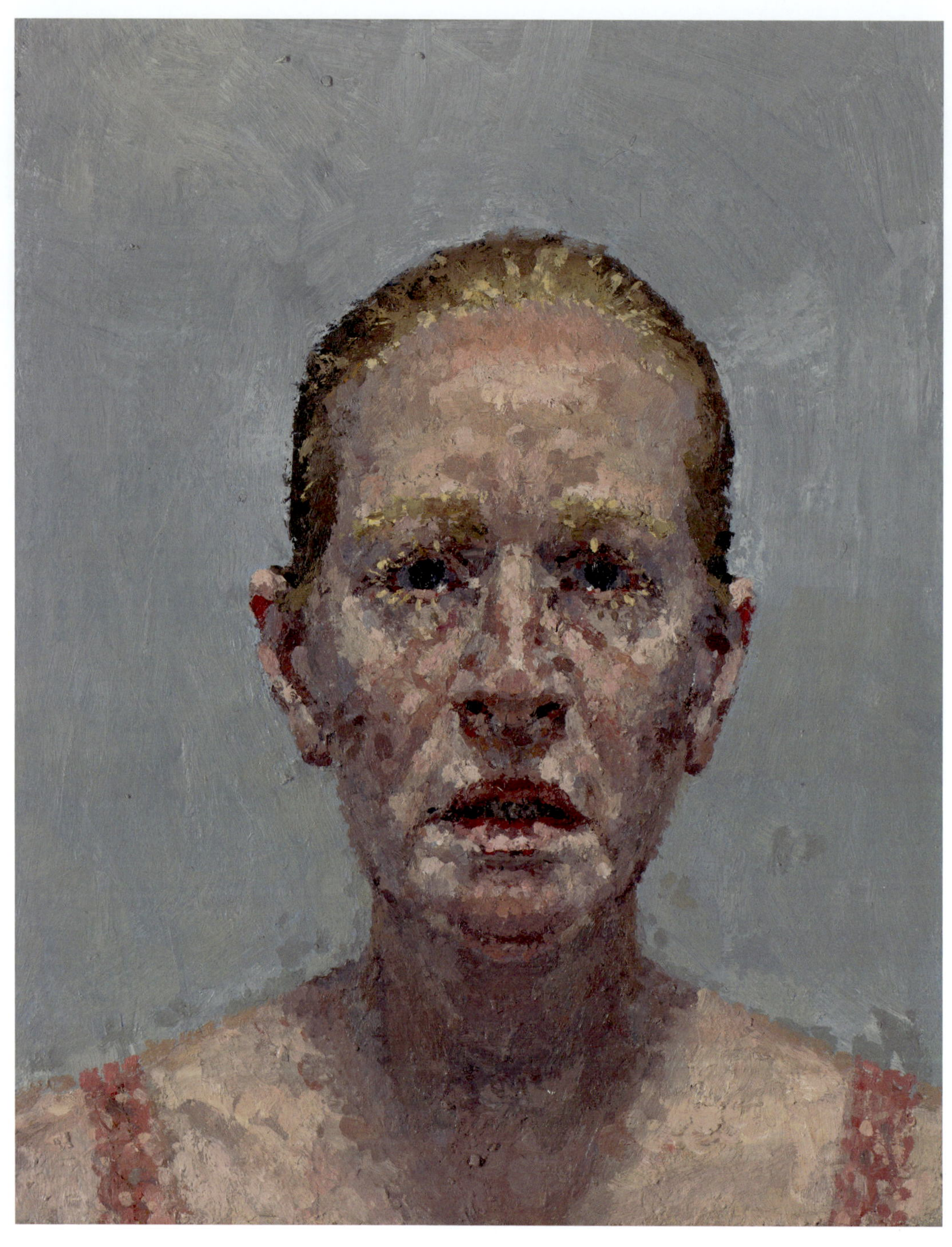

PLATES 8
Susanna Coffey
American, born New London, Connecticut, 1949;
active New York, New York
Self Portrait (for Roy Snow), 1993
Oil on linen
The Art Institute of Chicago, gift of the American Academy of Arts and Letters,
New York, from the Hassam, Speicher, Betts and Symons Funds, 1996

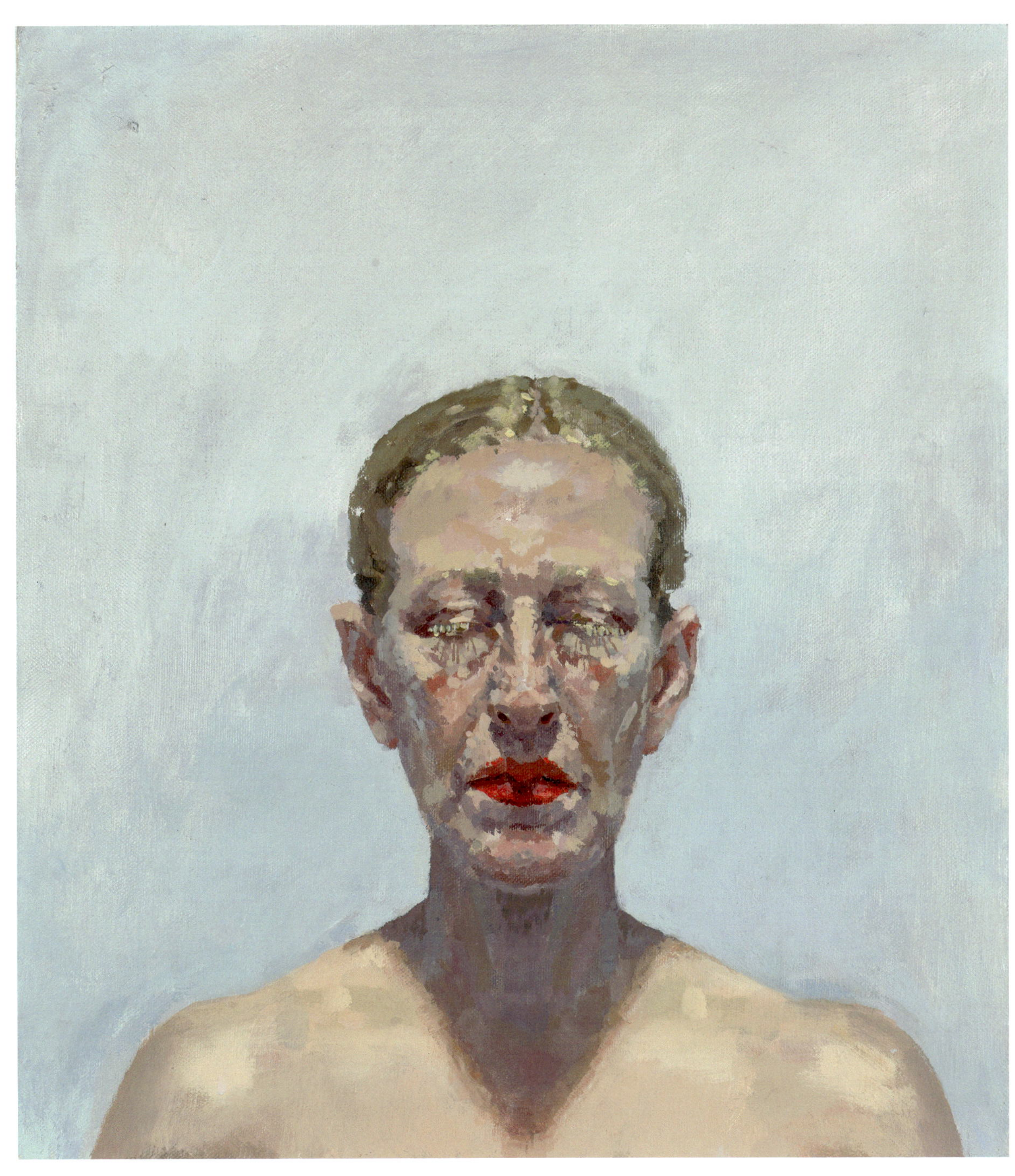

PLATES 9
Susanna Coffey
American, born New London, Connecticut, 1949;
active New York, New York
Self Portrait (Madonna's Lipstick), 1993
Oil on canvas
Courtesy of Marianne and Goran Strokirk

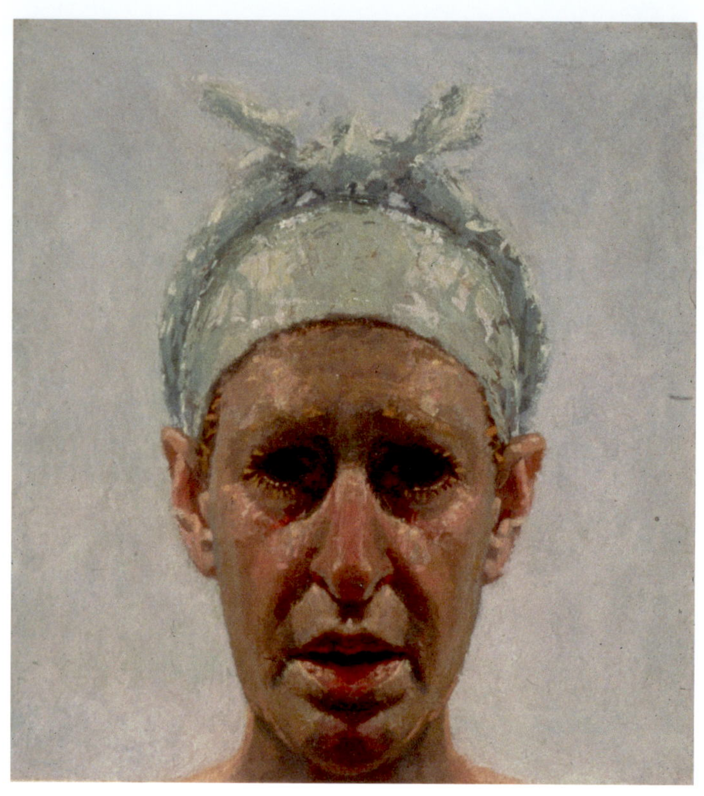

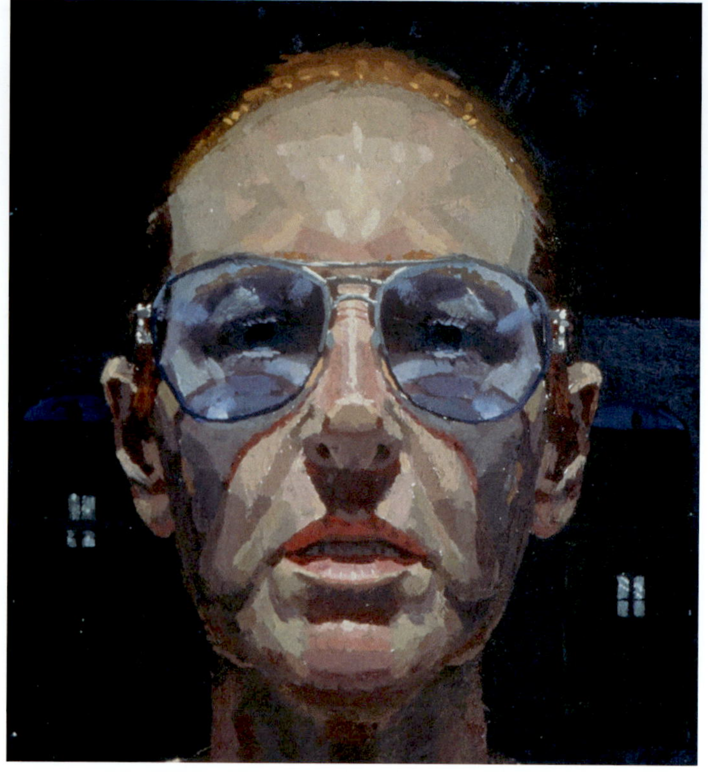

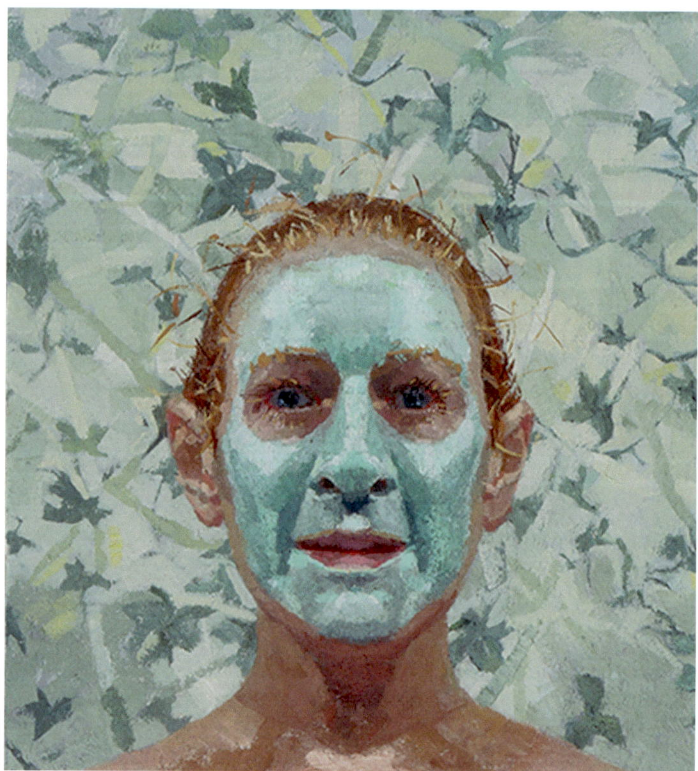

PLATES 10–12
Susanna Coffey
American, born New London, Connecticut, 1949;
active New York, New York

Self Portrait (Bay), 2001
Oil on linen
Courtesy of Linda Garrison

Self Portrait (Ice), 2001
Oil on linen
Courtesy of Linda Garrison

Self Portrait (Queen Helene), 2001
Oil on linen
Private collection, courtesy of Tibor
de Nagy Gallery, New York

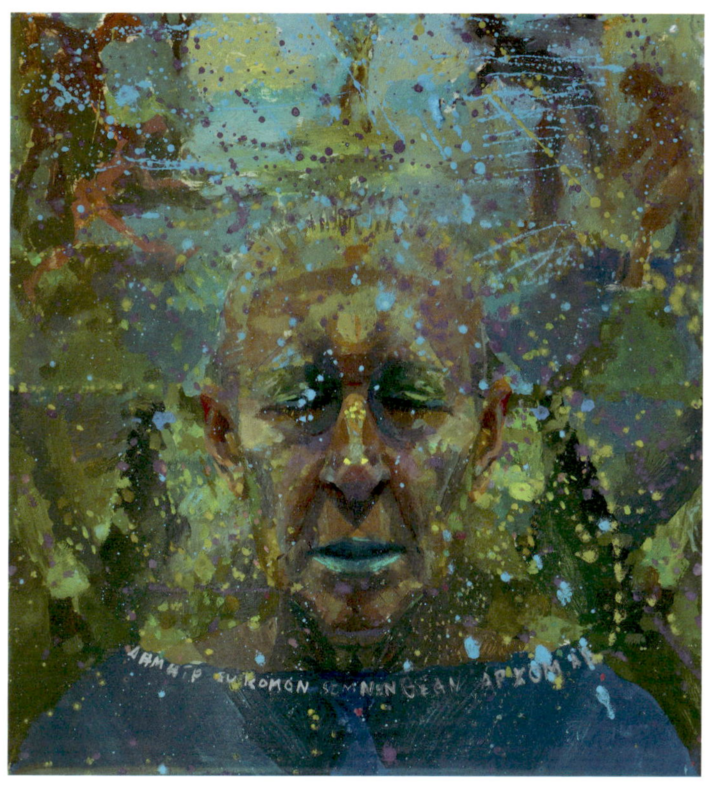

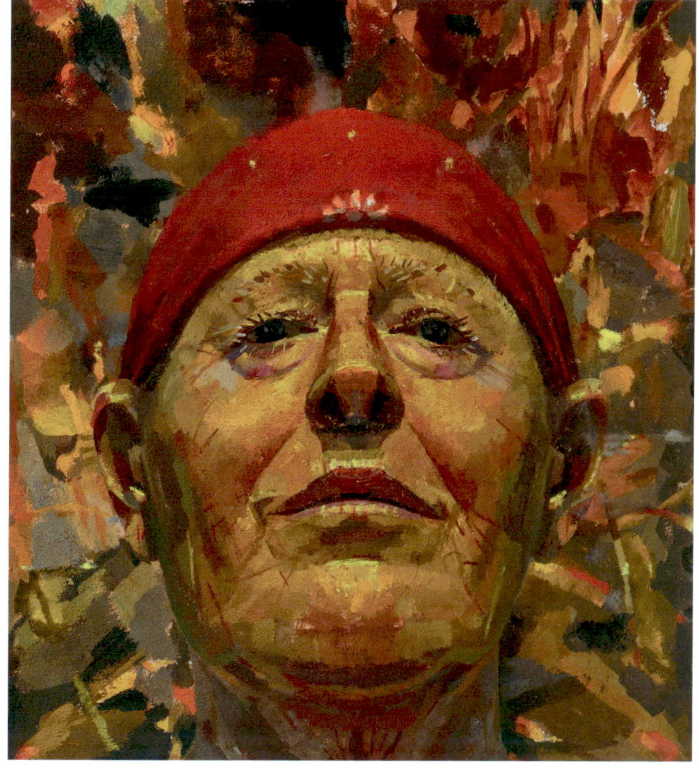

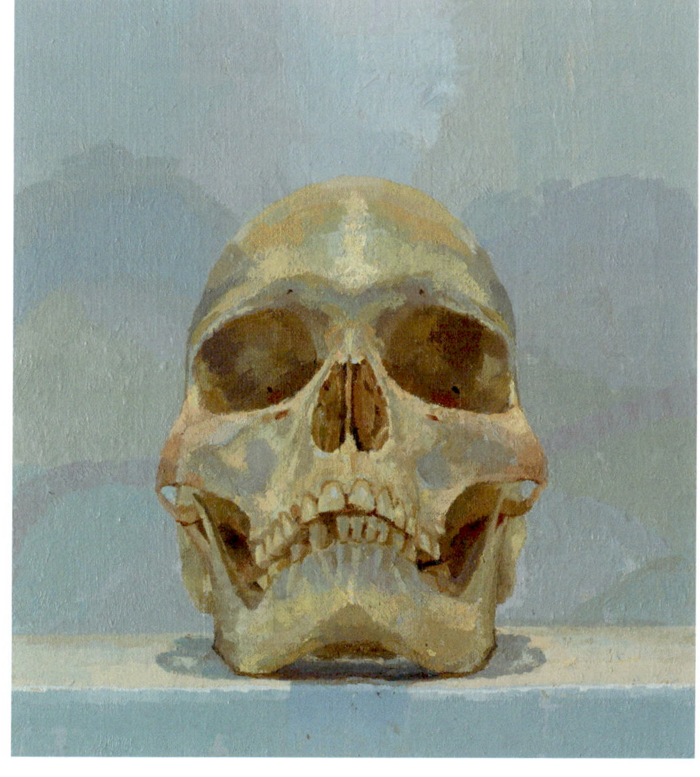

PLATES 13–15
Susanna Coffey
American, born New London, Connecticut, 1949;
active New York, New York

Telling, 2018
Oil on panel

Video et Tacio, 2018
Oil on panel

James' Woman's Skull One, 2015
Oil on panel

Courtesy of the artist

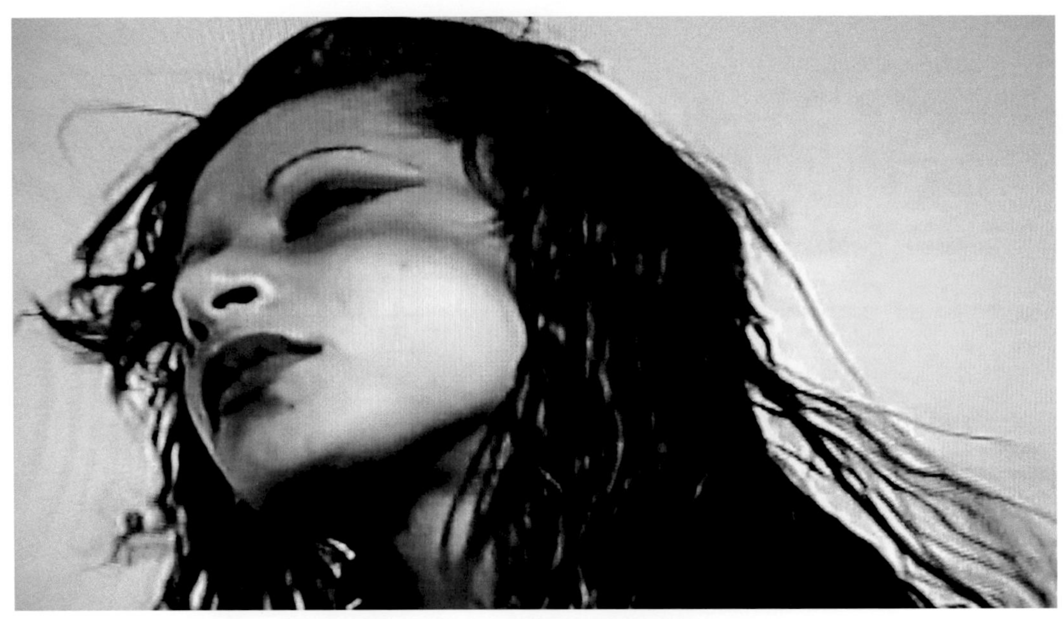

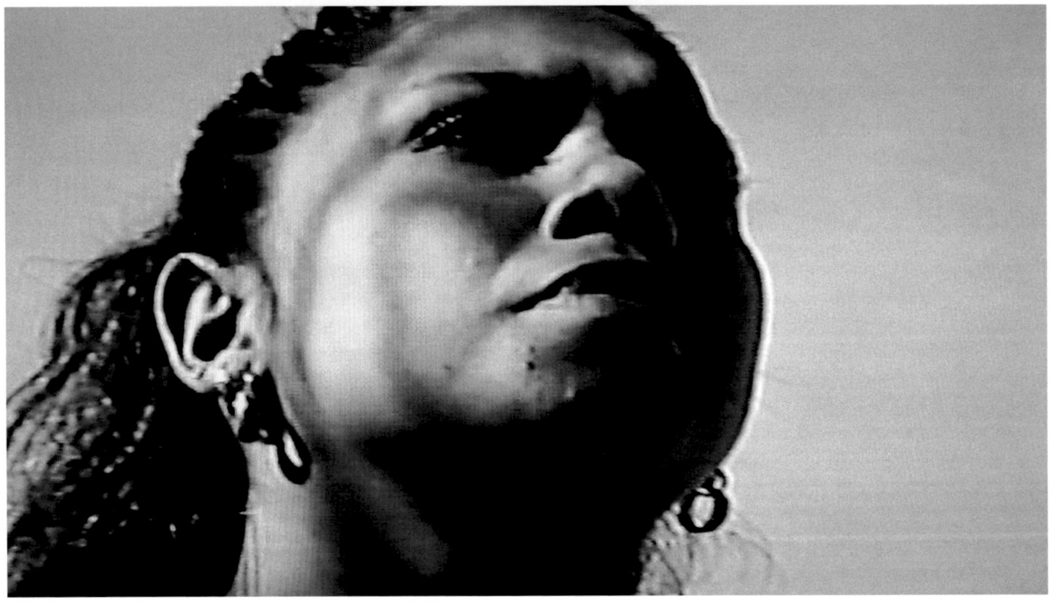

PLATE 16
James Drake
American, born Lubbock, Texas, 1946; active Santa Fe, New Mexico
Tongue-Cut Sparrows (Inside and Out), 2006–2007
Three-channel video
Running time: 30 minutes, 36 seconds
Courtesy of the artist

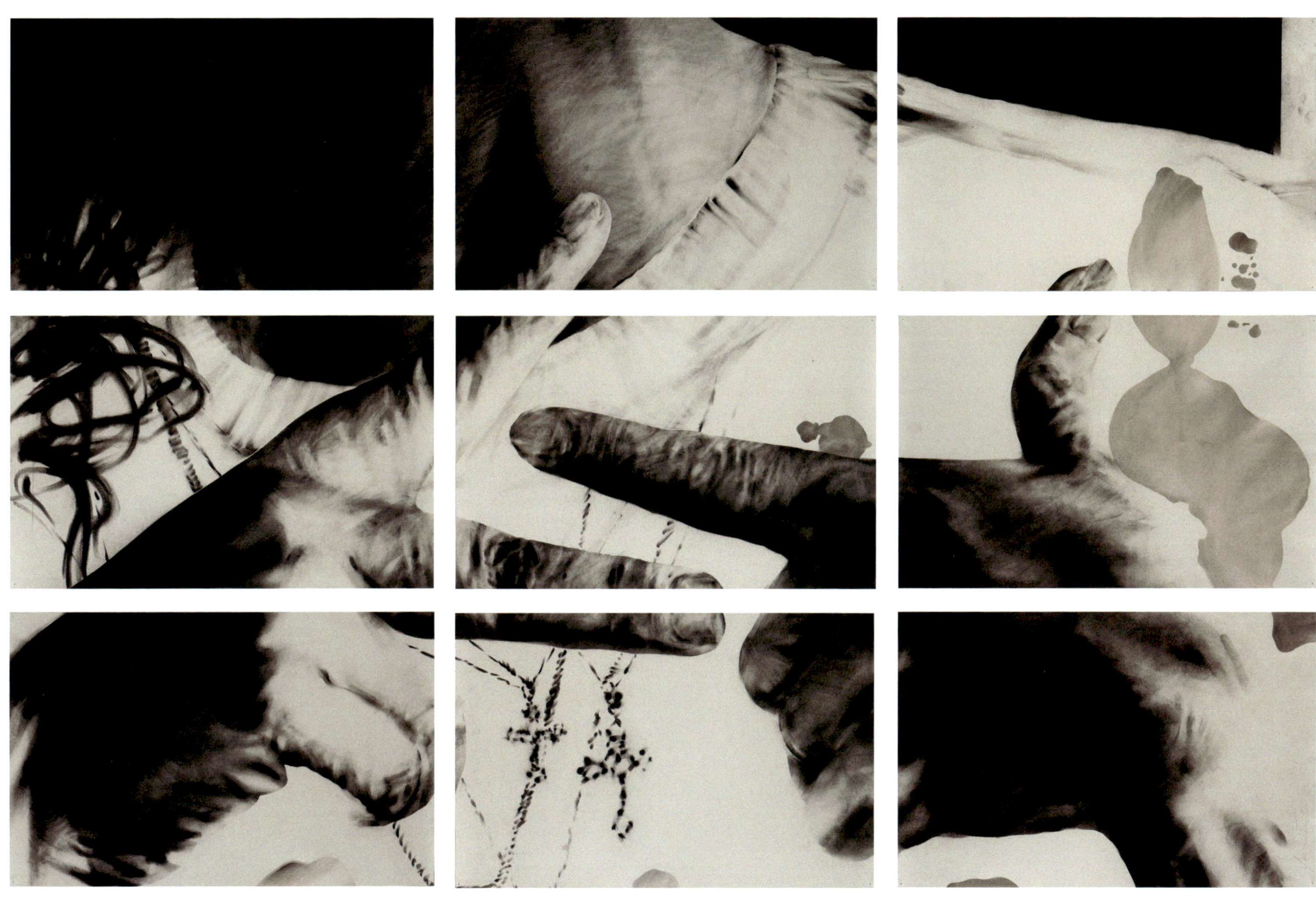

PLATE 17
James Drake
American, born Lubbock, Texas, 1946; active Santa Fe, New Mexico
Tongue-Cut Sparrows (Gabriella), 1996
Graphite on paper
Denver Art Museum, gift of Polly and Mark Addison, 2011.302A–I

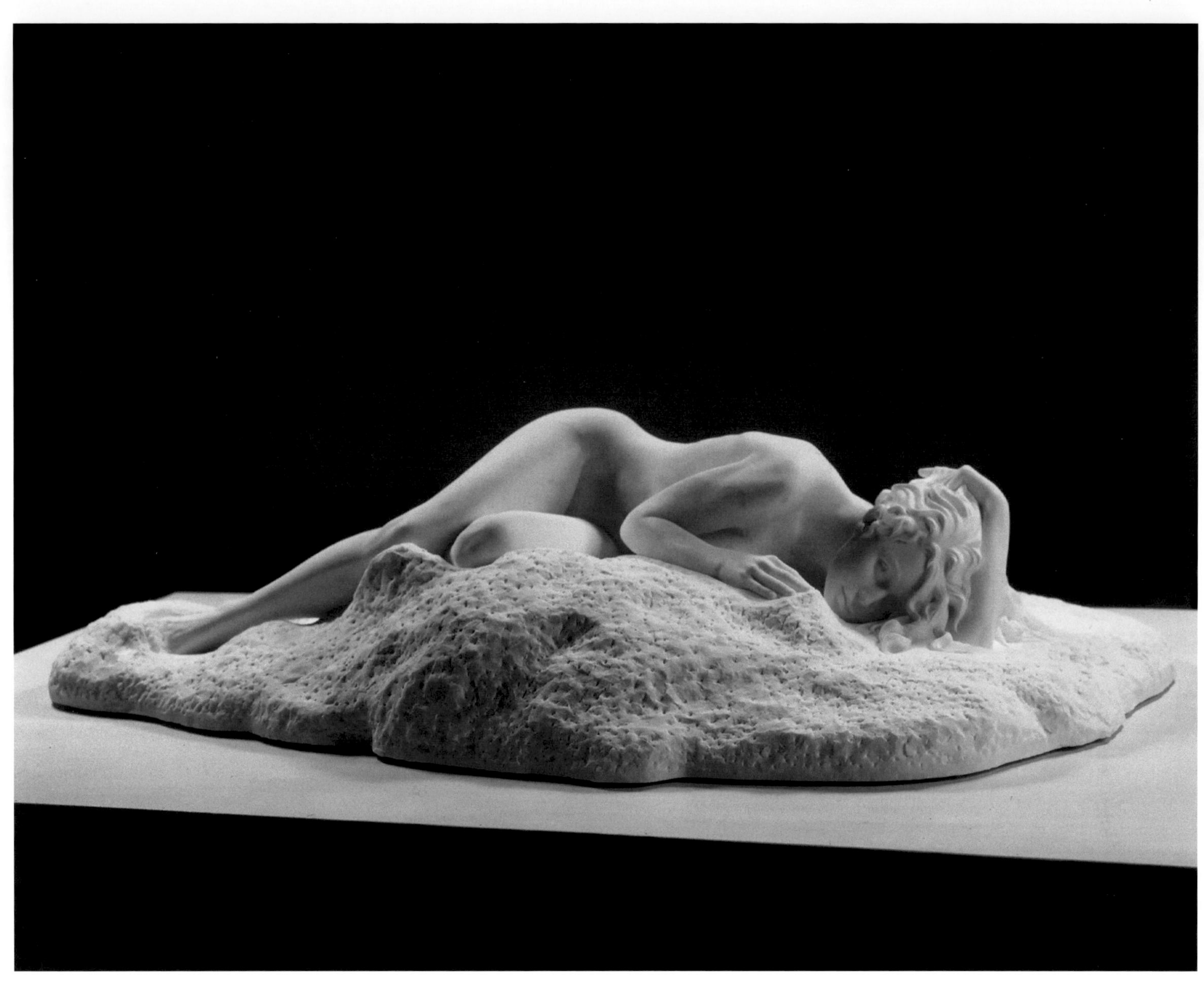

PLATE 18
Keith Edmier and Farrah Fawcett
Keith Edmier, American, born Chicago, Illinois, 1967; active New York, New York
Farrah Fawcett, American, born Corpus Christi, Texas, 1947; died Santa Monica, California, 2009
Keith Edmier and Farrah Fawcett, 2000, 2000–2002
Diptych; bronze, white marble, silver, and diamond
Courtesy of Keith Edmier and Petzel Gallery, New York

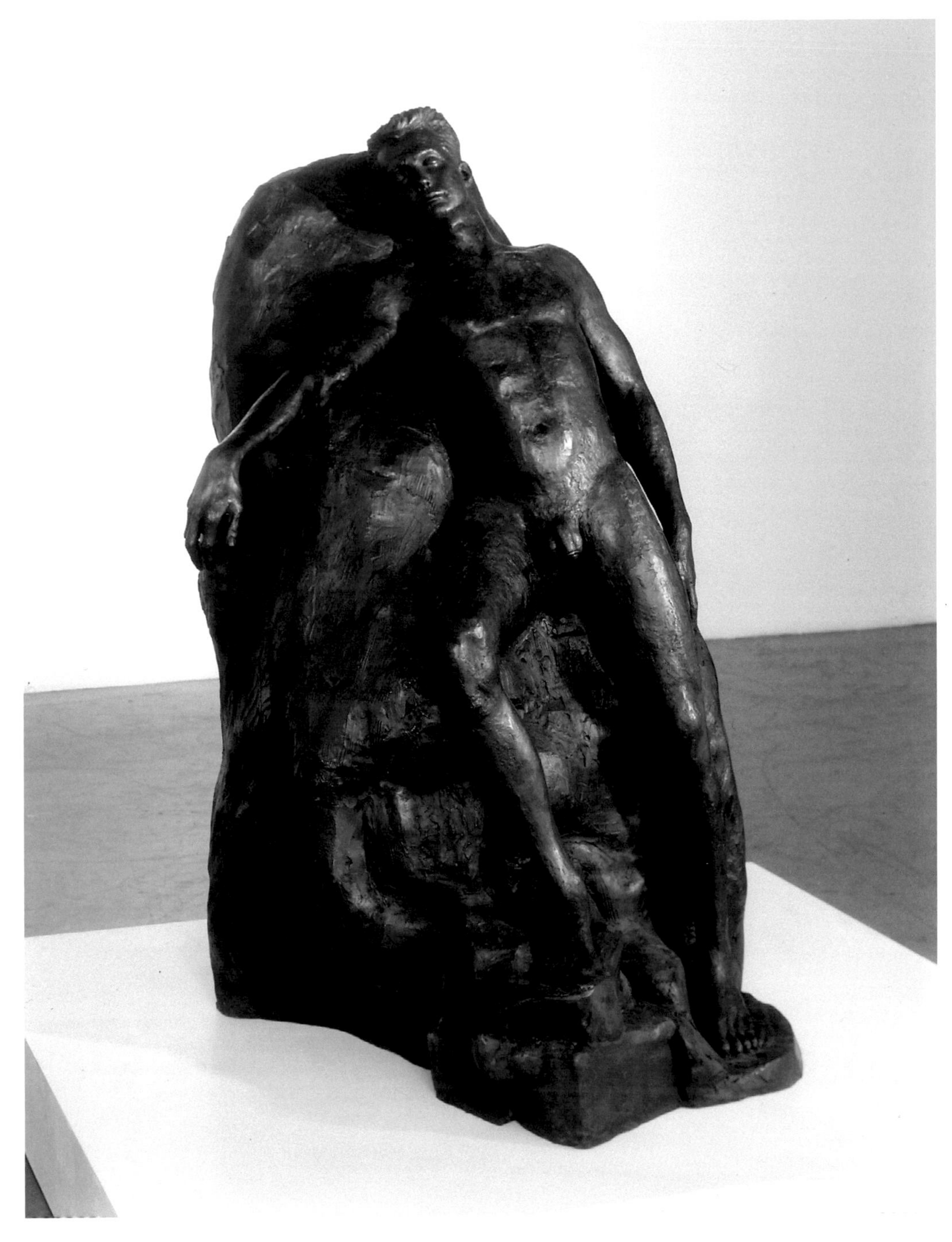

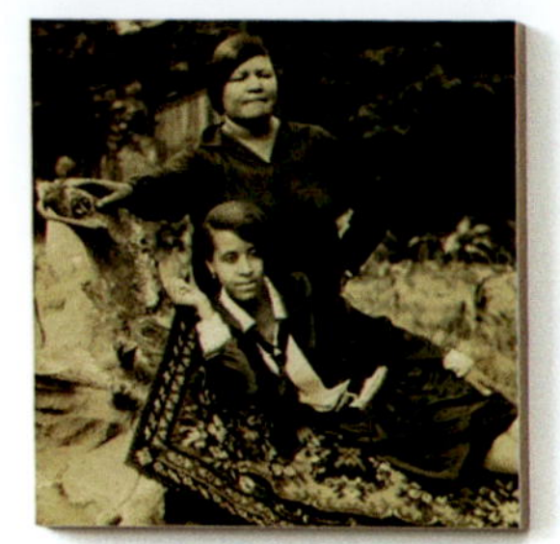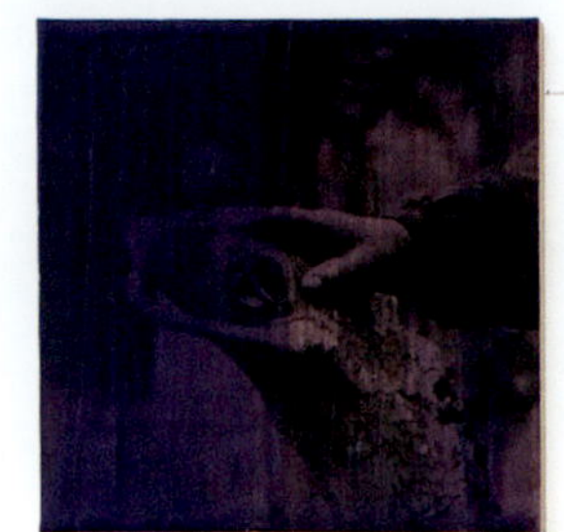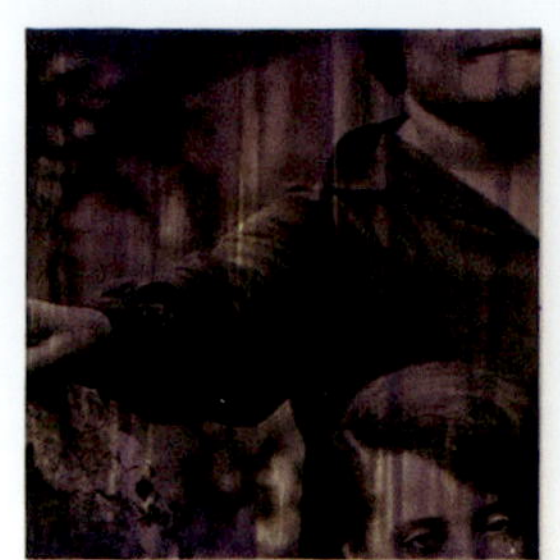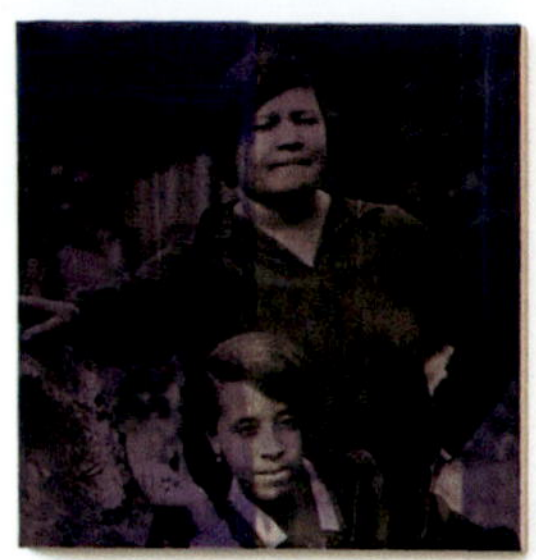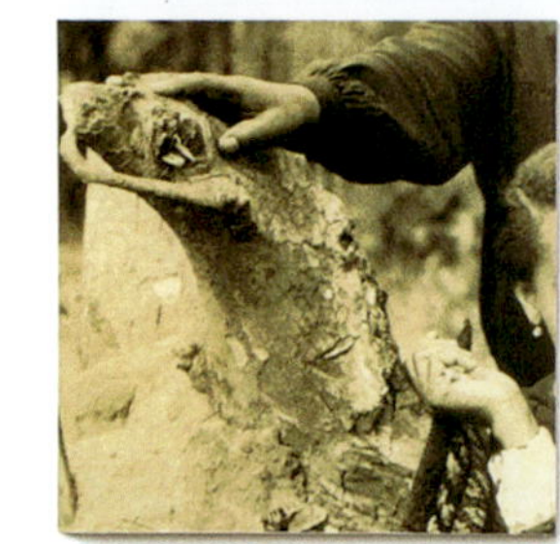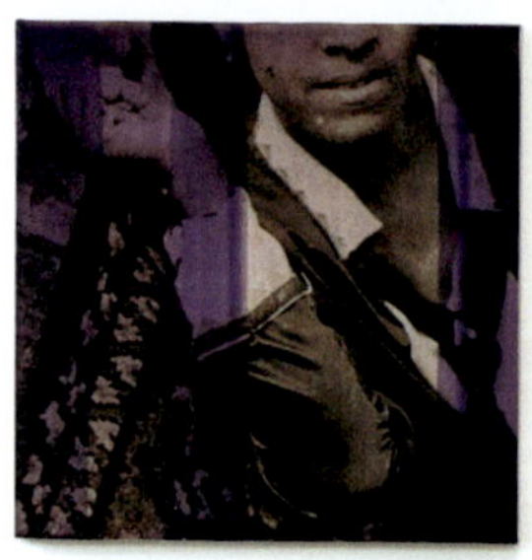

PLATE 19
Alanna Fields
American, born Marlboro, Maryland, 1990; active New York, New York
Our Love Was Deeply Purple, 2021
Pigment prints mounted on museum board; encaustic on panel
Courtesy of the artist

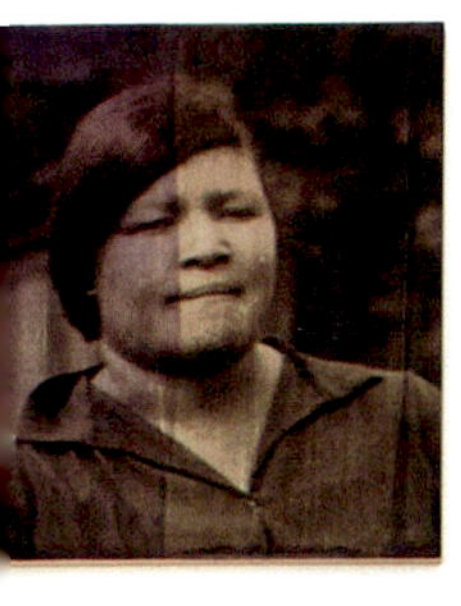
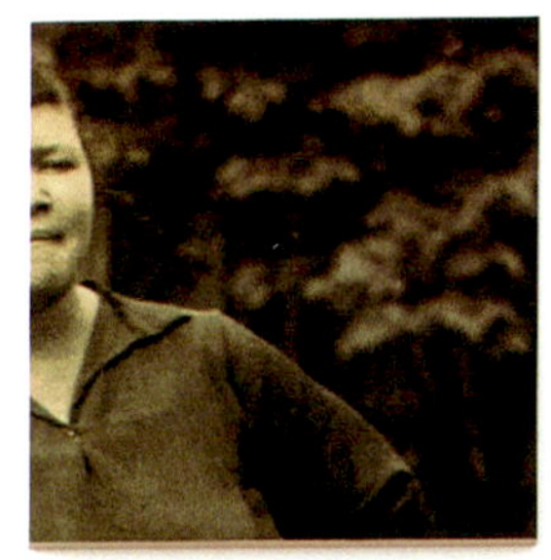
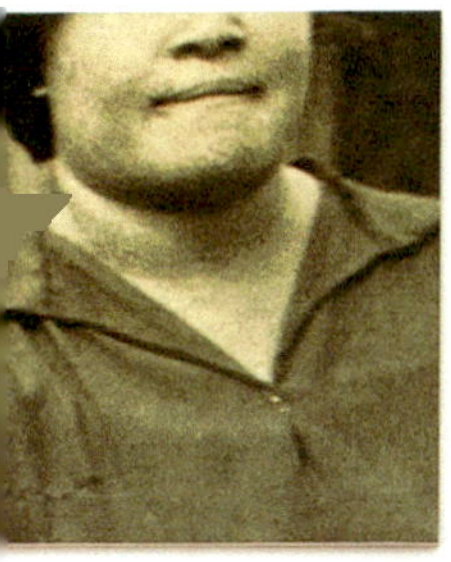
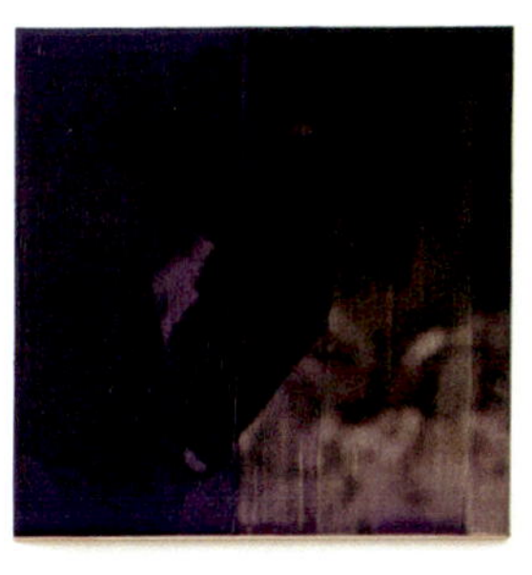
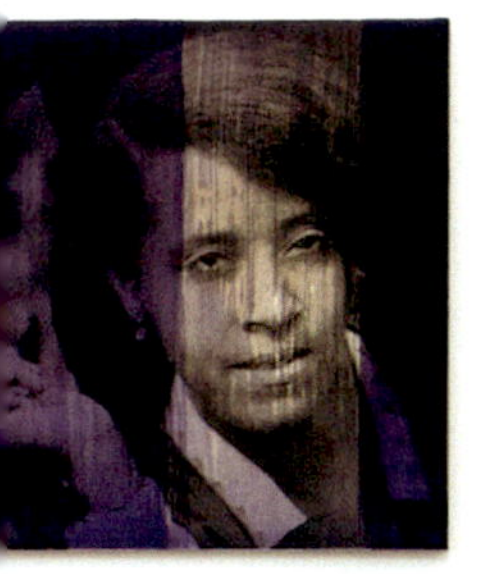
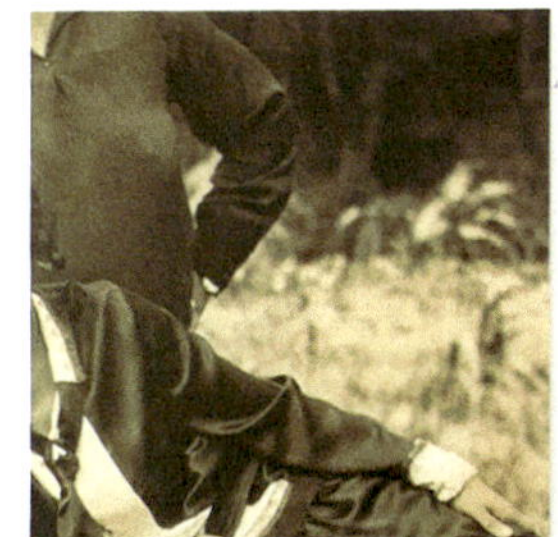
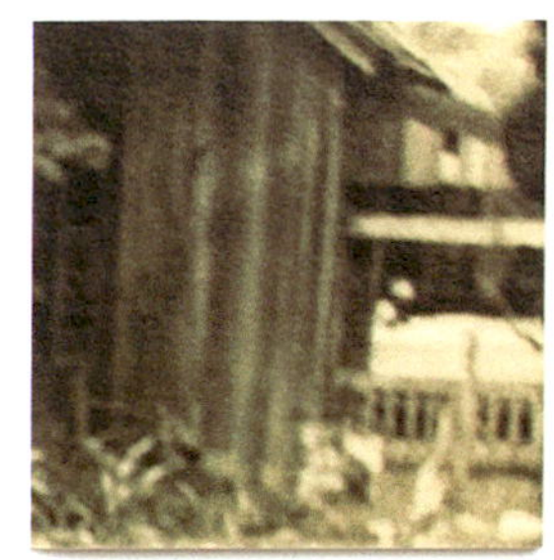
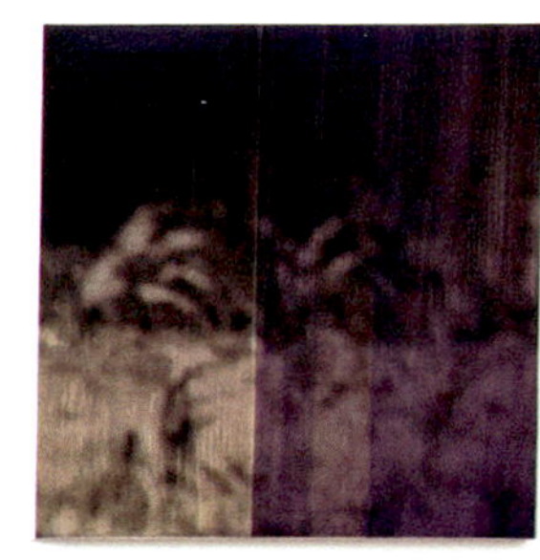
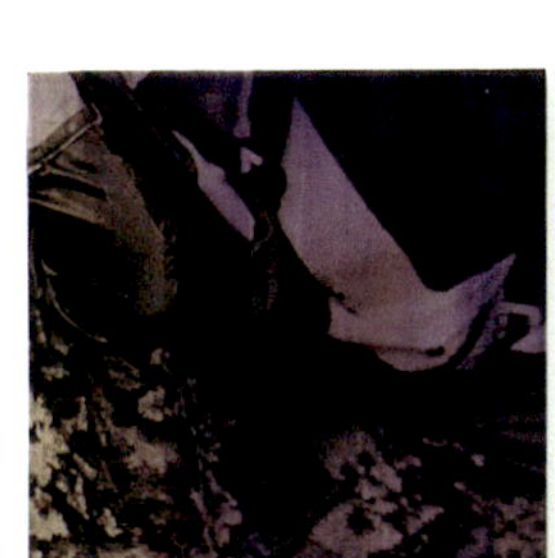
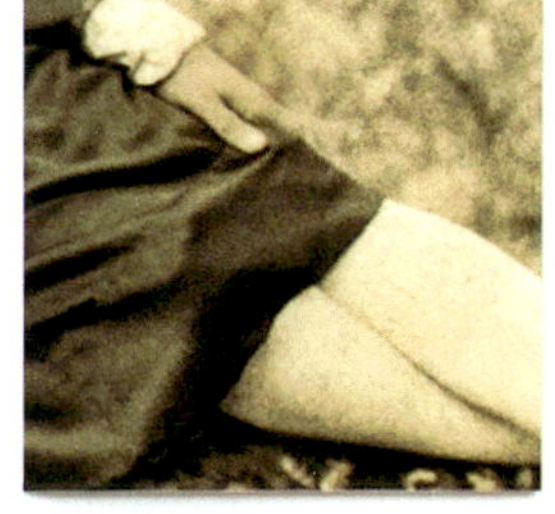
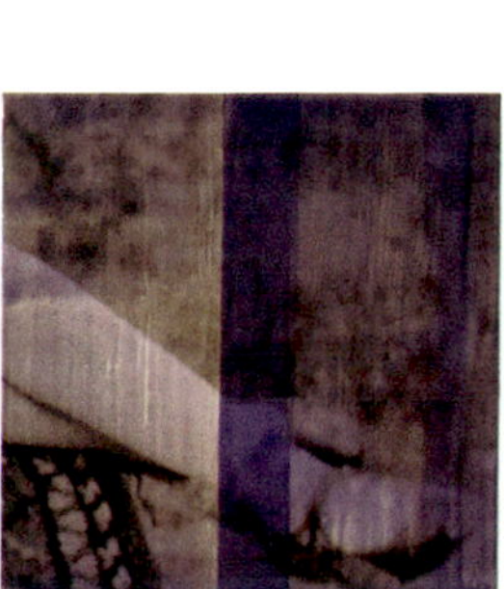
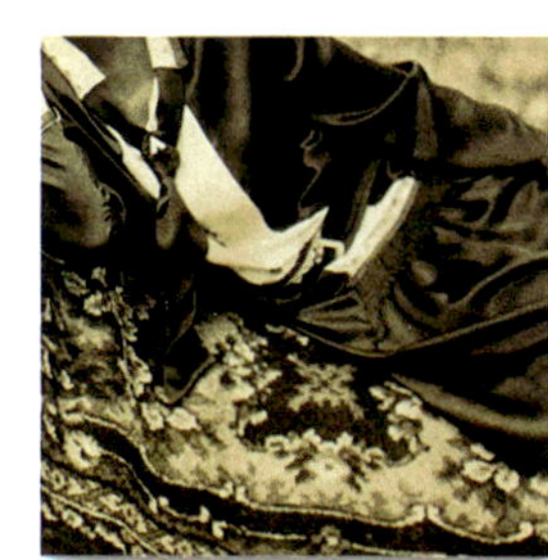
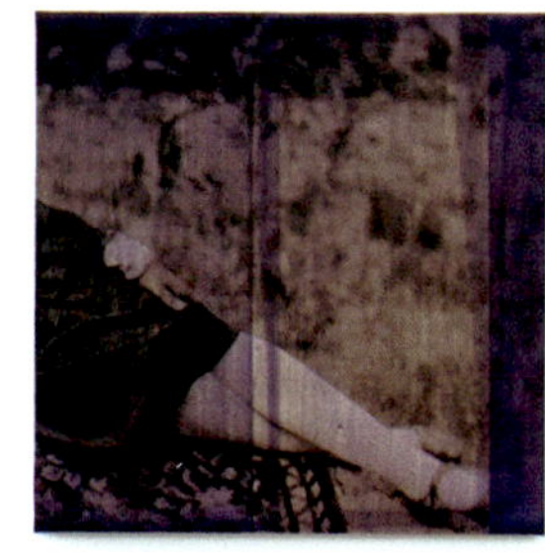

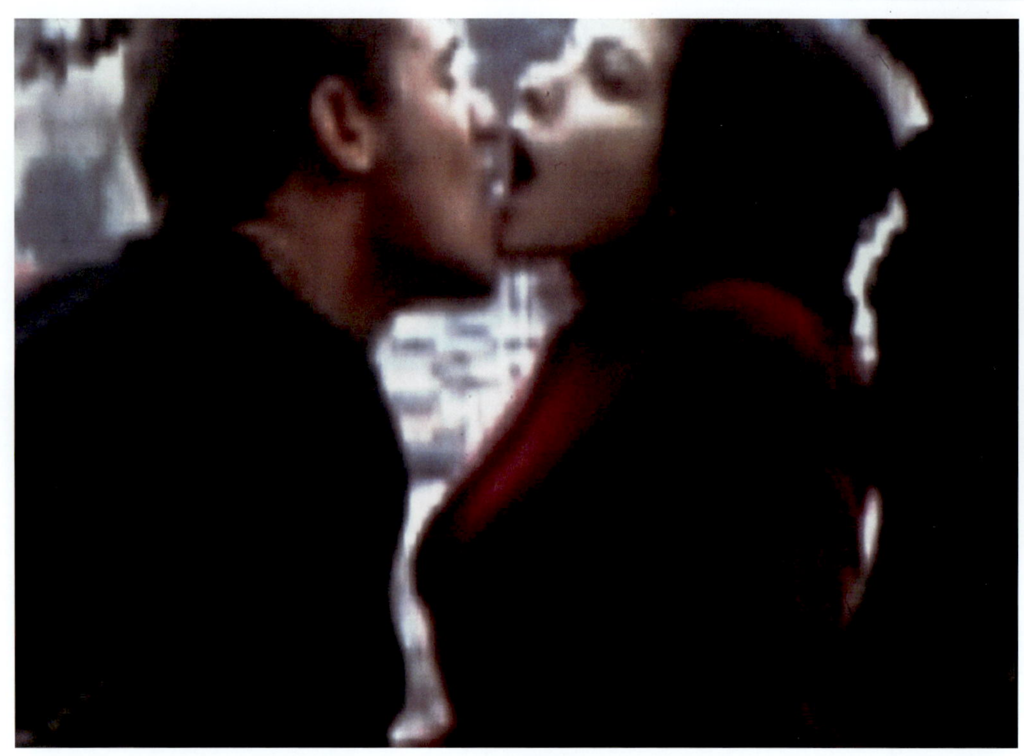

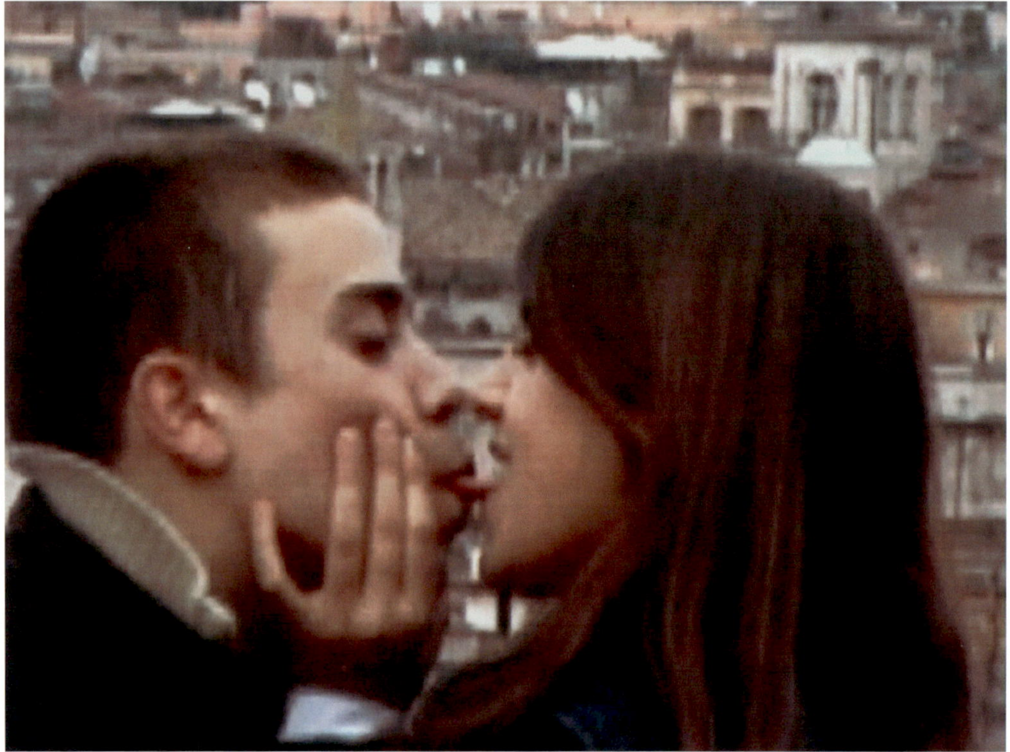

PLATE 20
Dara Friedman
German, born Bad Kreuznach, Germany, 1968; active Miami, Florida
Romance, 2001
Single-channel video
Courtesy of Pérez Art Museum Miami, gift of Mimi Floback

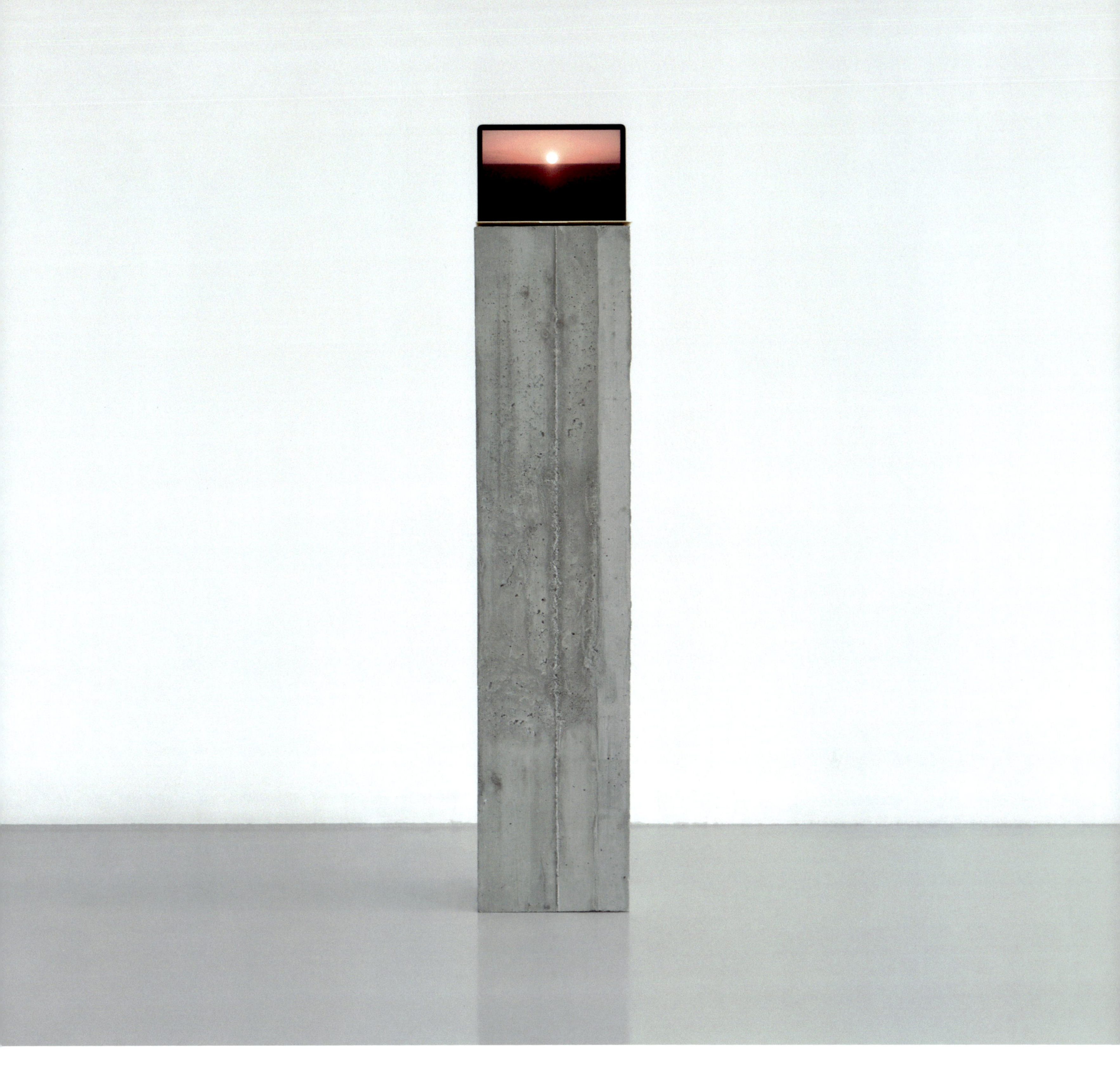

PLATE 21
Andrea Galvani
Italian, born Verona, Italy, 1973; active New York, New York,
and Mexico City, Mexico
The End (Action #5), 2015
16mm film transferred to video, displayed on MacBook Air on concrete pedestal
High Museum of Art, Atlanta, promised gift of the artist

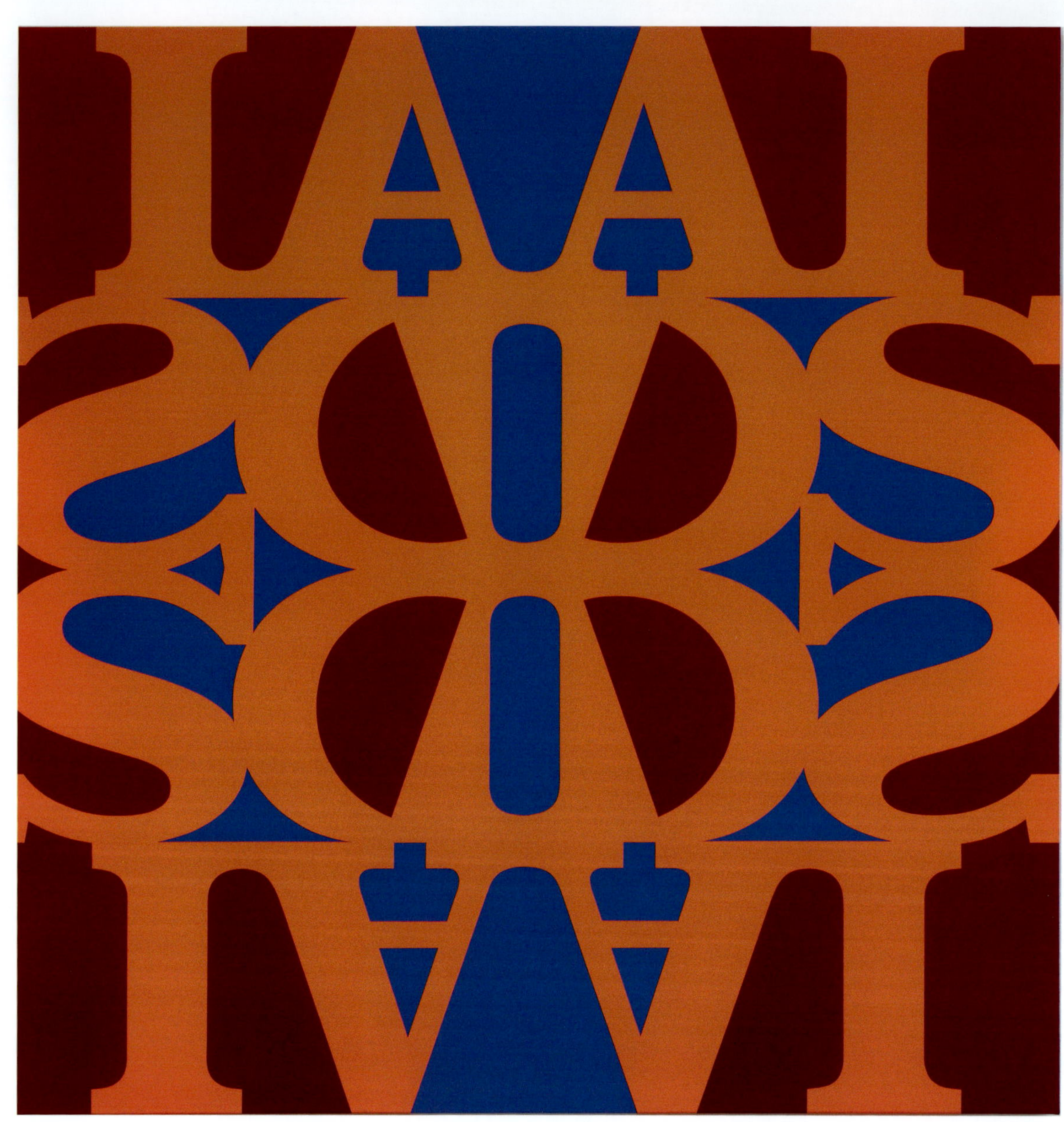

PLATE 22
General Idea (AA Bronson, born Michael Tims, Vancouver, British Columbia, Canada, 1946;
Felix Partz, born Ronald Gabe, Winnipeg, Manitoba, Canada, 1945–1994;
Jorge Zontal, born Slobodan Saia-Levy, Parma, Italy, 1944–1994), active 1967–1994
Great AIDS (Cadmium Orange Light), 1990/2019
Acrylic on linen
Courtesy of the Estate of General Idea and Mitchell-Innes & Nash, New York. © General Idea, Inc.

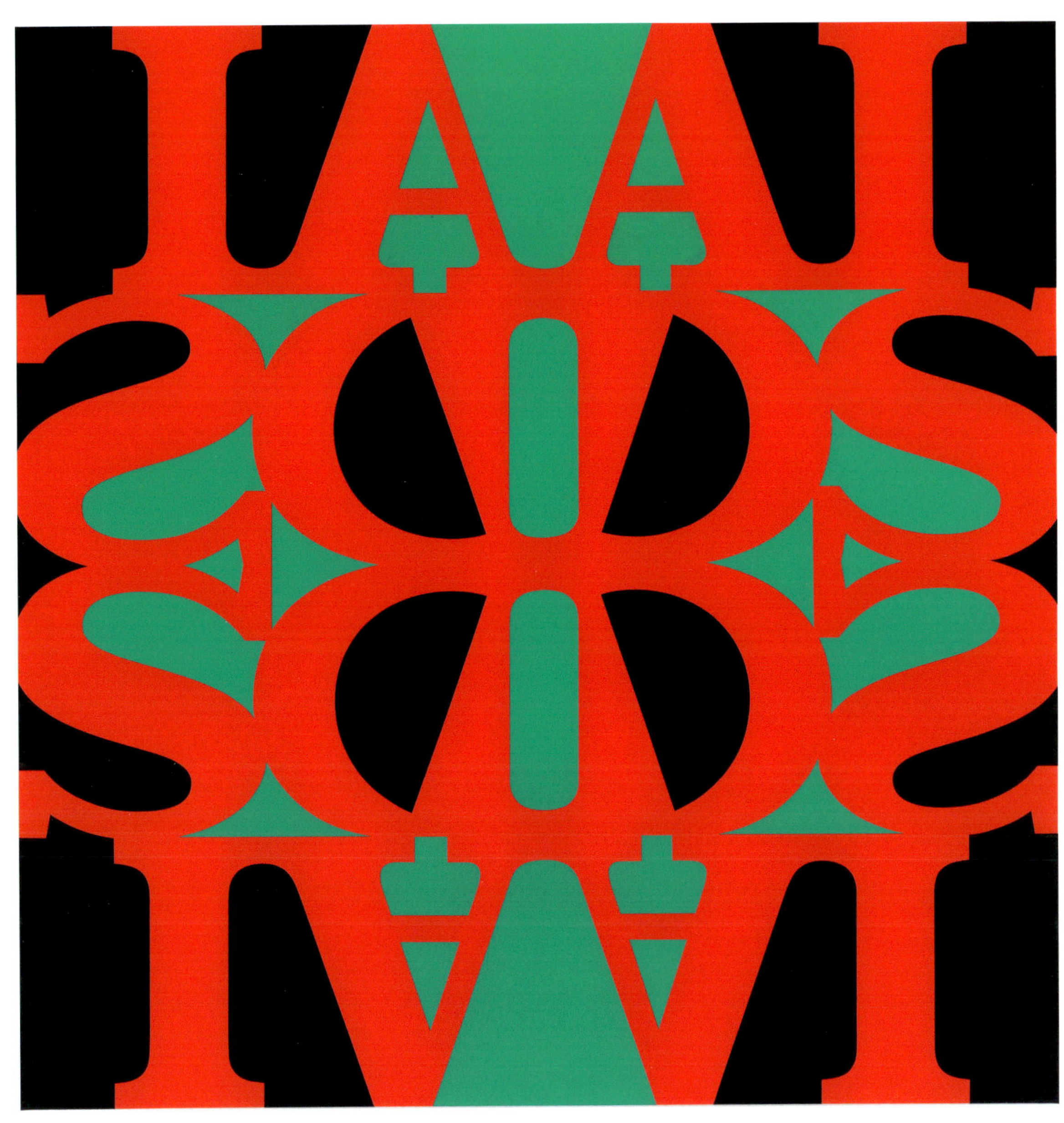

PLATE 23
General Idea (AA Bronson, born Michael Tims, Vancouver, British Columbia, Canada, 1946;
Felix Partz, born Ronald Gabe, Winnipeg, Manitoba, Canada, 1945–1994;
Jorge Zontal, born Slobodan Saia-Levy, Parma, Italy, 1944–1994), active 1967–1994
Great AIDS (Pyrrole Orange), 1990/2019
Acrylic on linen
Courtesy of the Estate of General Idea and Mitchell-Innes & Nash, New York. © General Idea, Inc.

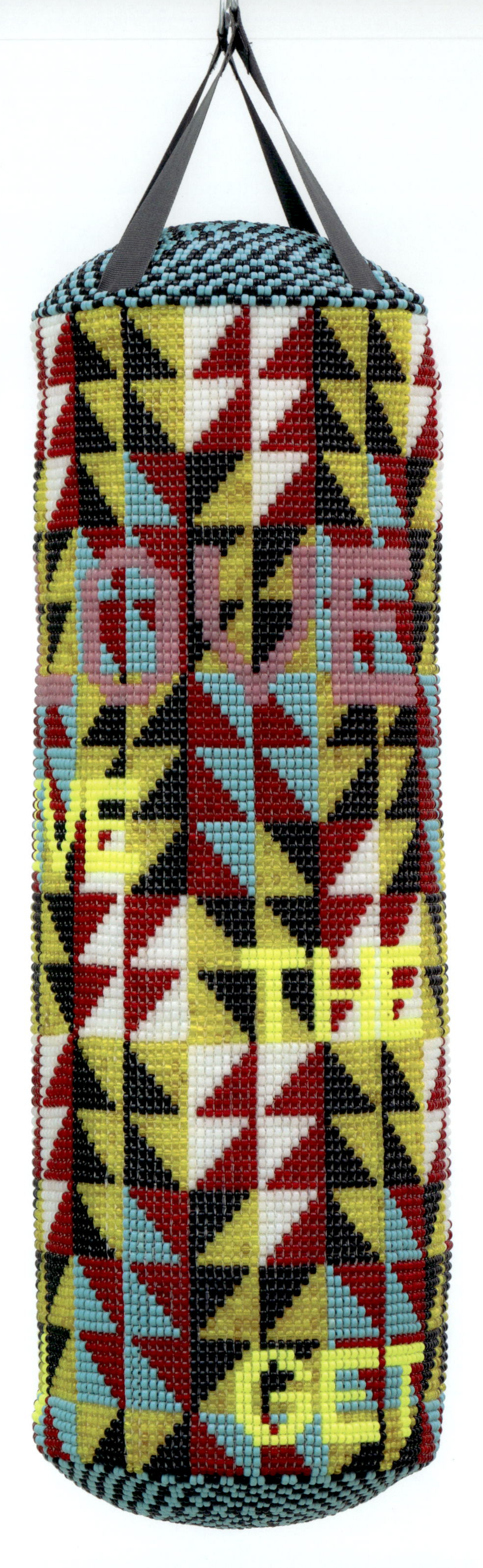
OF
THE
GET

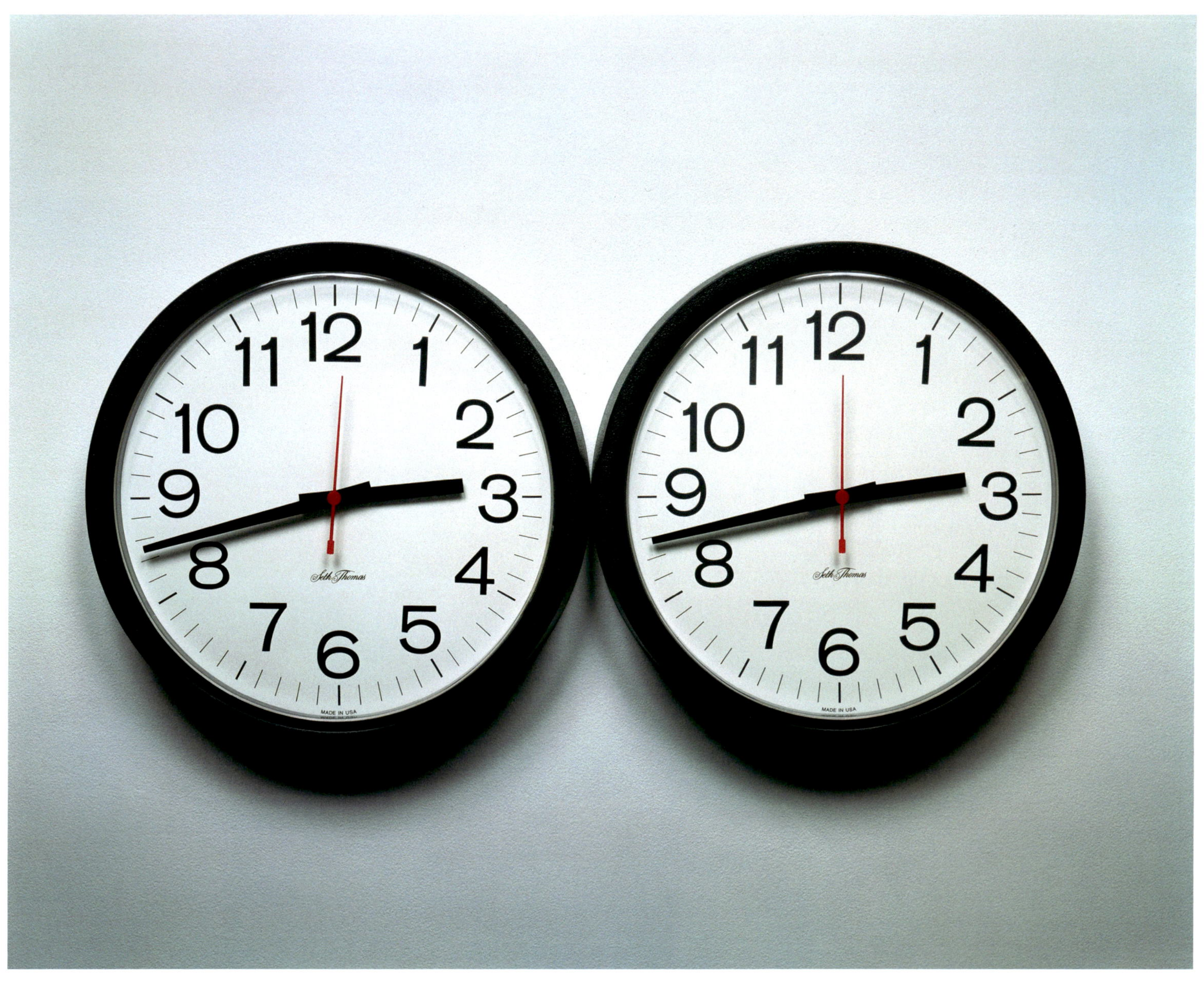

PLATE 24
Jeffrey Gibson
American, Mississippi Choctaw-Cherokee,
born Colorado Springs, Colorado, 1972; active Hudson, New York
The Love You Give Is the Love You Get, 2020
Punching bag, glass beads, artificial sinew, and acrylic felt
High Museum of Art, Atlanta, promised gift of John Auerbach

PLATE 25
Felix Gonzalez-Torres
American, born Guáimaro, Cuba, 1957; died Miami, Florida, 1996
"Untitled" (Perfect Lovers), 1987–1990
Wall clocks
Dallas Museum of Art, fractional gift of The Rachofsky Collection

PLATE 26
Kahlil Robert Irving
American, born San Diego, California, 1992; active St. Louis, Missouri
My Grandmother's Cupboard (Artifact) (detail), 2020
Glazed ceramics and wooden cabinet
Courtesy of the artist

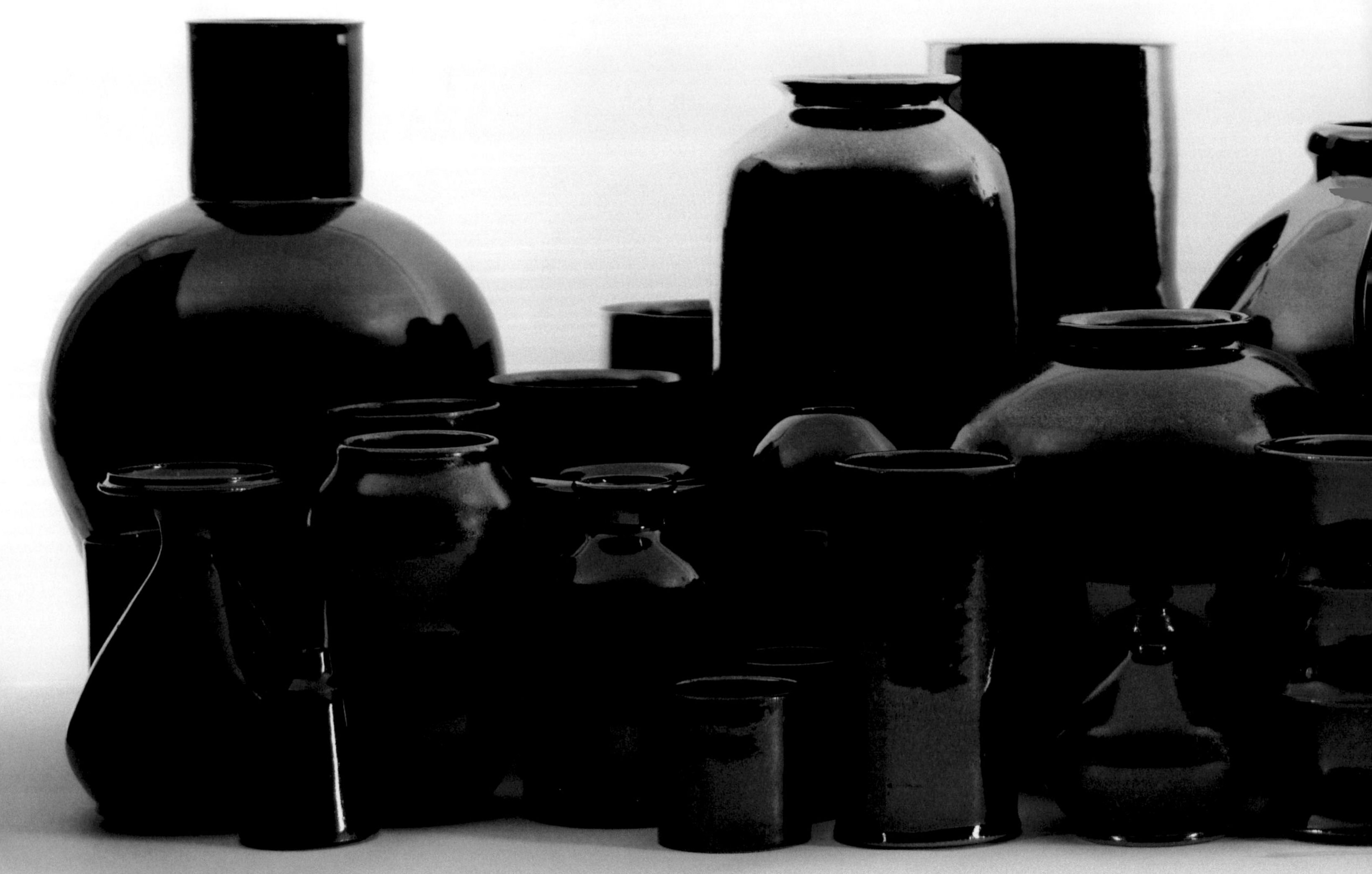

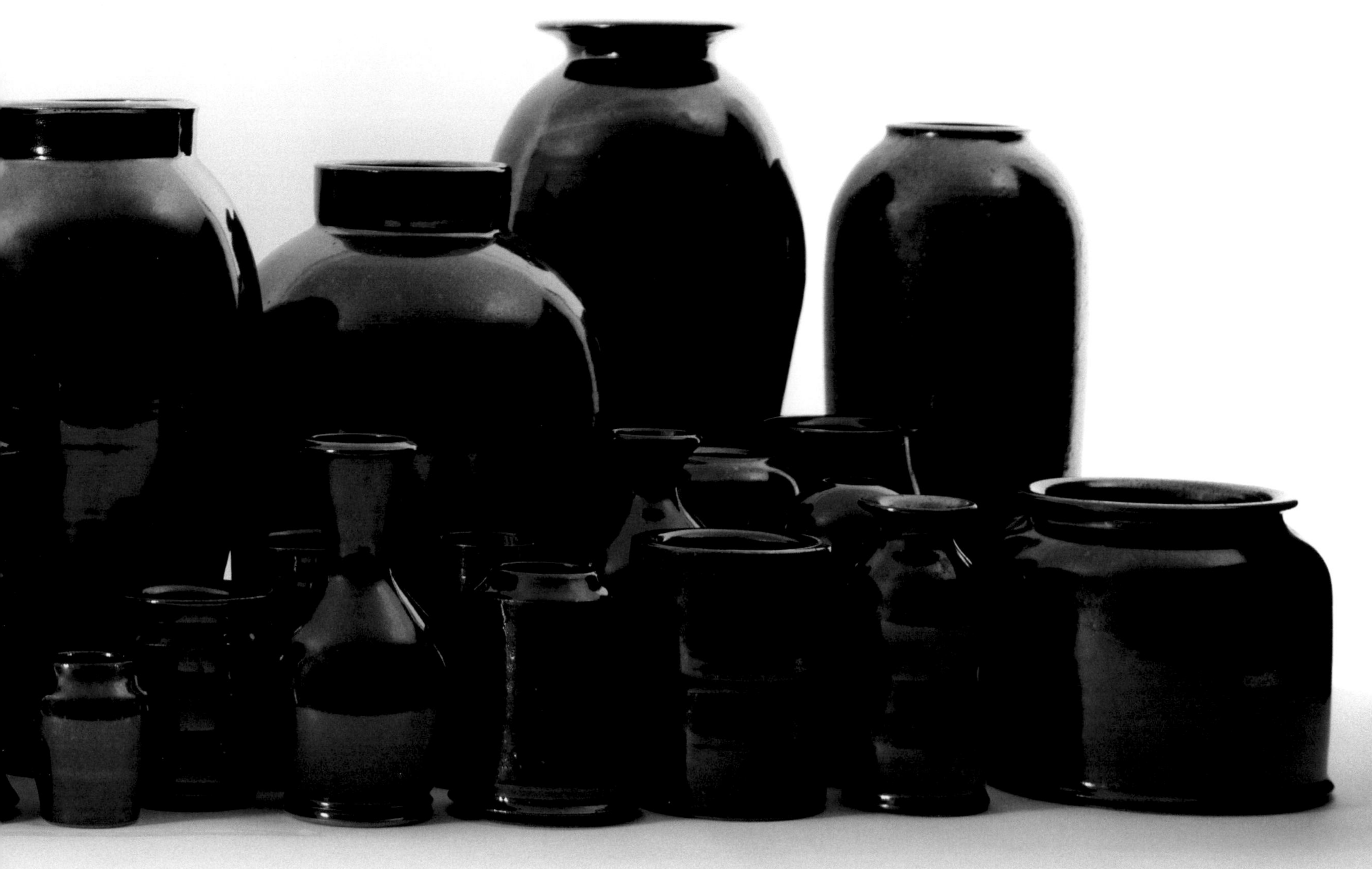

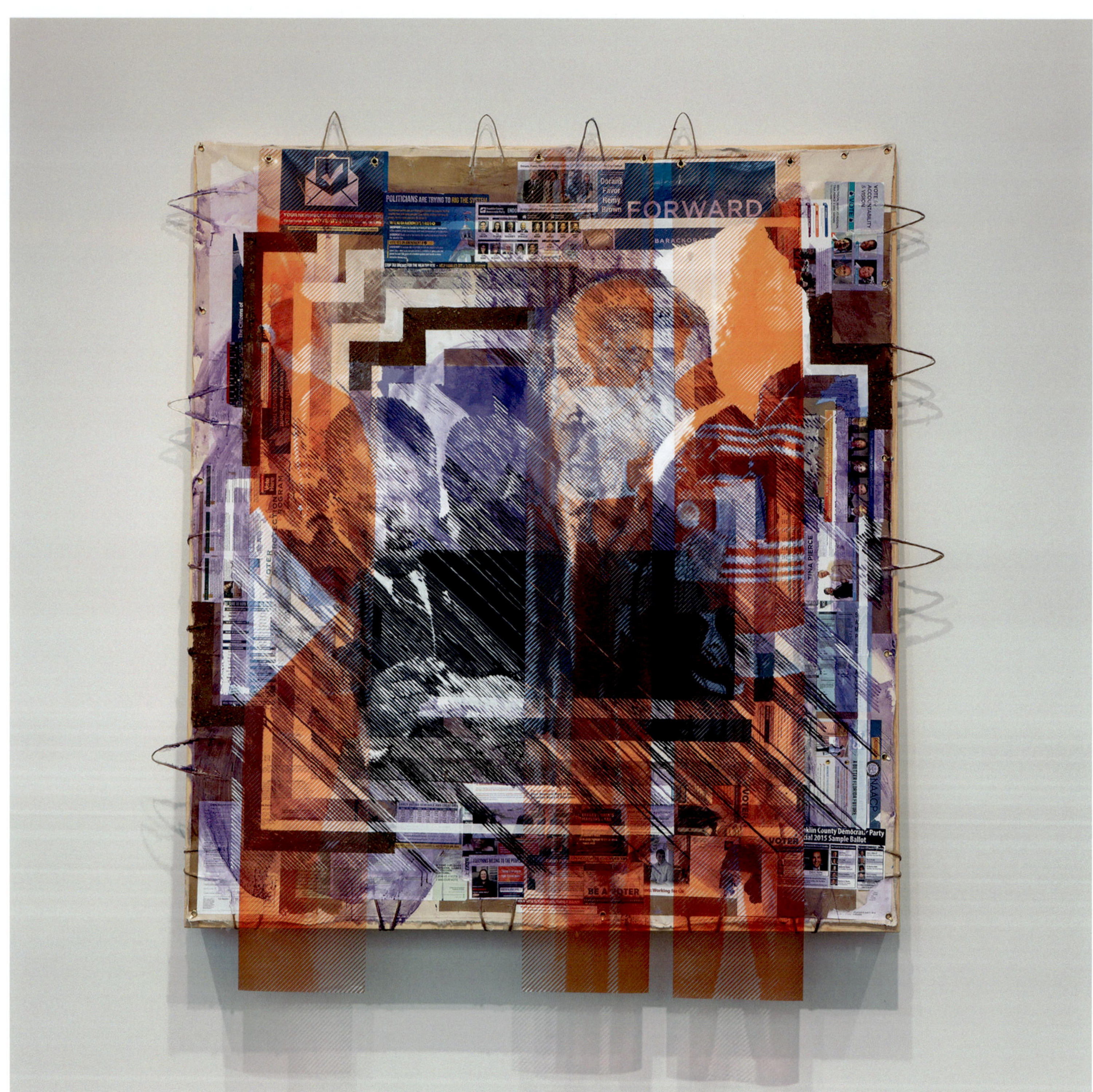

PLATE 27
Tomashi Jackson
American, born Houston, Texas, 1980; active Cambridge, Massachusetts
Love Rollercoaster (2016 Butler County Line) (1965 John Lewis Accepts
Voting Rights Act Signing Pen from LBJ), 2020
Acrylic, Pentelic marble, Ohio Underground Railroad site soil,
American electoral ephemera, and paper bags on canvas and fabric
Collection of Suzanne McFayden

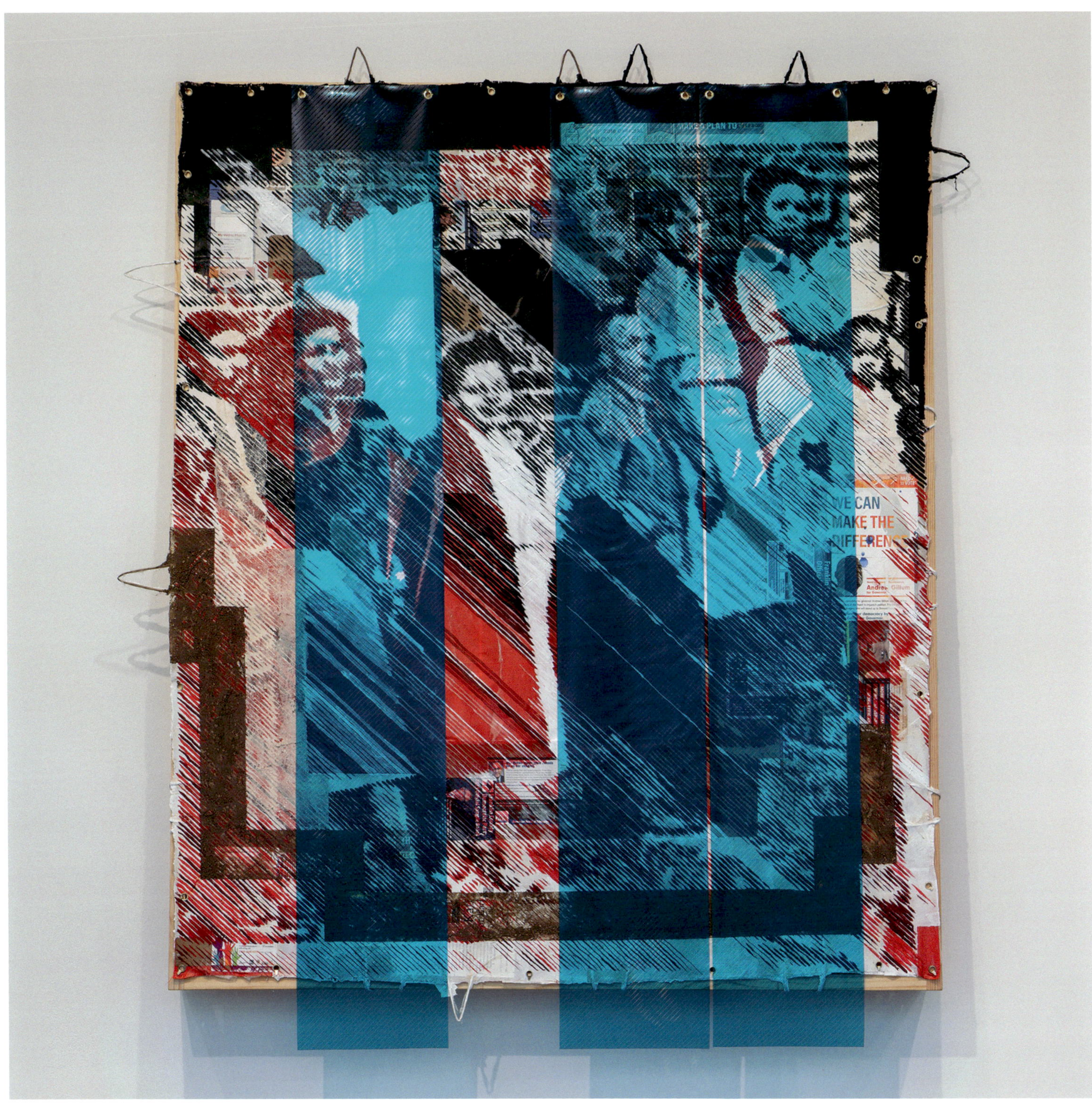

PLATE 28
Tomashi Jackson
American, born Houston, Texas, 1980; active Cambridge, Massachusetts
Is Anybody Gonna Be Saved? (1948 Middle of Voter Registration Line) (1965 Abernathy and King Watch the Signing of the Act), 2020
Acrylic, Pentelic marble, Ohio Underground Railroad site soil, American electoral ephemera, and paper bags on canvas and fabric
Courtesy of the artist and Tilton Gallery, New York

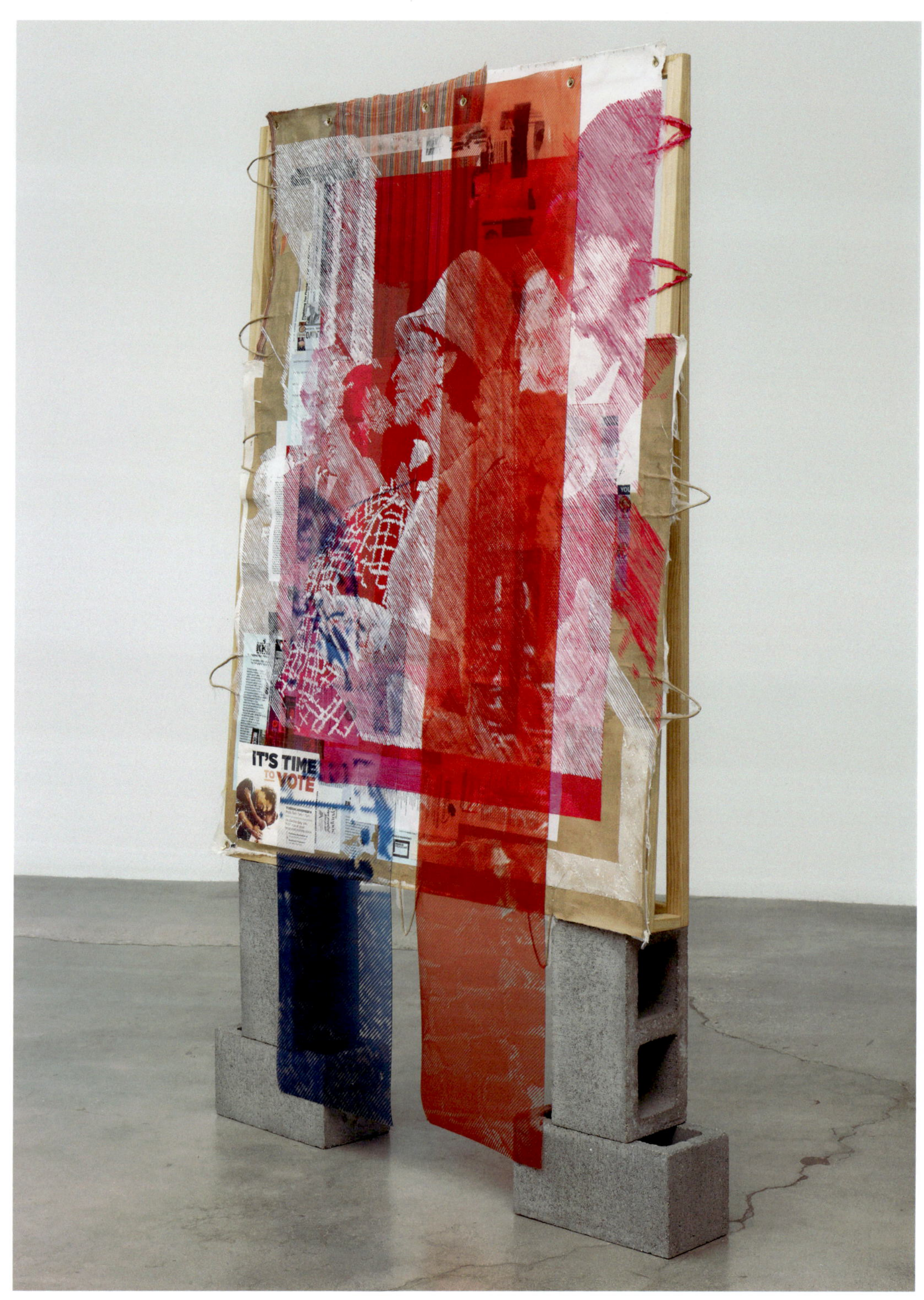

PLATE 29
Tomashi Jackson
American, born Houston, Texas, 1980; active Cambridge, Massachusetts
Ecology of Fear (Abrams for Governor of Georgia) (Negro Women Wait to Congratulate LBJ), 2020
Archival prints on PVC marine vinyl, Pentelic marble dust, acrylic paint, American election flyers, Greek ballot papers, paper bags, and muslin
Collection of Arthur Lewis and Hau Nguyen

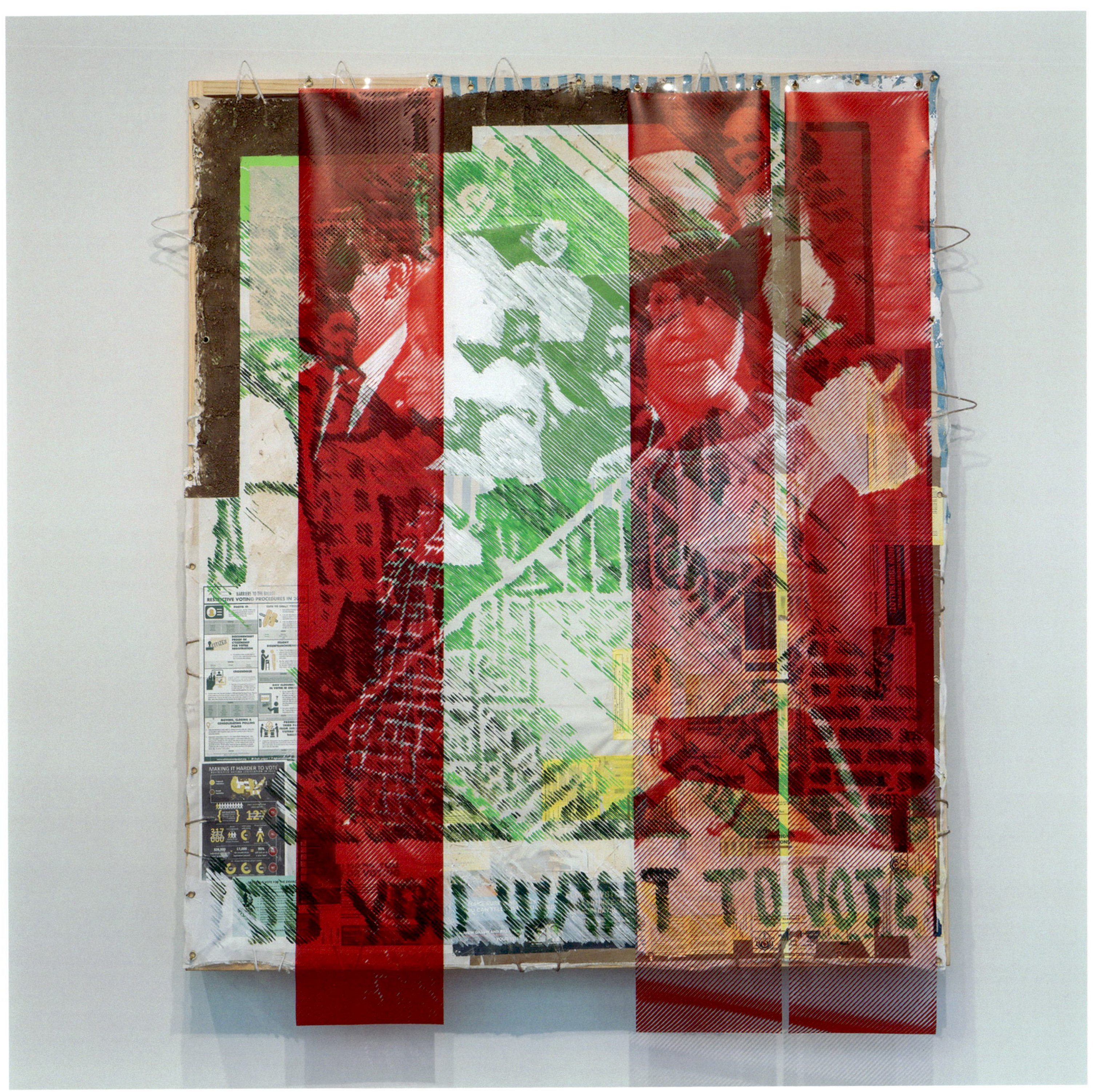

PLATE 30
Tomashi Jackson
American, born Houston, Texas, 1980; active Cambridge, Massachusetts
Contradiction (1948 Head of Voter Registration Line) (1965 Clarence Mitchell,
Patricia Roberts Harris, and Others Watch the Signing of the Act), 2020
Acrylic, Pentelic marble, Ohio Underground Railroad site soil, American
electoral ephemera, and paper bags on canvas and fabric
Pizzuti Collection

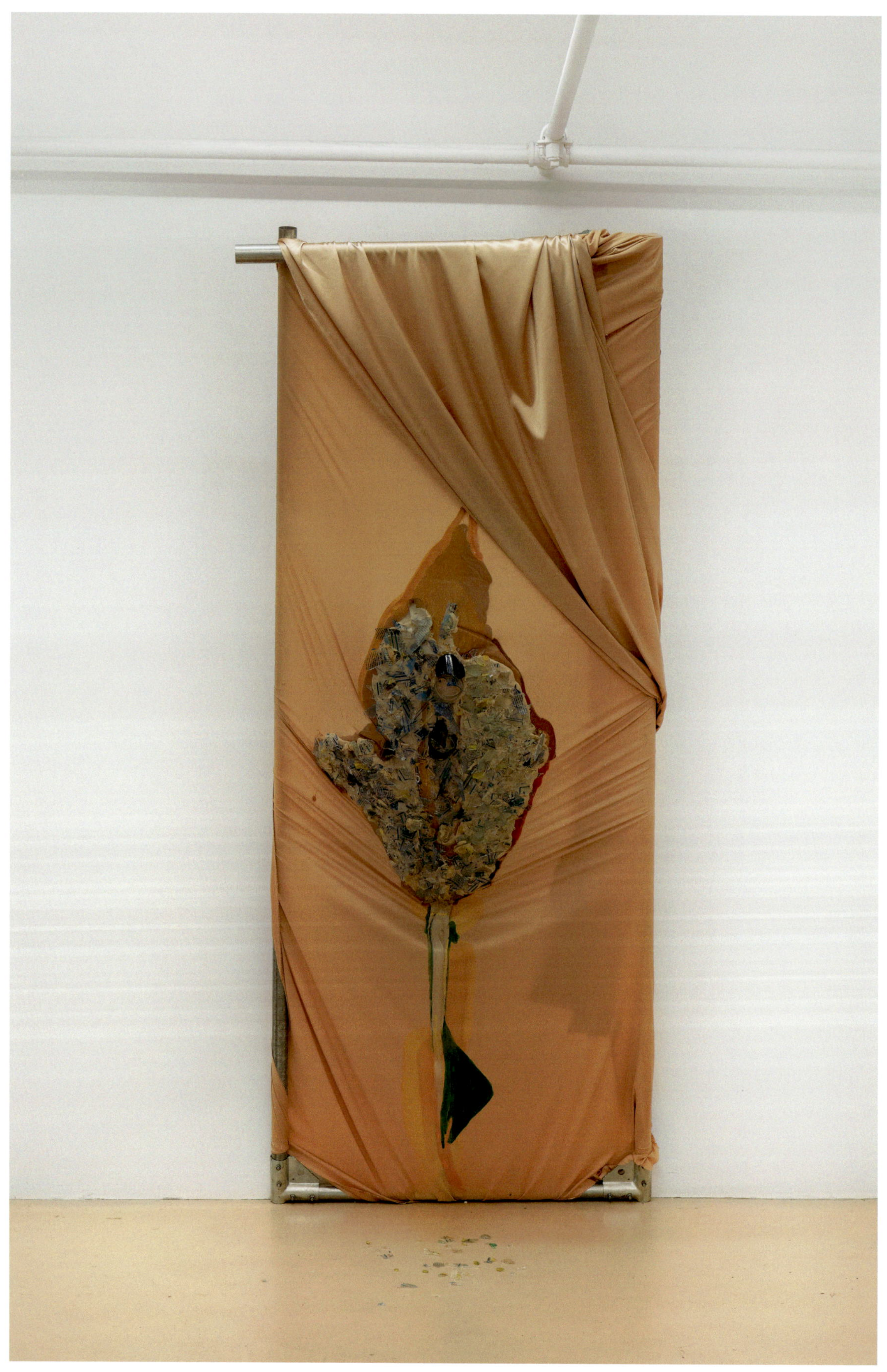

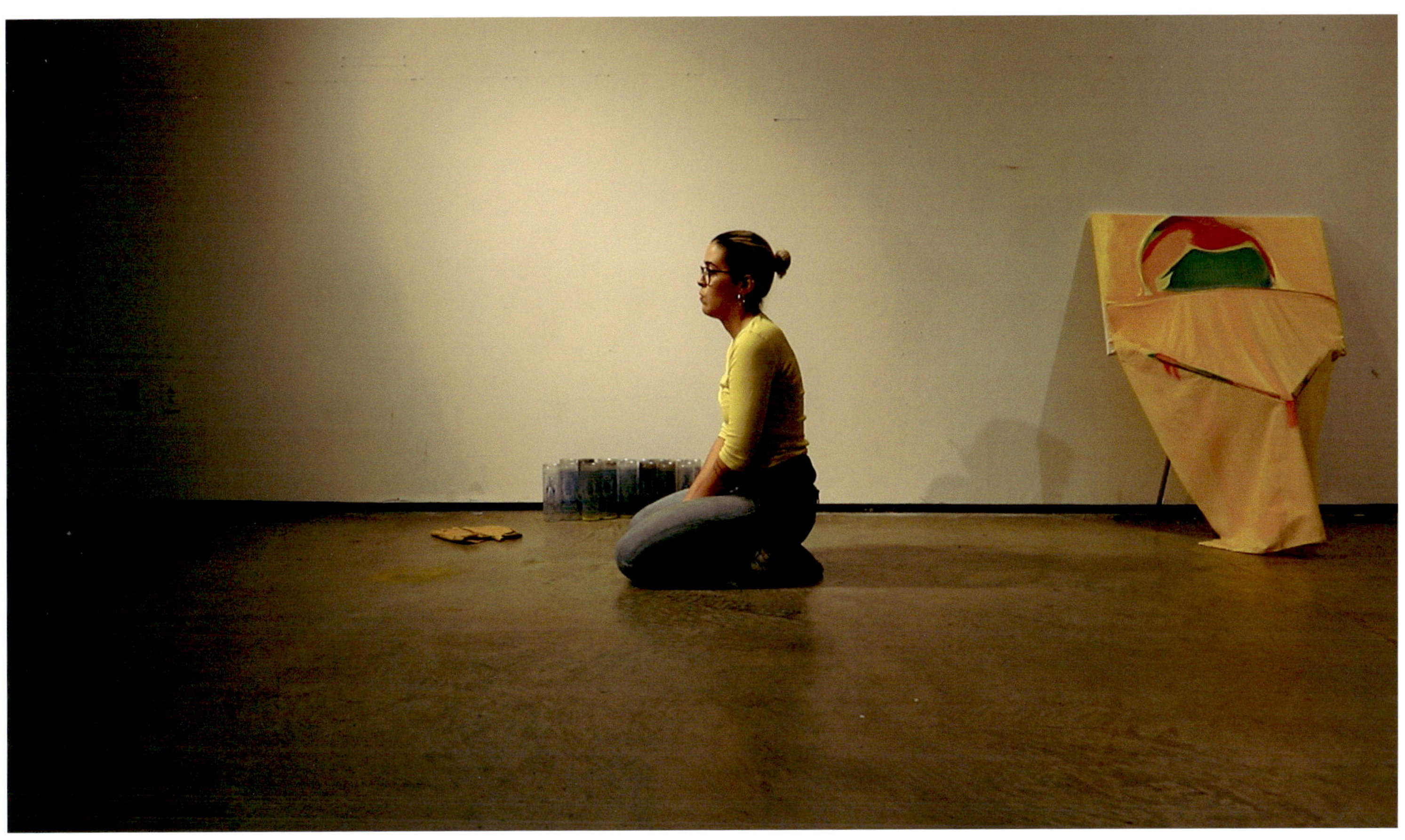

PLATE 31
María de los Angeles Rodríguez Jiménez
Cuban, born Holguín, Cuba, 1992; active Miami, Florida
Caridad, 2019
Oil, rubber, and glass on satin over fence post structure,
hung with wire on wall; acrylic paint and glass on floor
Courtesy of the artist and David Castillo

PLATE 32
María de los Angeles Rodríguez Jiménez
Cuban, born Holguín, Cuba, 1992; active Miami, Florida
Glass, Yale University, December 14, 2018, 2018
Single-channel video
Running time: 3 minutes, 34 seconds
Courtesy of the artist and David Castillo

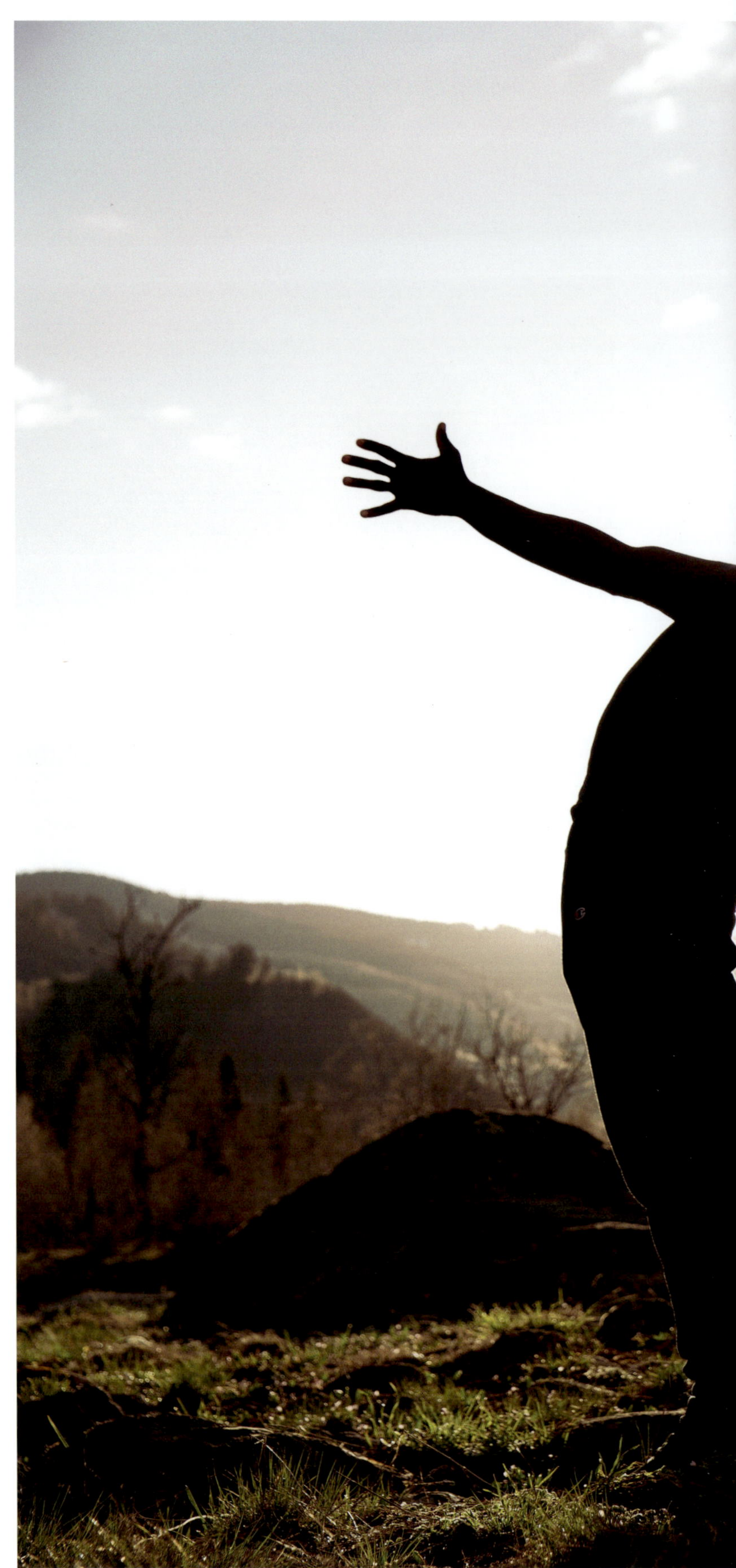

PLATE 33
Rashid Johnson
American, born Chicago, Illinois, 1977;
active New York, New York
The Hikers, 2019
16mm film transferred to digital video with sound
Running time: 7 minutes, 14 seconds
High Museum of Art, Atlanta, anonymous gift, 2021.171

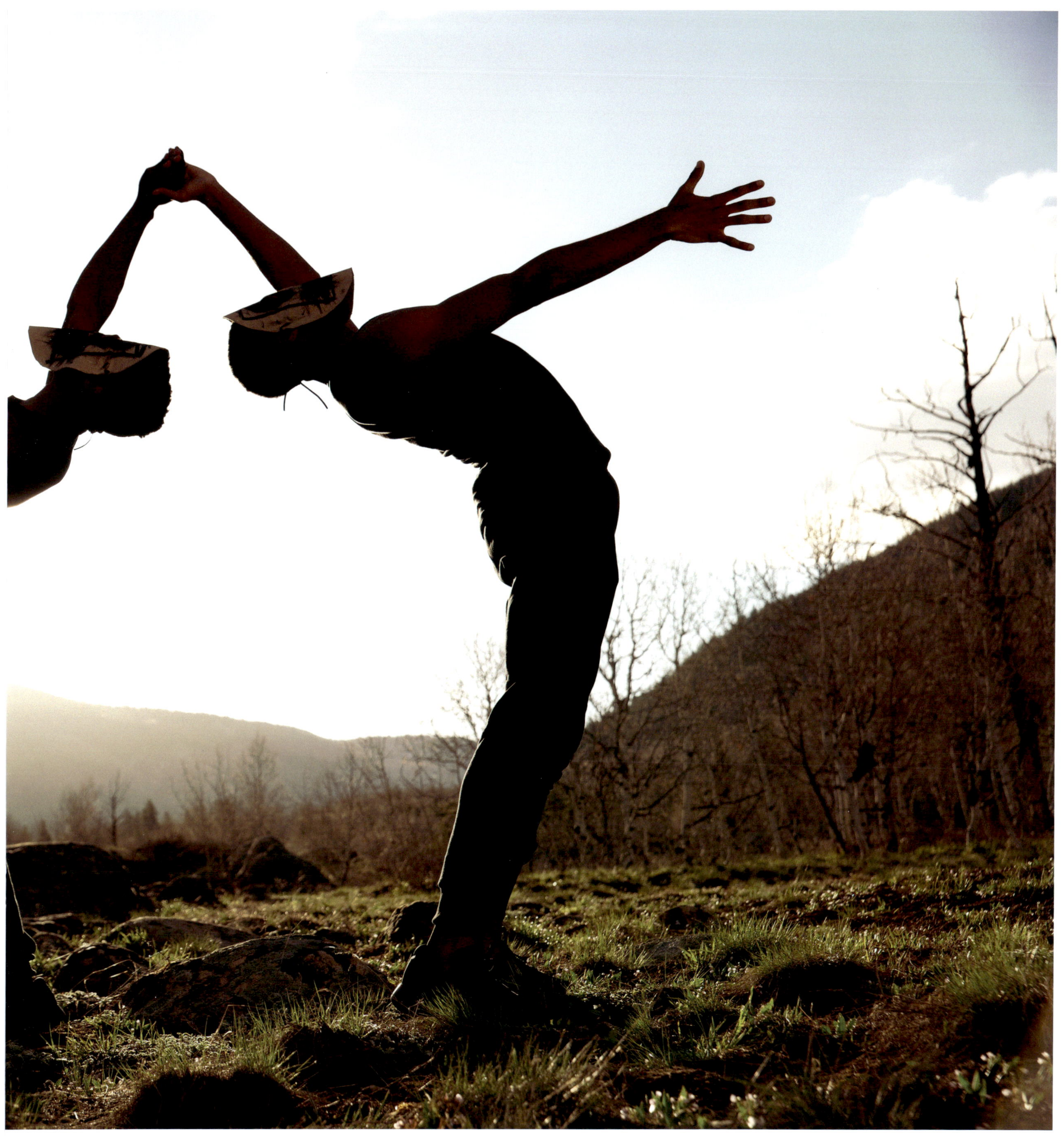

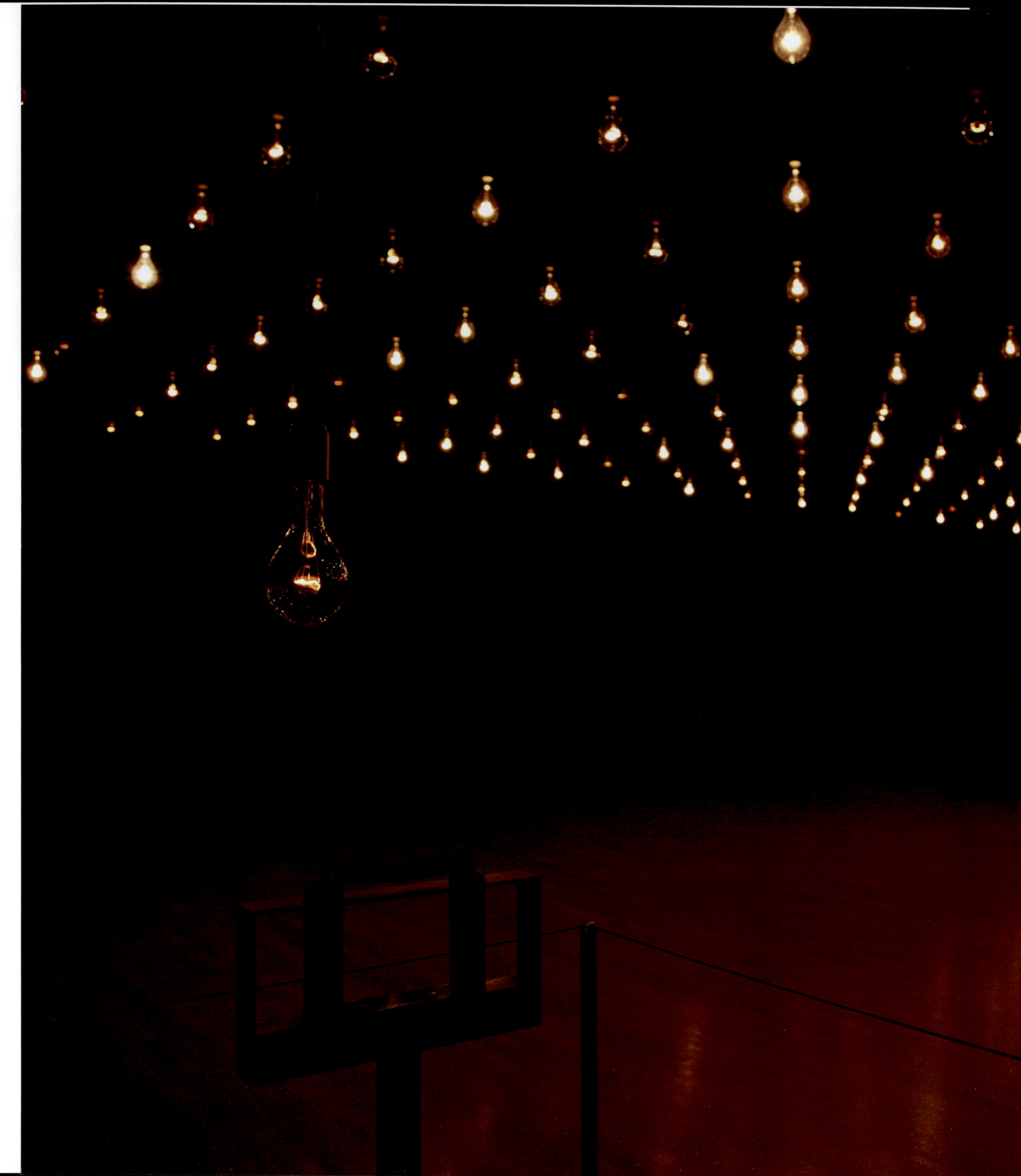

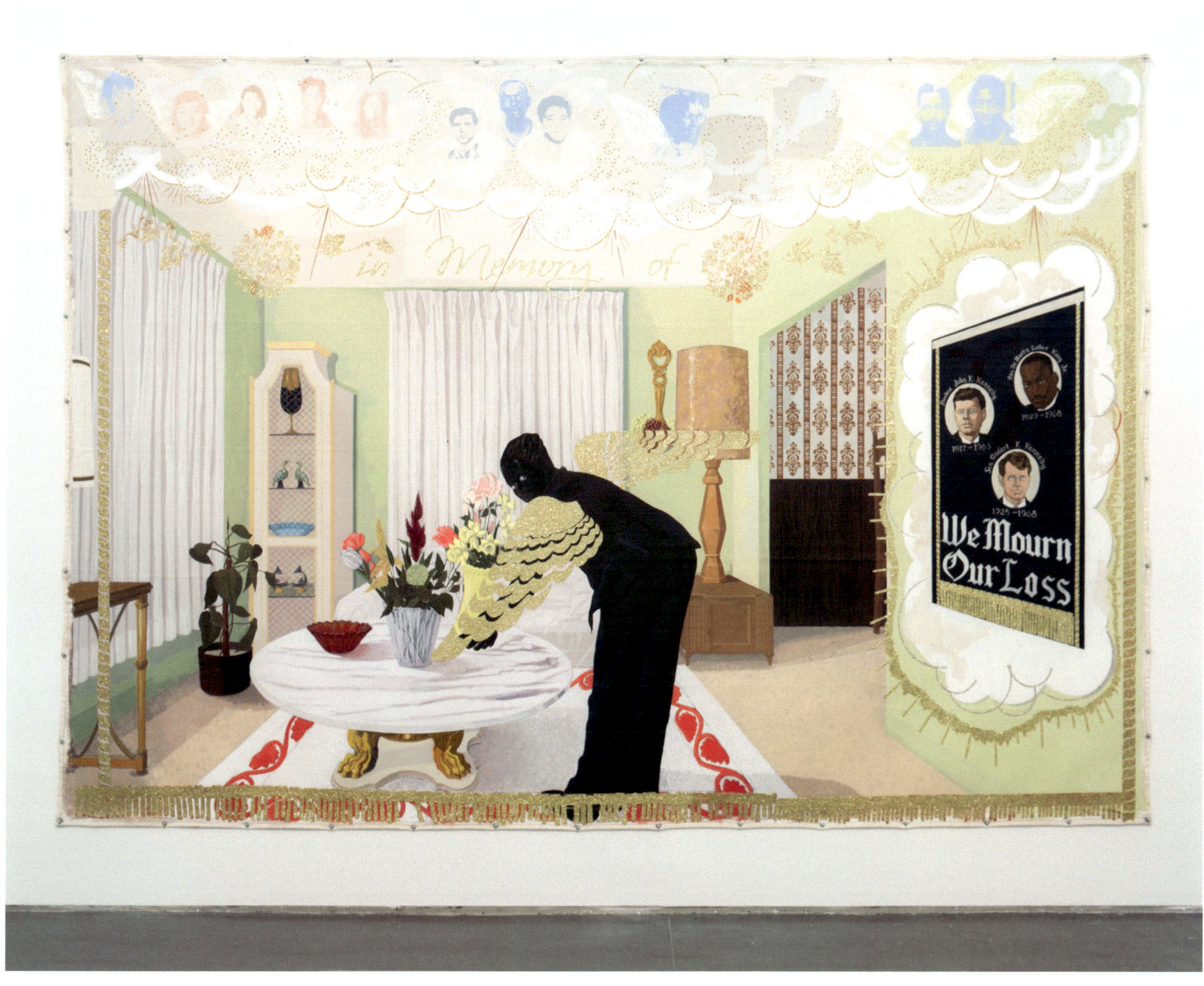

PLATE 36
Rafael Lozano-Hemmer
Mexican, born Mexico City, Mexico, 1967; active Montréal, Canada
Pulse Room, 2006
Incandescent light bulbs, voltage controllers,
heart rate sensors, computer, metal, and sound
Museum of Modern Art, New York, gift of Karin Srb, 213.2014

PLATE 37
Kerry James Marshall
American, born Birmingham, Alabama, 1955; active Chicago, Illinois
Souvenir I, 1997
Acrylic, collage, and glitter on canvas
Museum of Contemporary Art Chicago, Bernice and Kenneth
Newberger Fund, 1997.73

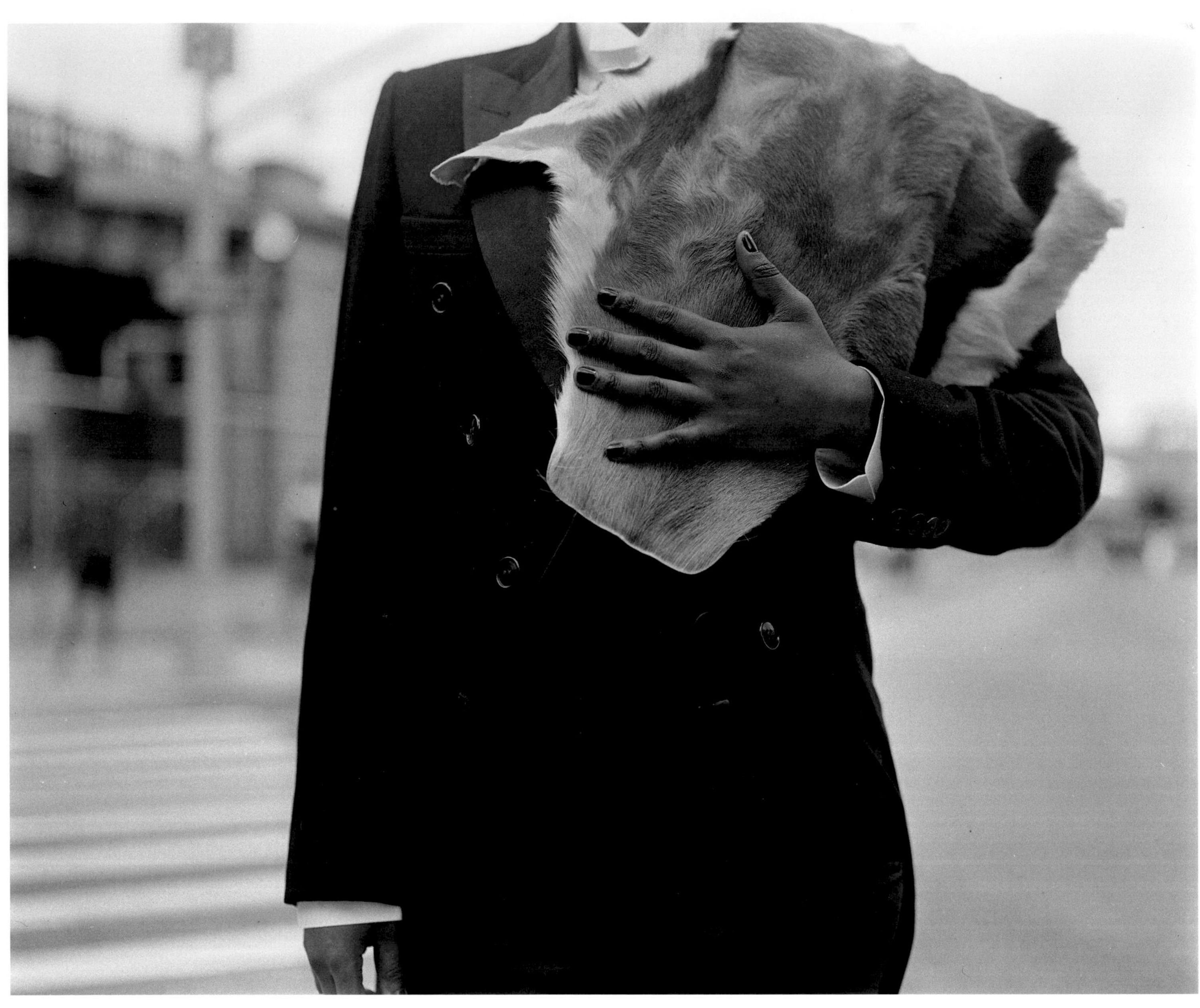

PLATE 38
Felicita Felli Maynard
American, born Brooklyn, New York, 1989;
active New Orleans, Louisiana
Angelo Lwazi Owenzayo from the series
Ole Dandy, the Tribute, 2018
Gelatin silver print
Courtesy of the artist

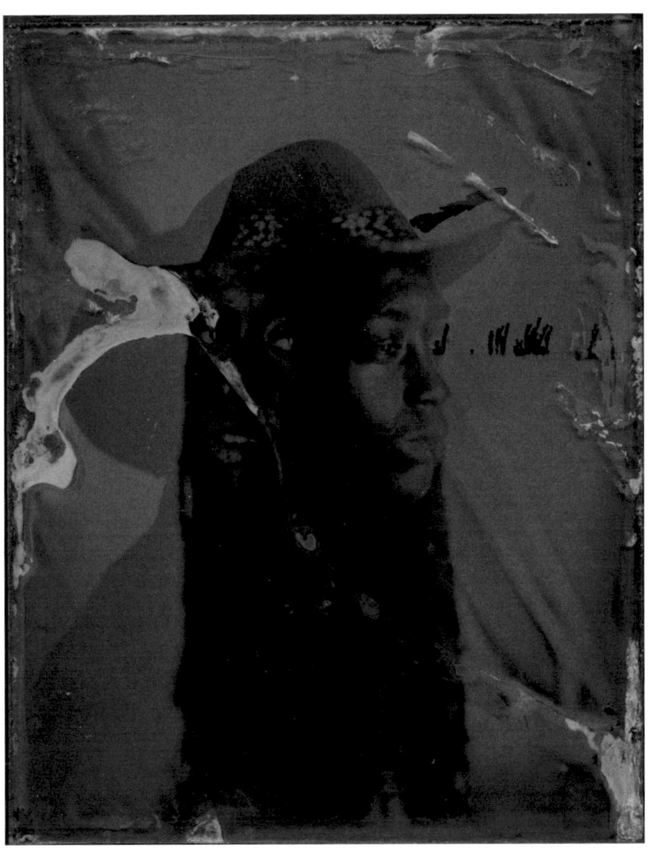

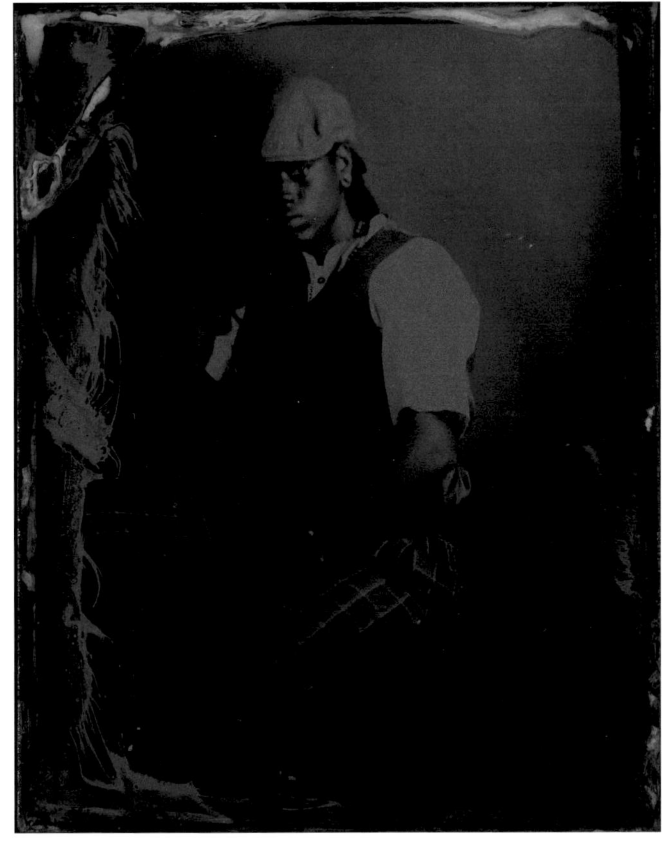

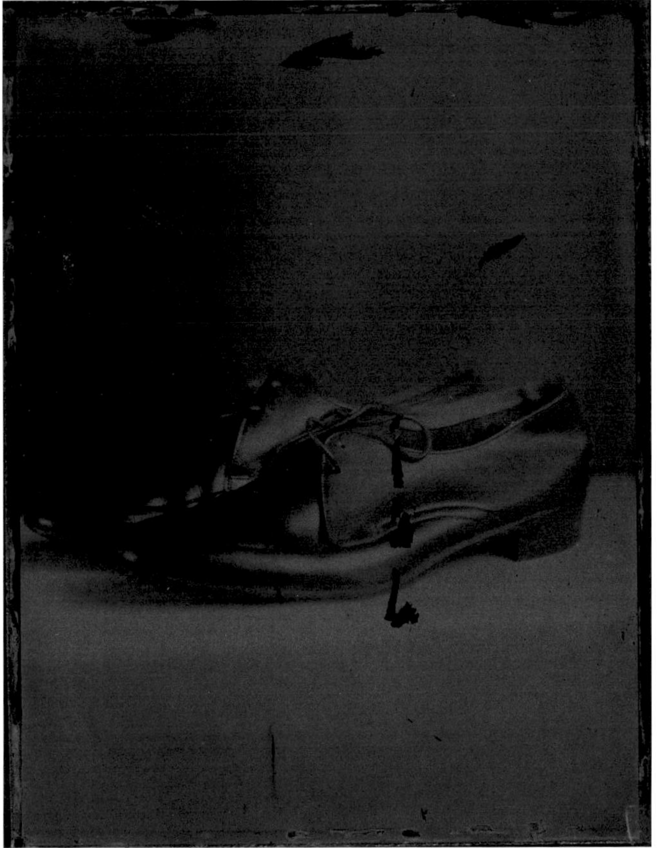

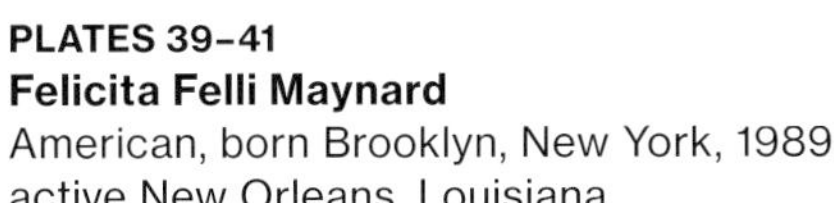

PLATES 39–41
Felicita Felli Maynard
American, born Brooklyn, New York, 1989;
active New Orleans, Louisiana

Vueltiao from the series *Ole Dandy, the Tribute*, 2017
Tintype and ambrotype

Jean Loren Feliz in the Studio from the series
Ole Dandy, the Tribute, 2019
Ambrotype

Angelo's Shoes from the series
Ole Dandy, the Tribute, 2019
Ambrotype

Courtesy of the artist

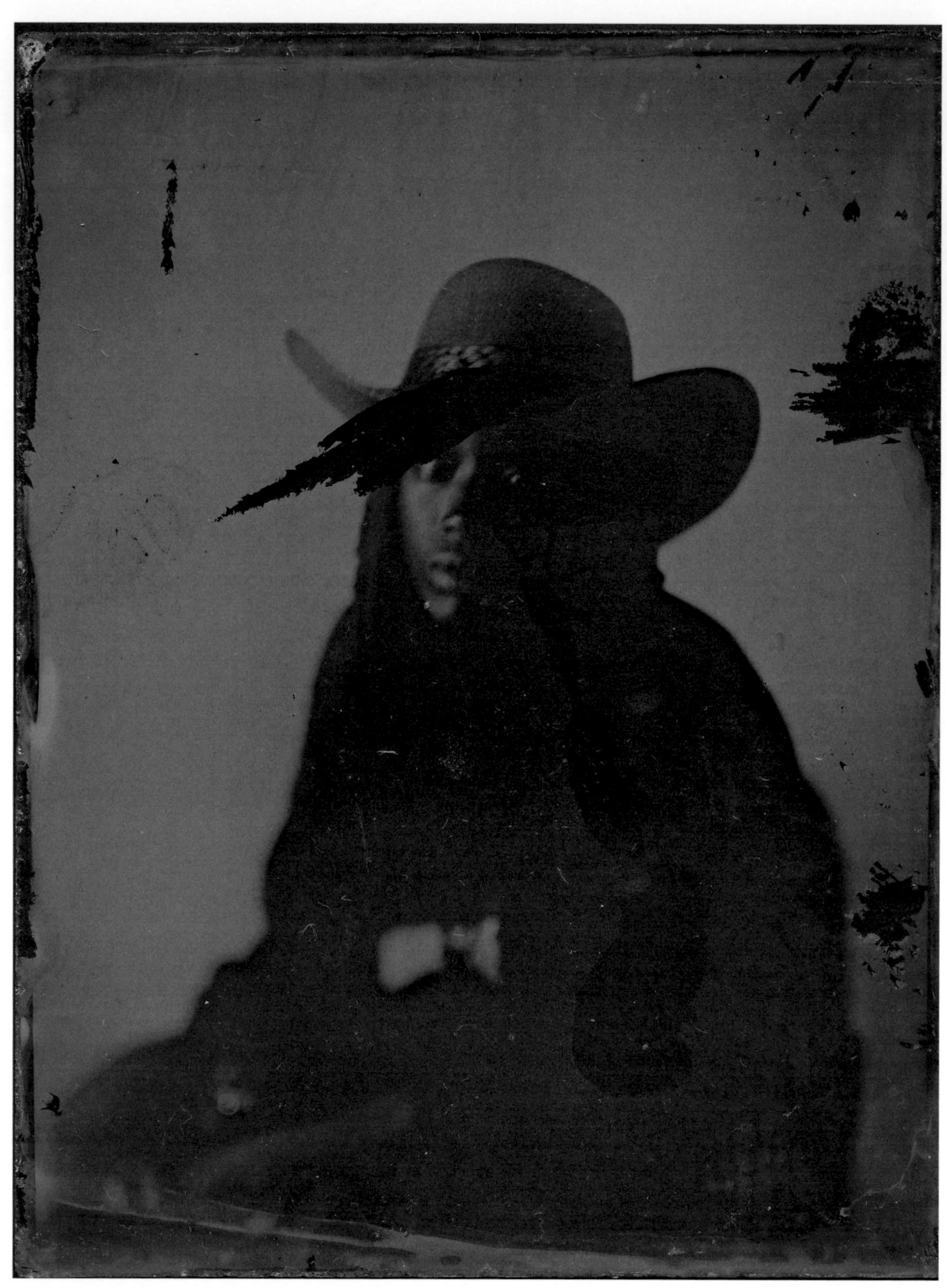

Felicita Felli Maynard
American, born Brooklyn, New York, 1989;
active New Orleans, Louisiana

Pre-Jean from the series
Ole Dandy, the Tribute, 2018
Ambrotype

Jean with Hands Up from the series
Ole Dandy, the Tribute, 2019
Ambrotype

Jean Loren Feliz from the series
Ole Dandy, the Tribute, 2019
Ambrotype

Courtesy of the artist

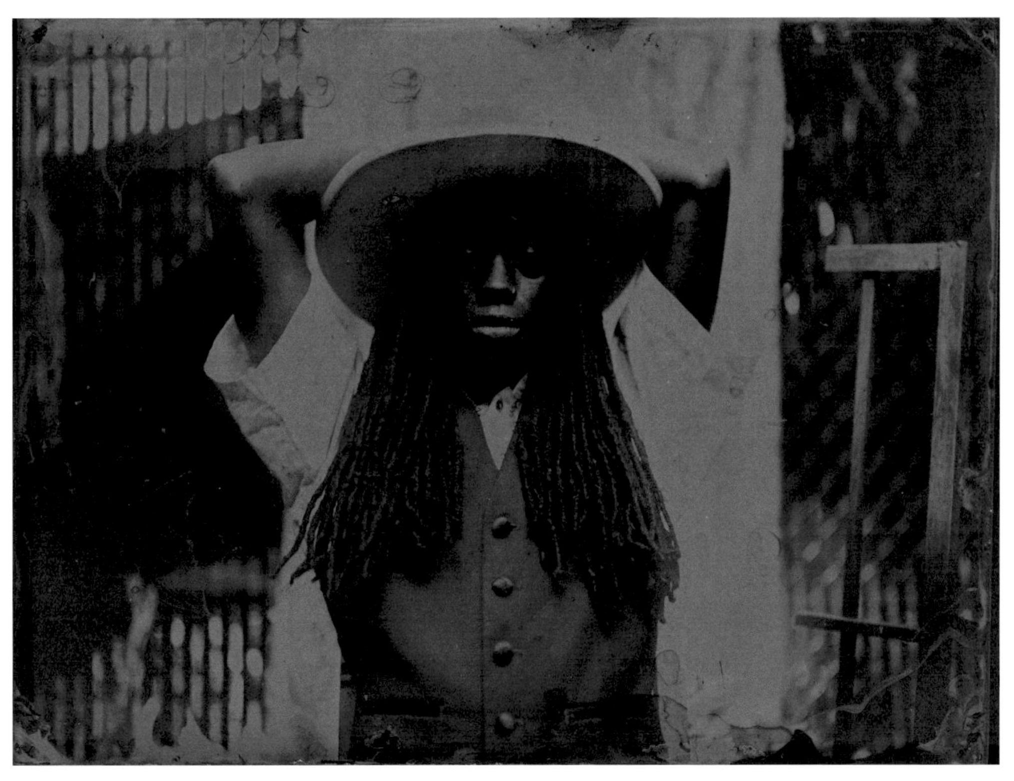

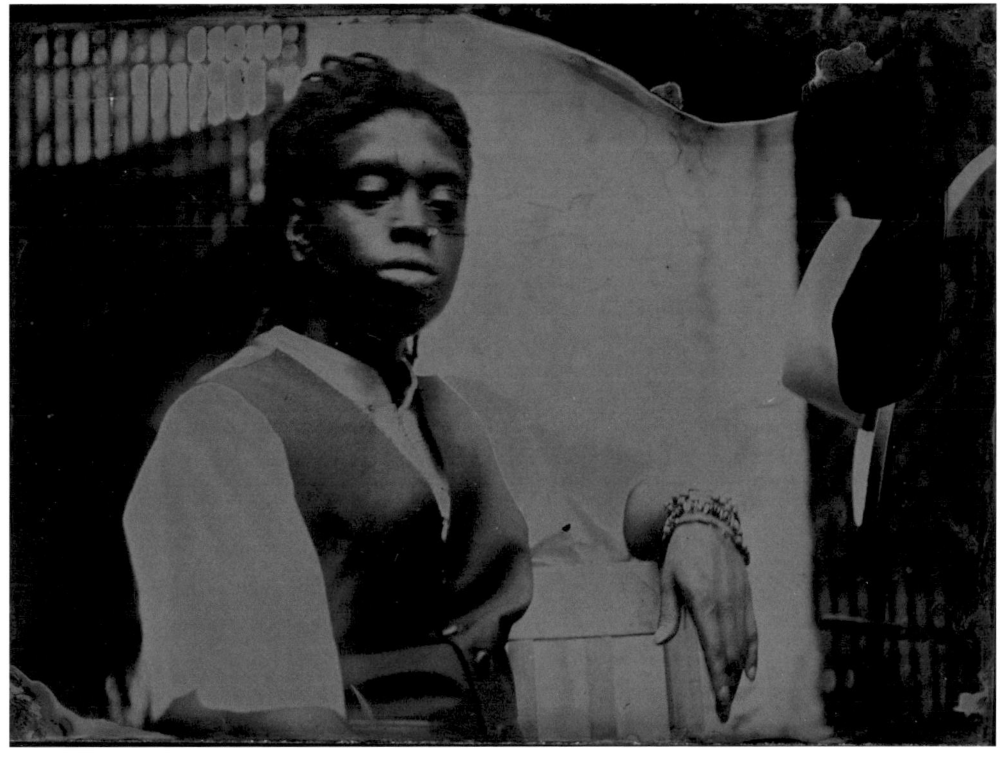

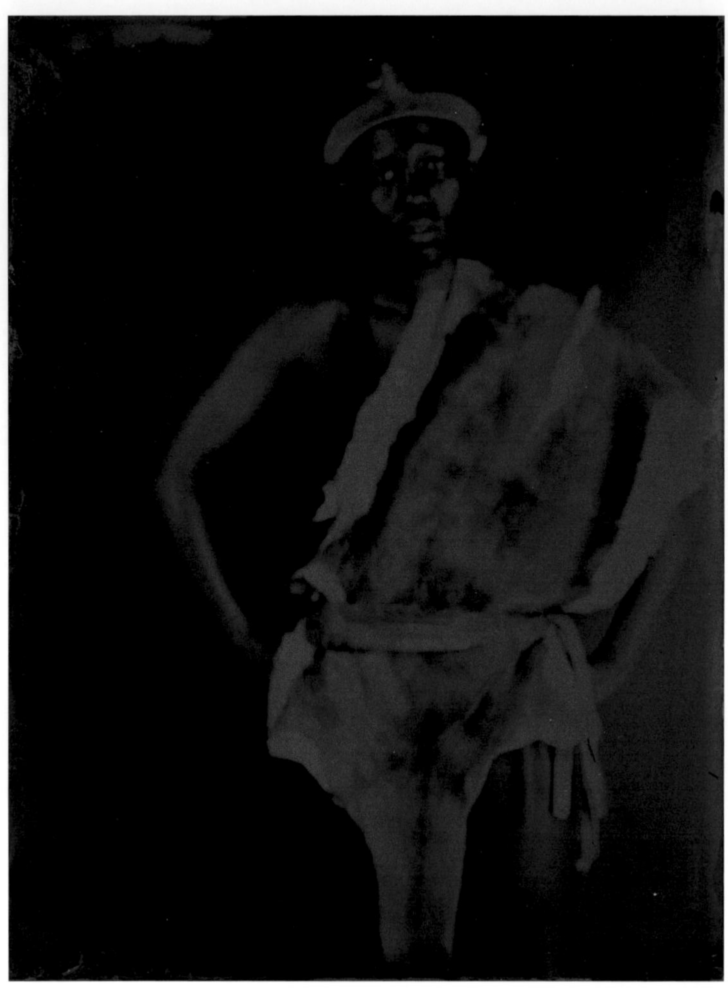

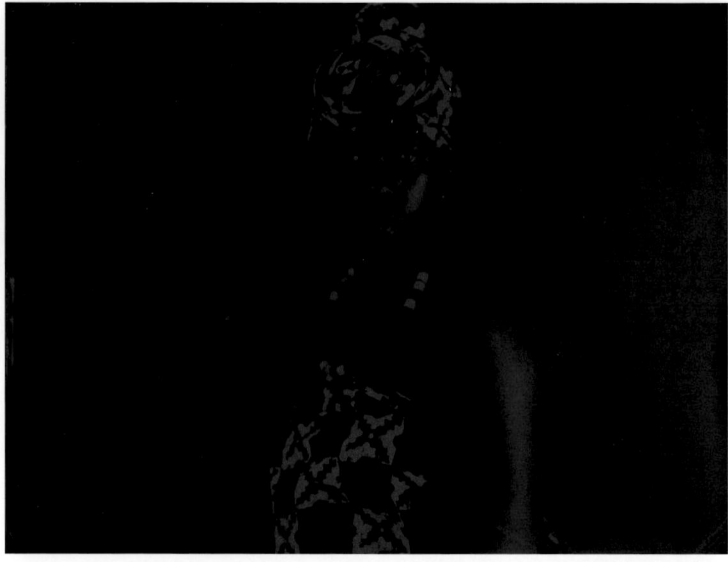

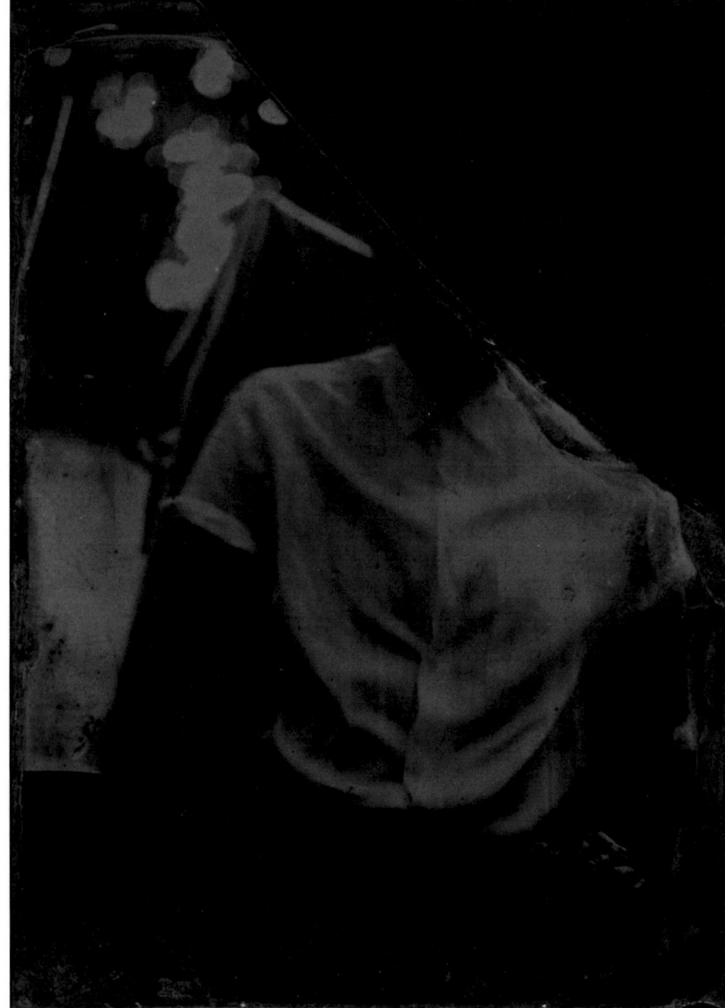

PLATES 45–47
Felicita Felli Maynard
American, born Brooklyn, New York, 1989;
active New Orleans, Louisiana

Pre Angelo, Zulu XY from the series
Ole Dandy, the Tribute, 2018
Tintype

Pre Angelo, Zulu XX from the series
Ole Dandy, the Tribute, 2018
Tintype

Untitled V, Angelo Lwazi Owenzayo
from the series *Ole Dandy, the Tribute*, 2020
Ambrotype

Courtesy of the artist

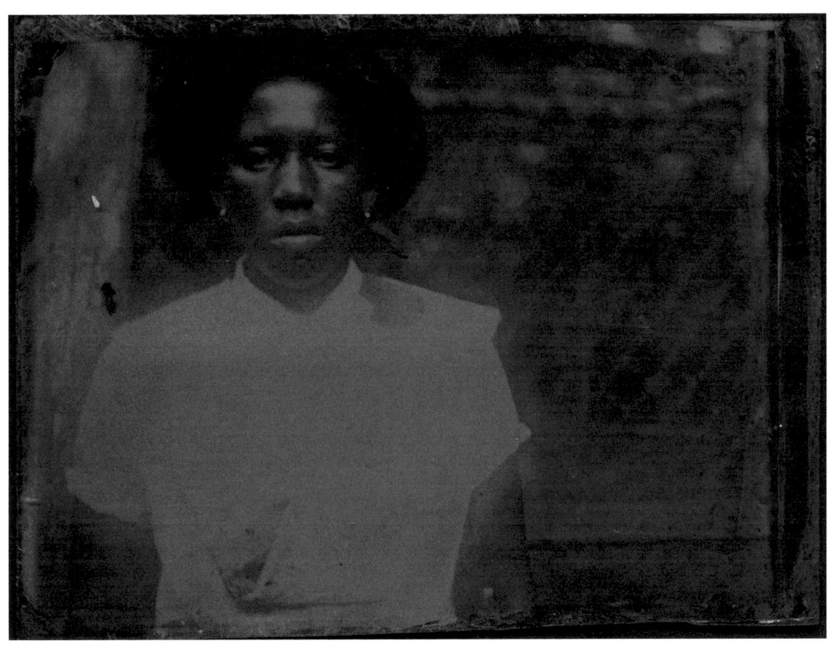

PLATES 48–49
Felicita Felli Maynard
American, born Brooklyn, New York, 1989;
active New Orleans, Louisiana

Untitled IV, Angelo Lwazi Owenzayo from the series
Ole Dandy, the Tribute, 2020
Ambrotype

Untitled, Angelo Lwazi Owenzayo from the series
Ole Dandy, the Tribute, 2020
Ambrotype

Courtesy of the artist

PLATE 50
Wangechi Mutu
Kenyan, born Nairobi, Kenya, 1972; active Brooklyn, New York
Sisters, 2019
Bronze
Courtesy of the artist

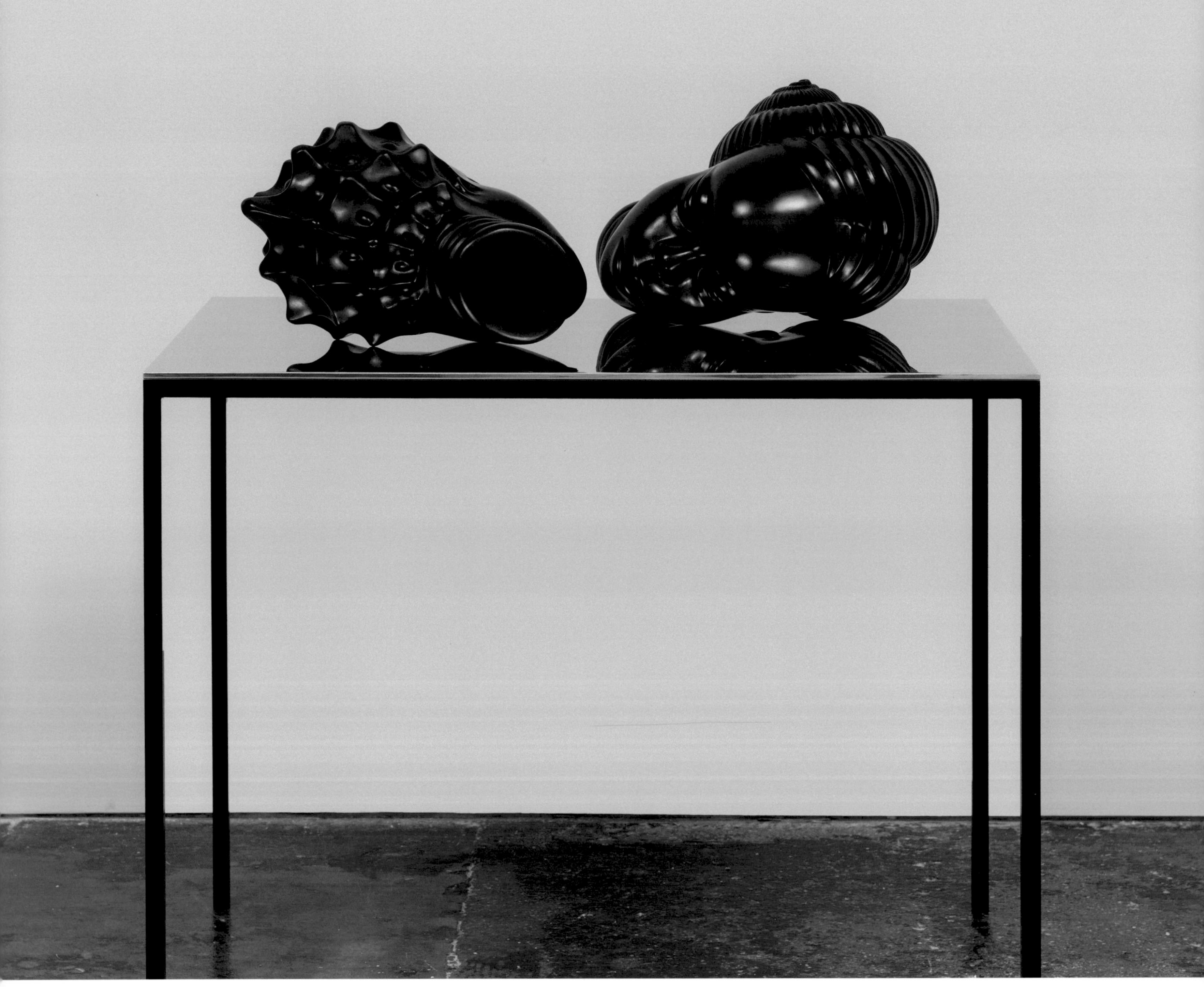

90

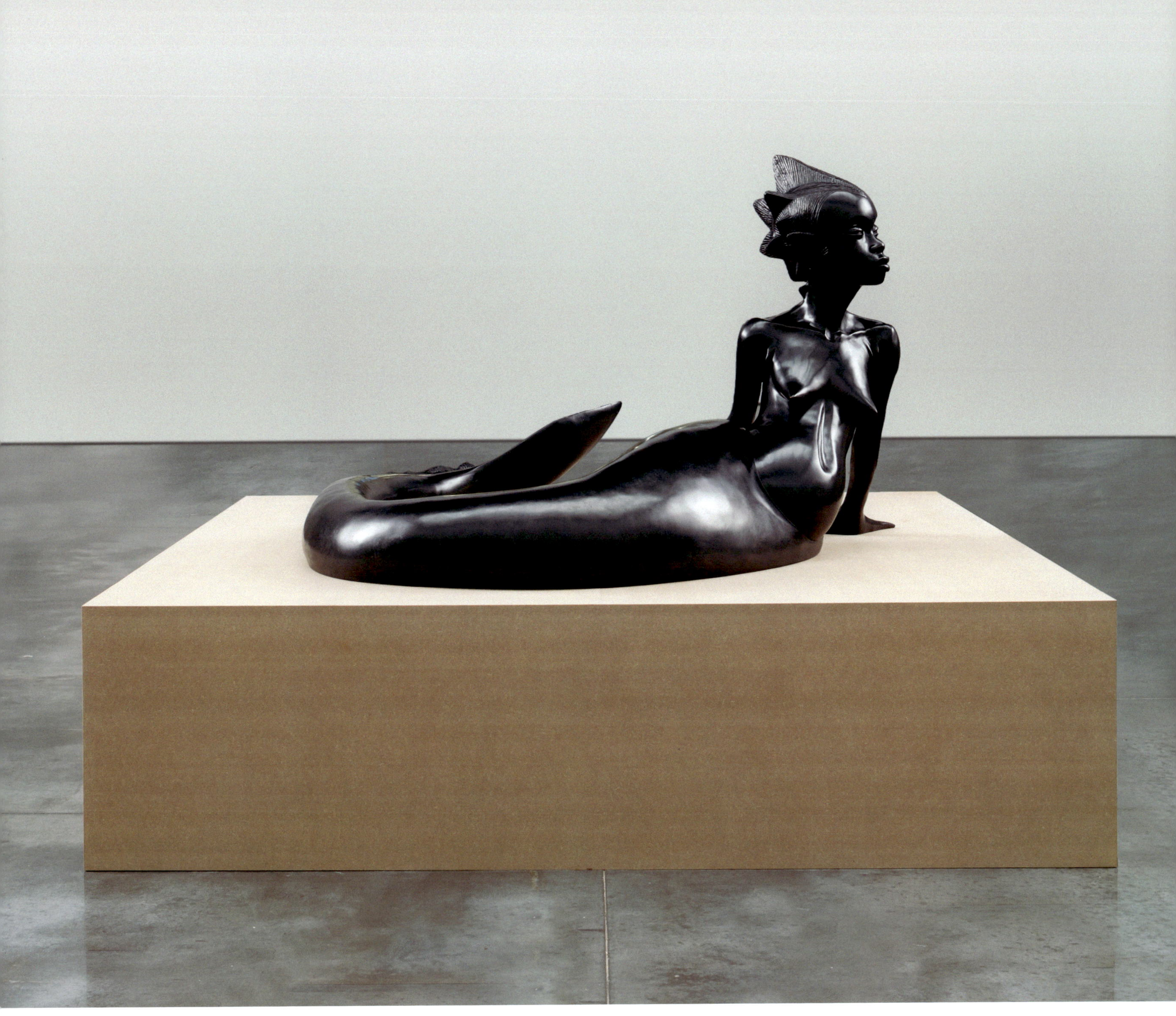

PLATE 51
Wangechi Mutu
Kenyan, born Nairobi, Kenya, 1972; active Brooklyn, New York
Water Woman, 2017
Bronze
Courtesy of the artist

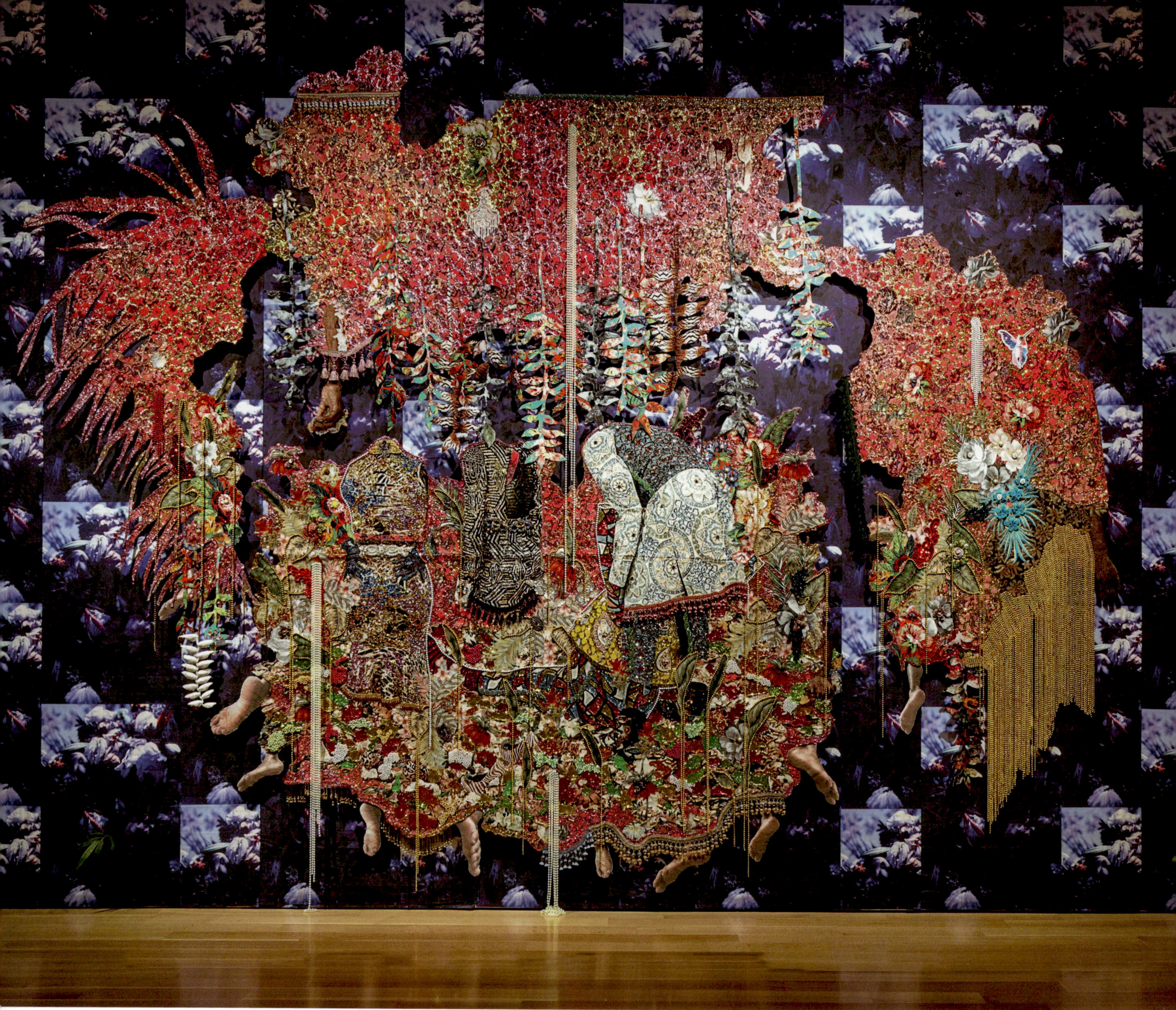

PLATE 52
Ebony G. Patterson
Jamaican, born Kingston, Jamaica, 1981; active Chicago, Illinois
. . . they stood in a time of unknowing . . .
for those who bear/bare witness, 2018
Hand-cut jacquard woven photo tapestry with glitter,
appliques, pins, embellishments, fabric, tassels, brooches,
acrylic, glass pearls, beads, and hand-cast heliconias
Courtesy of the artist and Monique Meloche Gallery, Chicago

92

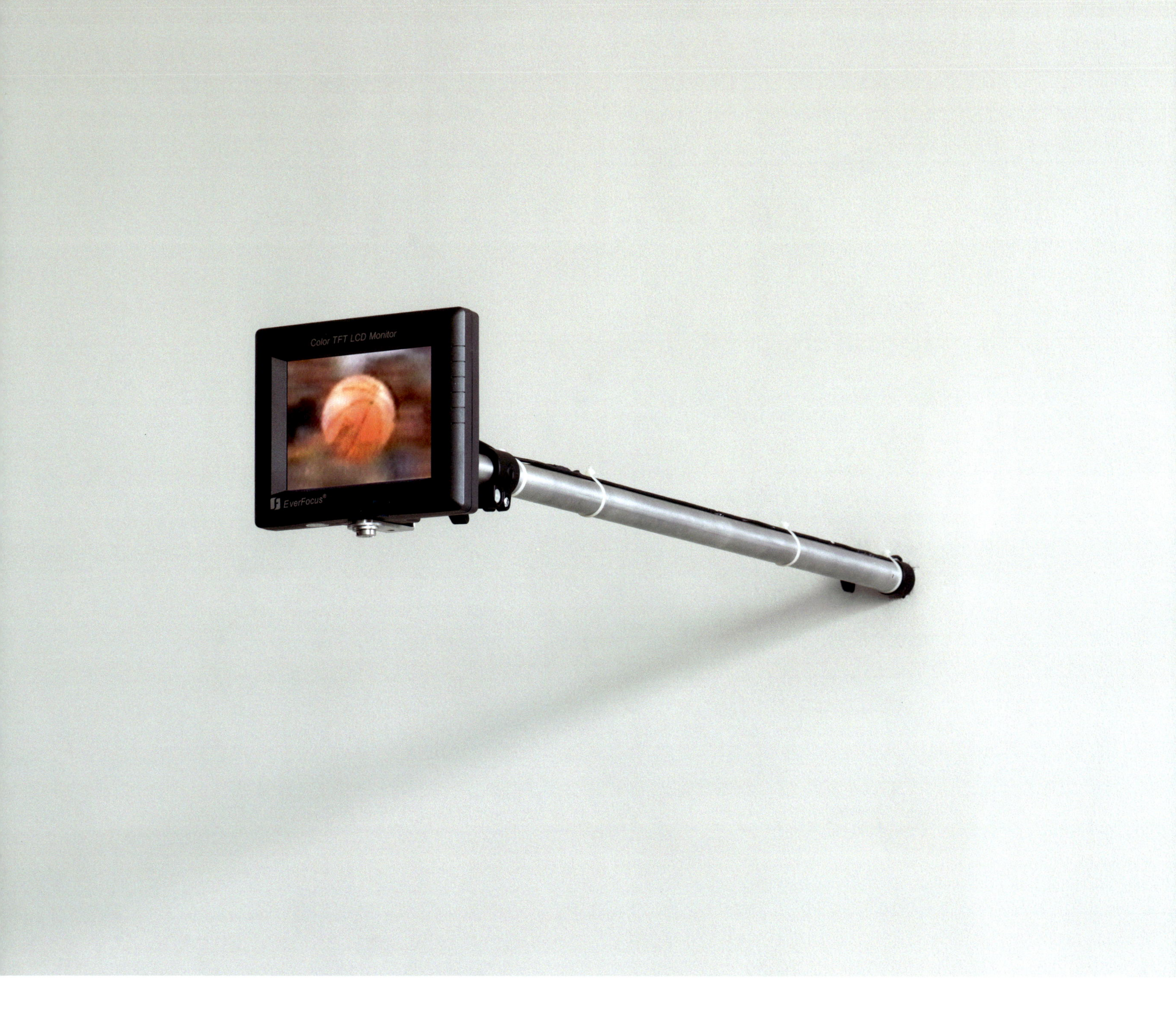

PLATE 53
Paul Pfeiffer
American, born Honolulu, Hawaii, 1966;
active New York, New York
John 3:16, 2000
Digital video loop, metal armature, and LCD monitor
Running time: 2 minutes, 7 seconds
Courtesy of the artist and Paula Cooper Gallery, New York

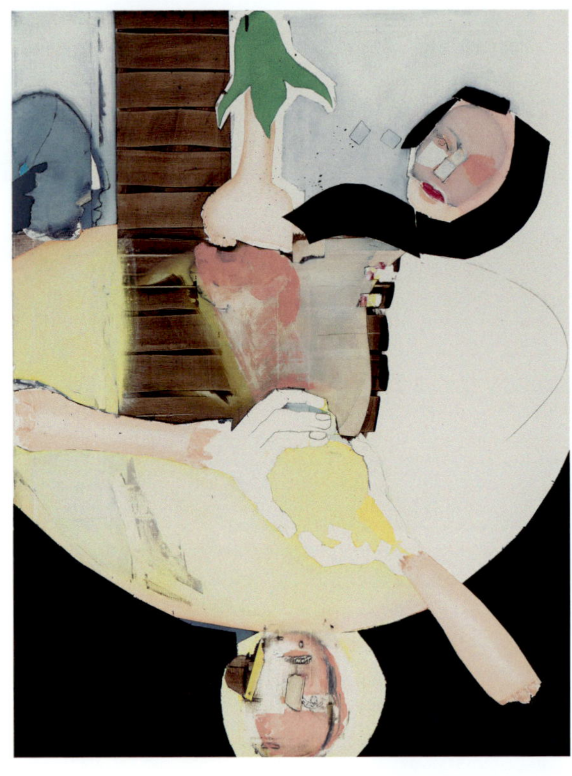
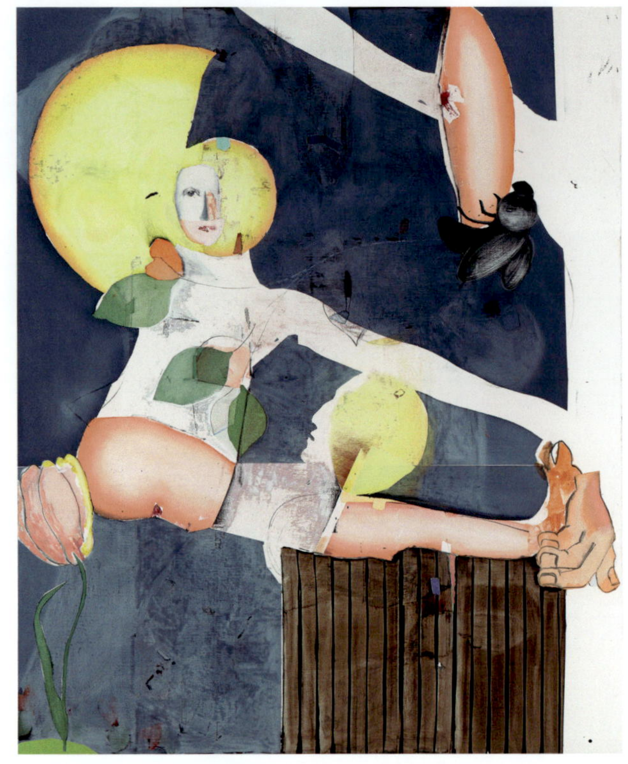
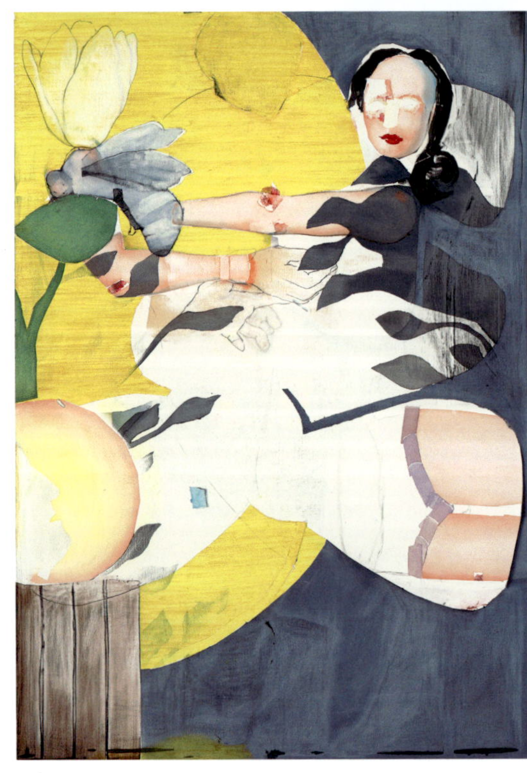
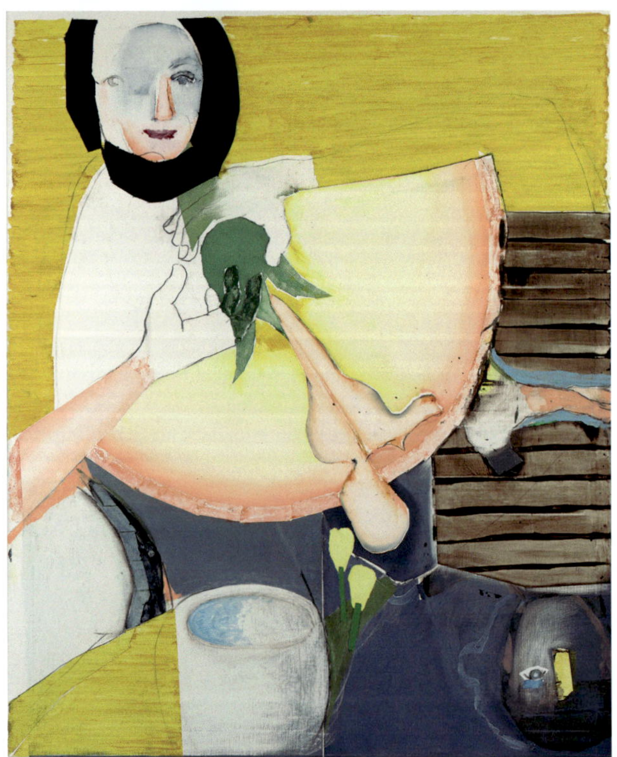

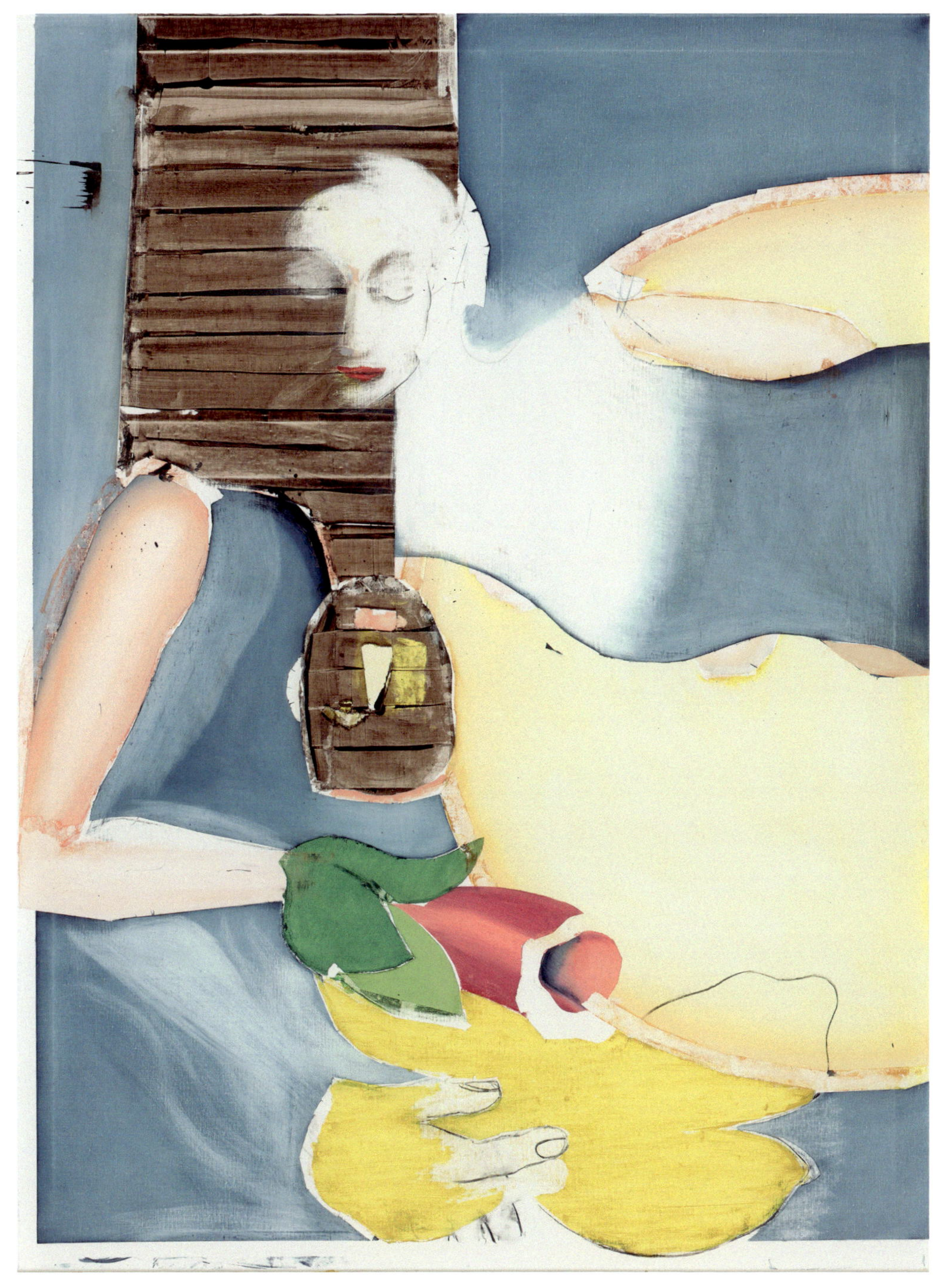

PLATES 54–58
Magnus Plessen
German, born Hamburg, Germany, 1967; active Berlin, Germany

Untitled (Fig. 6), 2019
Untitled (Fig. 11), 2020
Untitled (Fig. 13), 2020
Untitled (Fig. 16), 2020
Untitled (Fig. 20), 2021

Oil and charcoal on canvas
Courtesy of the artist and White Cube

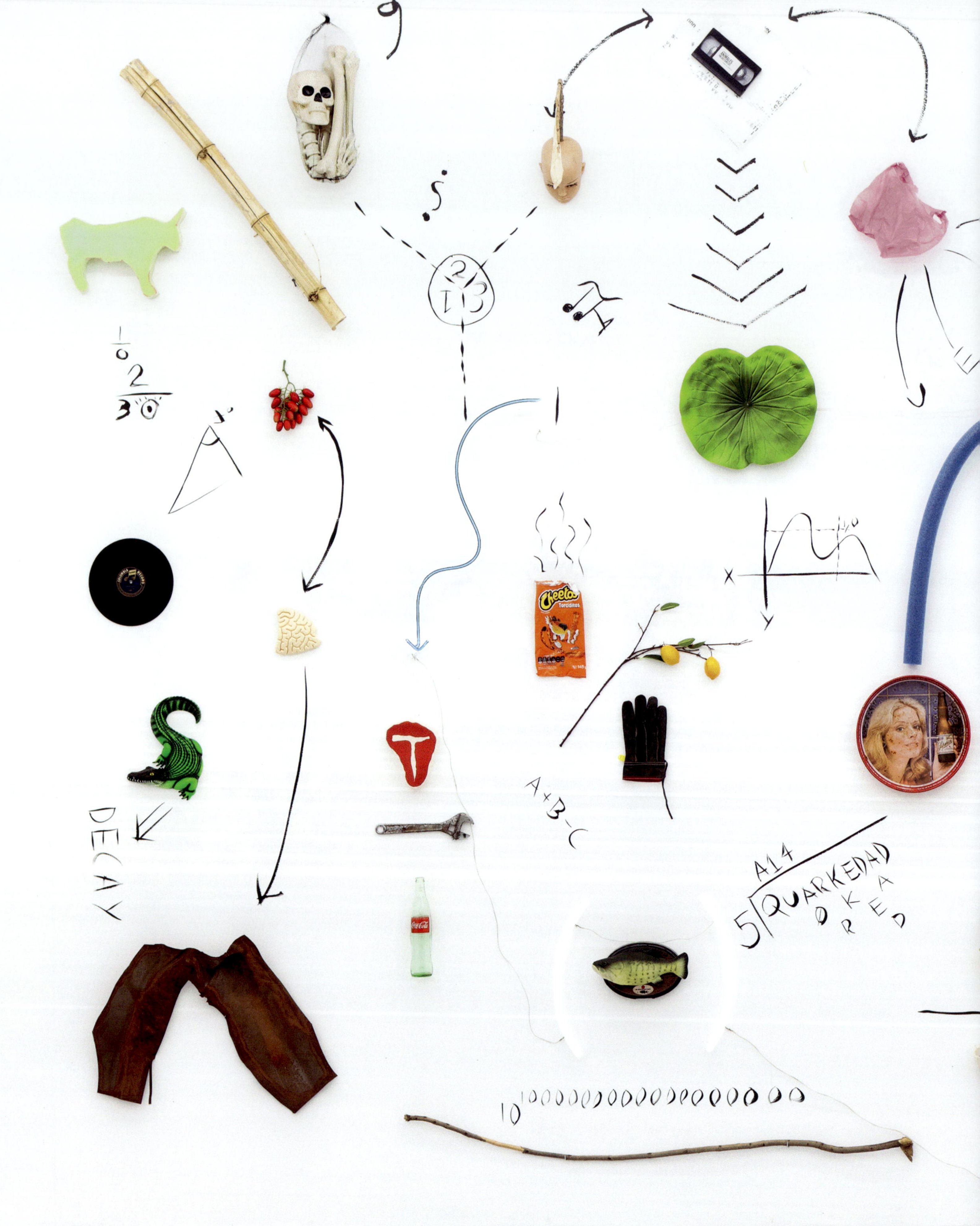
9
DECAY
A+B=C
QUARKEDAD
A14
5
10

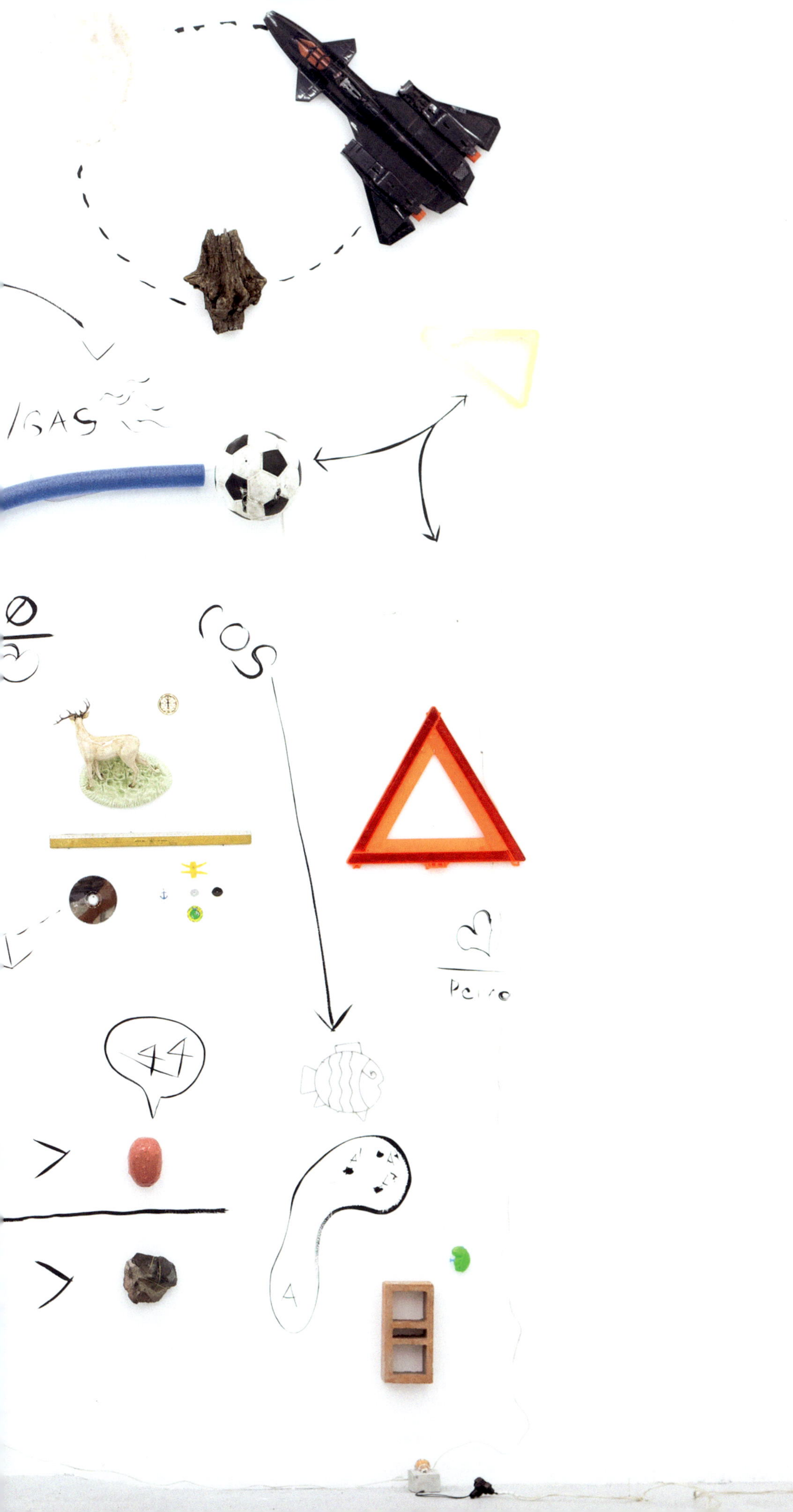

PLATE 59
Gabriel Rico
Mexican, born Lagos de Moreno, Mexico, 1980;
active Guadalajara, Mexico
*VI Mural from the series Reducción objetiva
orquestada*, 2021
Mixed media, acrylic paint, and neon
Courtesy of the artist and Perrotin

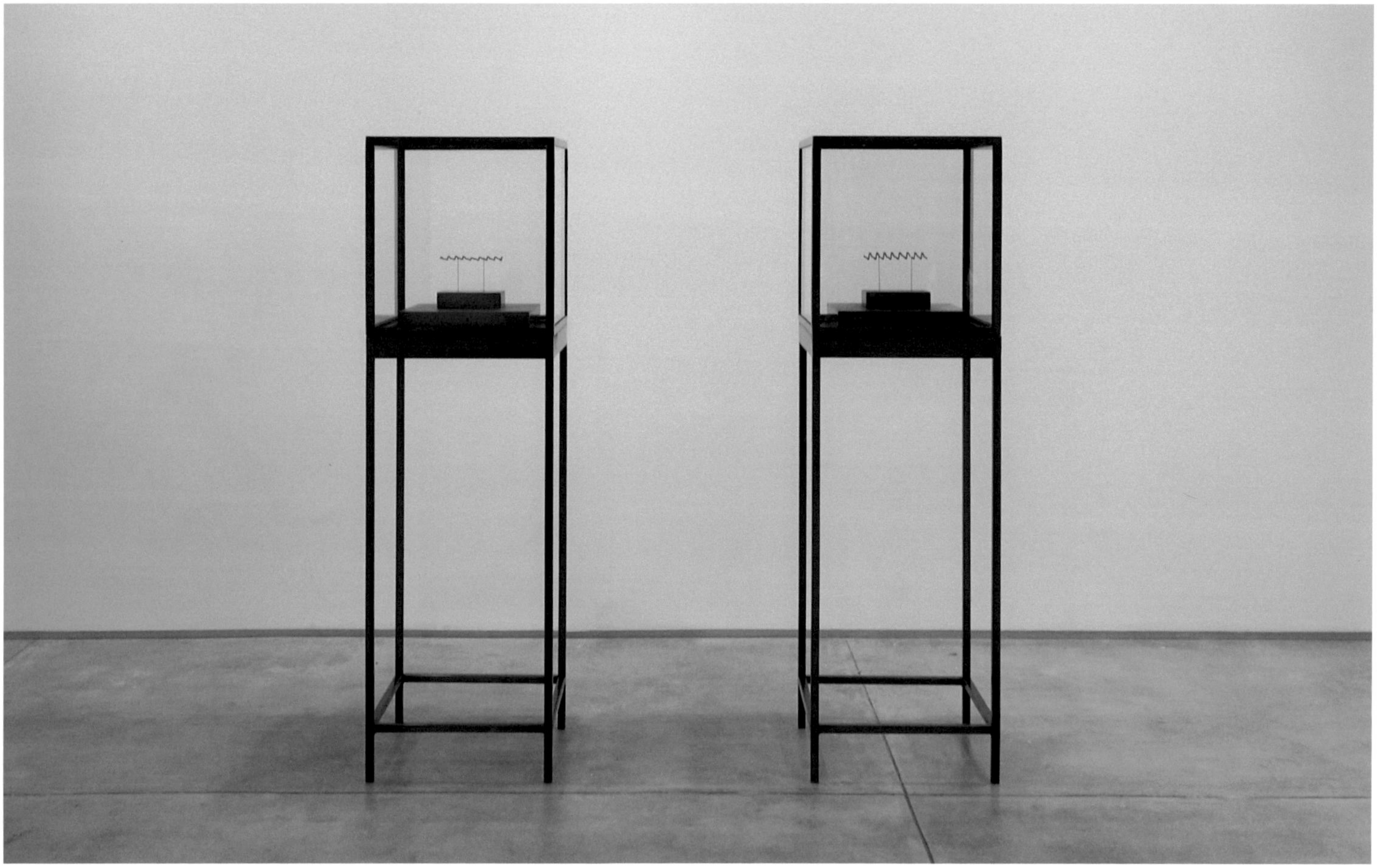

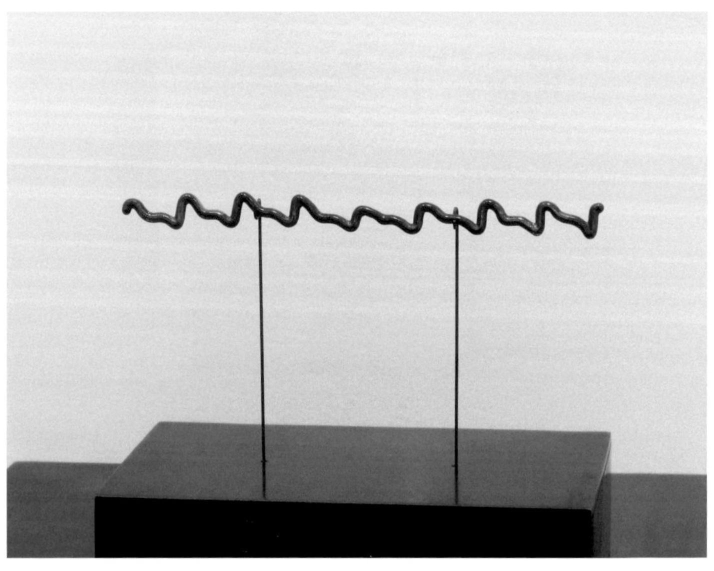

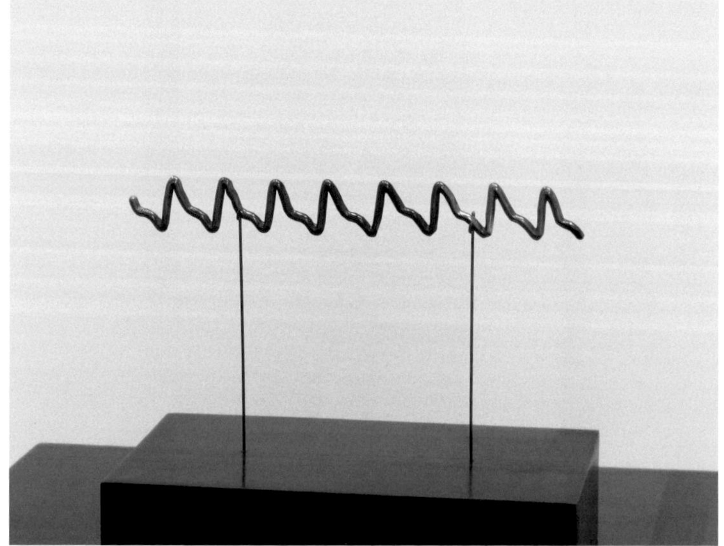

PLATE 60
Dario Robleto
American, born San Antonio, Texas, 1972; active Houston, Texas
Love, Before There Was Love (detail), 2018
Earliest waveform recordings of blood flowing from the heart
both before and during an emotional state (1870), rendered and
3D printed in brass-plated stainless steel, brushed steel, and glass
Courtesy of the artist and Inman Gallery, Houston, Texas

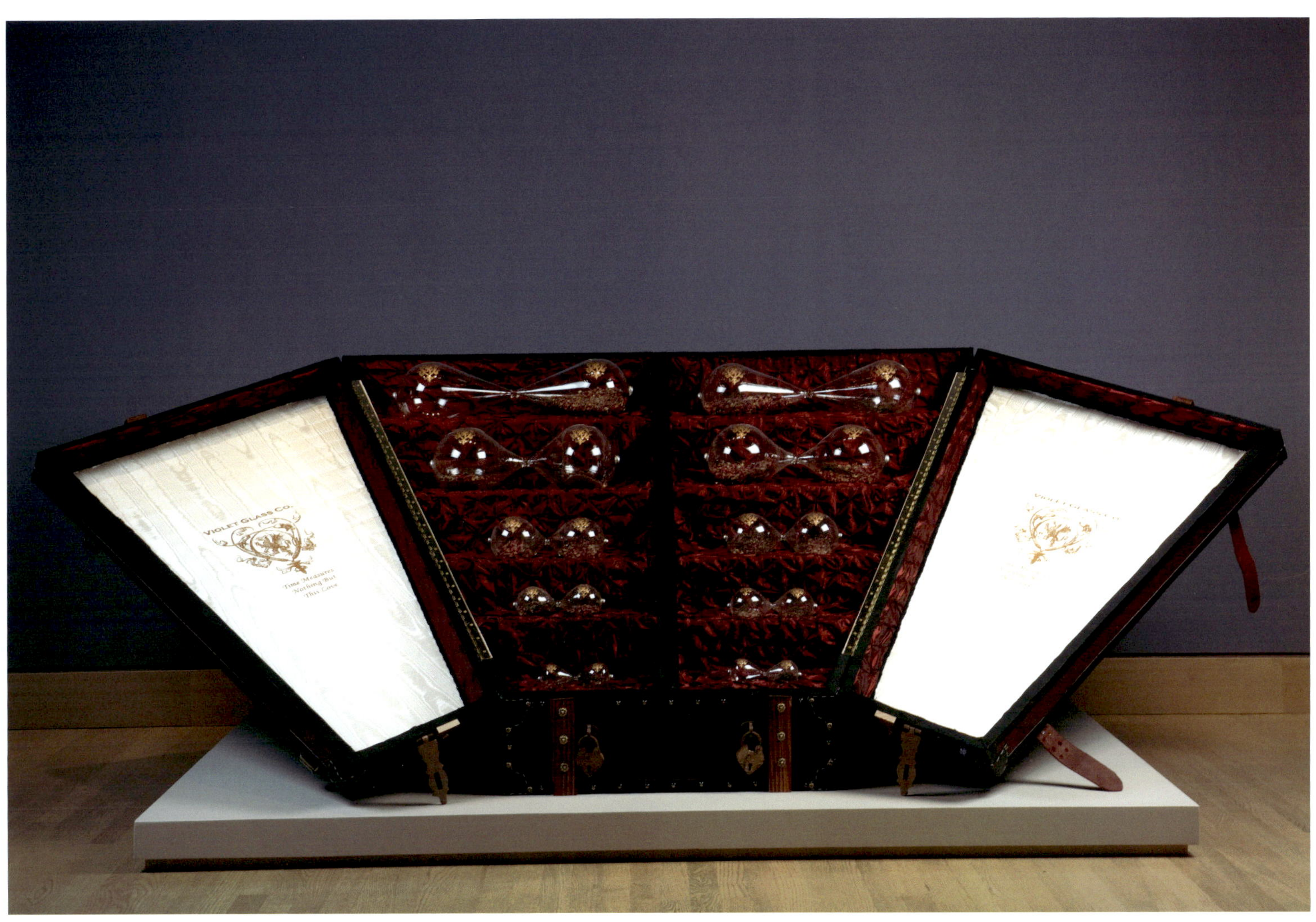

PLATE 61
Dario Robleto
American, born San Antonio, Texas, 1972; active Houston, Texas
Time Measures Nothing But This Love, 2008
Handblown glass beakers, stretched audiotape of field
recordings of the world's oldest married couple (80 years),
stretched and pulled audiotape of the earliest recording of time
(experimental clock, 1878), ground resurrection plant, ground
rosebuds and rosehips, silk, satin, leather, brass, iron, fir, typeset
Courtesy of the artist and Inman Gallery, Houston, Texas

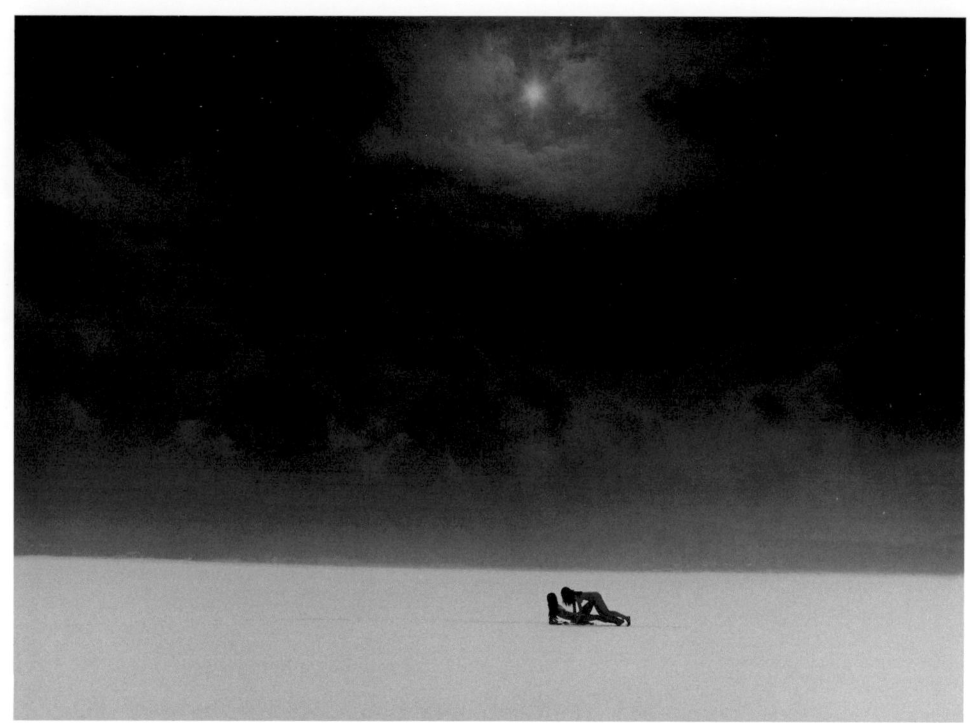

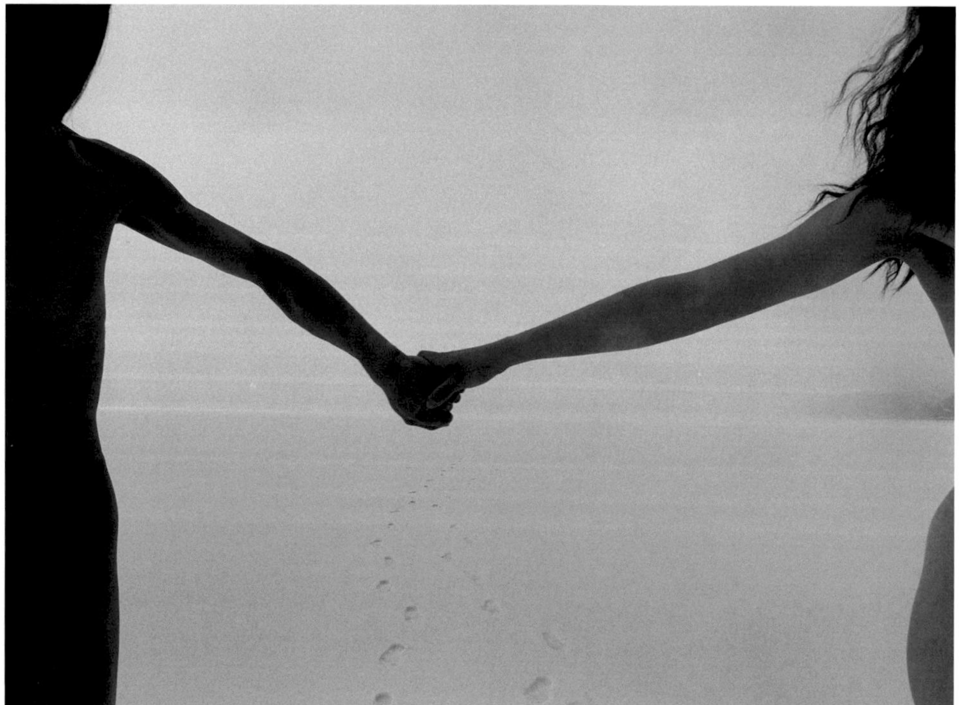

PLATE 62
RongRong&inri, active Beijing, China
RongRong, born Zhangzhou, Fujian Province, China, 1968
inri, born Kanagawa Prefecture, Japan, 1973
In Fujisan, Japan (detail), 2001
Silver gelatin and color photograph, set of sixteen prints
Collection of Charles Jing

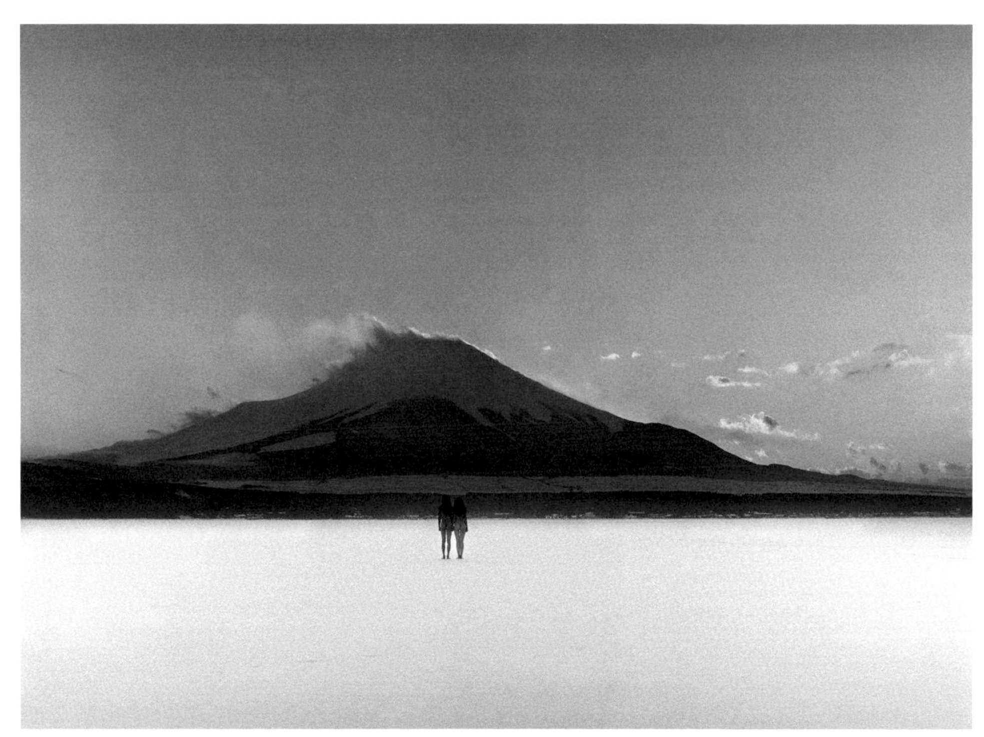

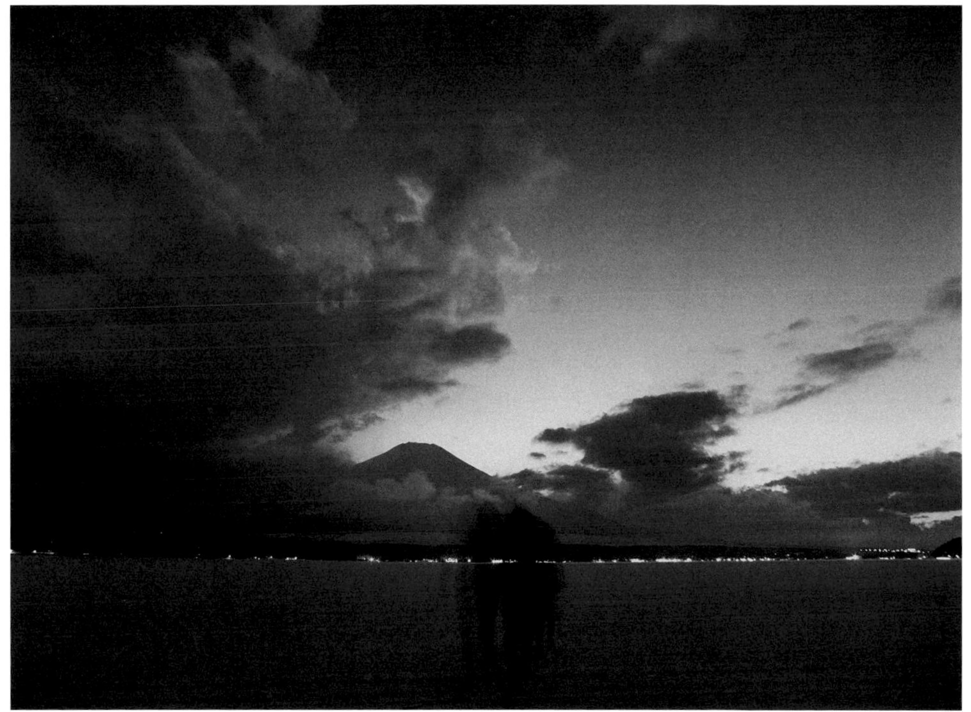

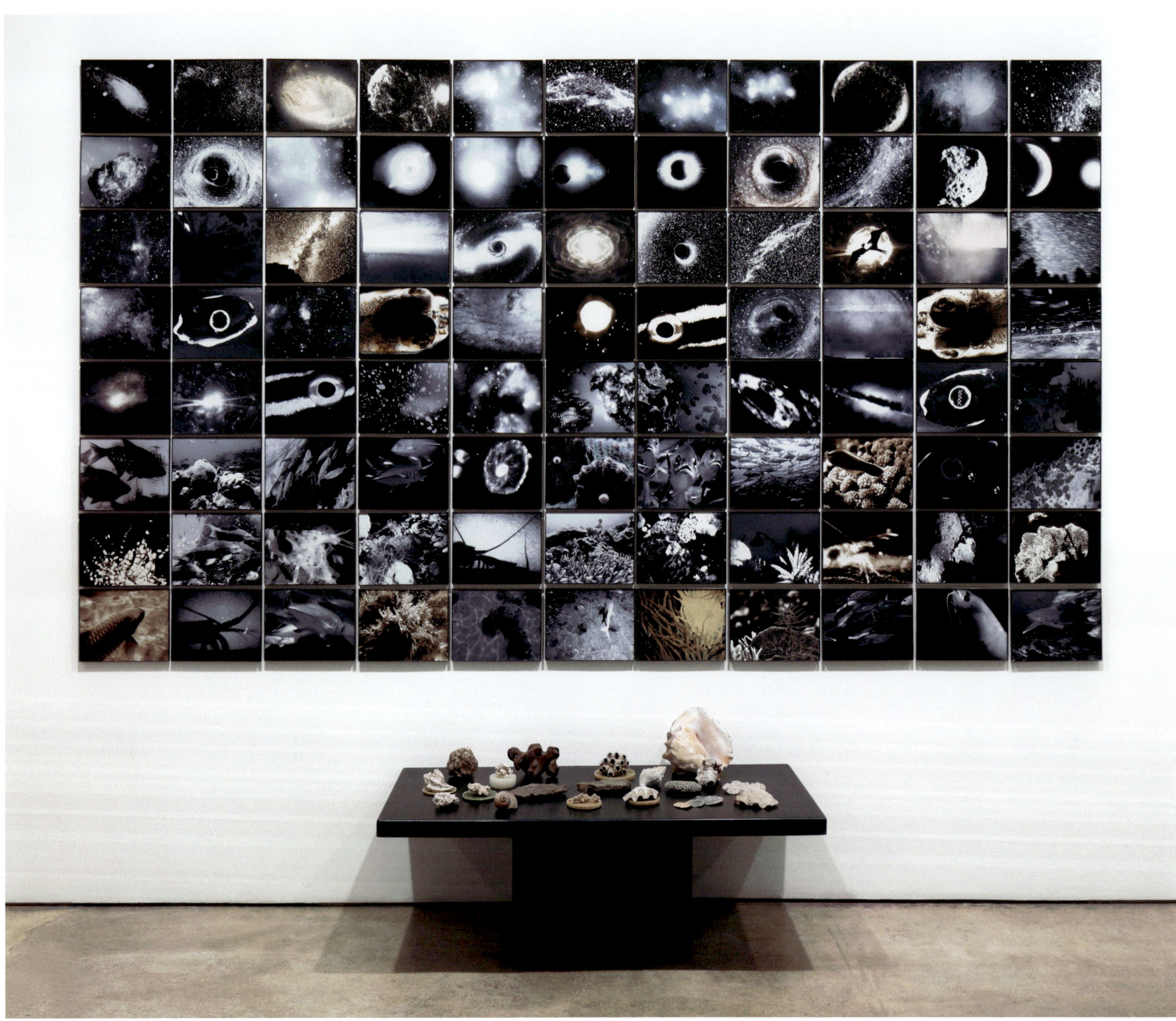

American, born Los Angeles, California, 1933; active New York, New York
In the Beginning: Time and Dark Matter, 2016–2020
Archival pigment prints, metal and wood table, shells, and beeswax plates
Courtesy of the artist and Galerie Lelong & Co., New York

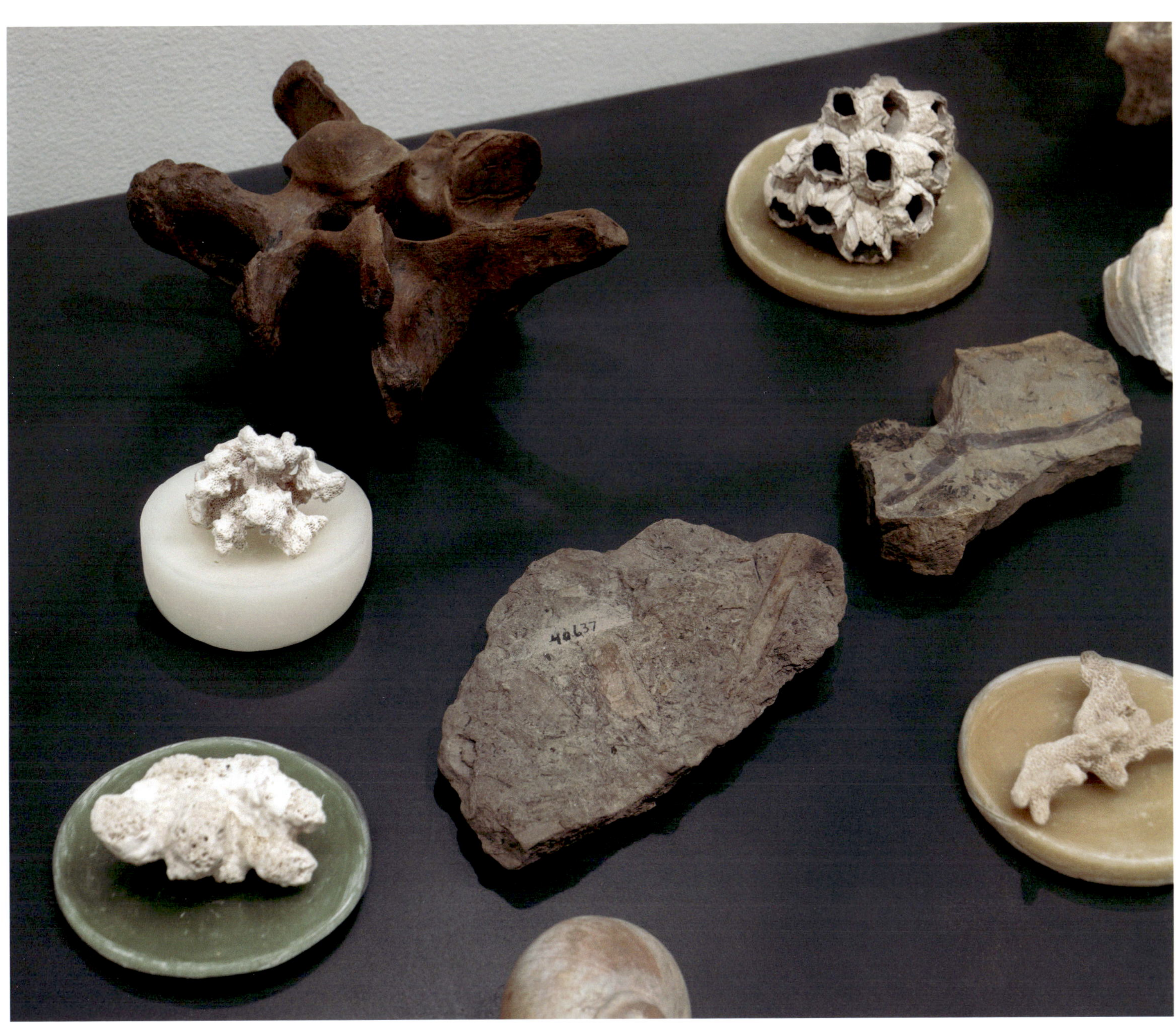

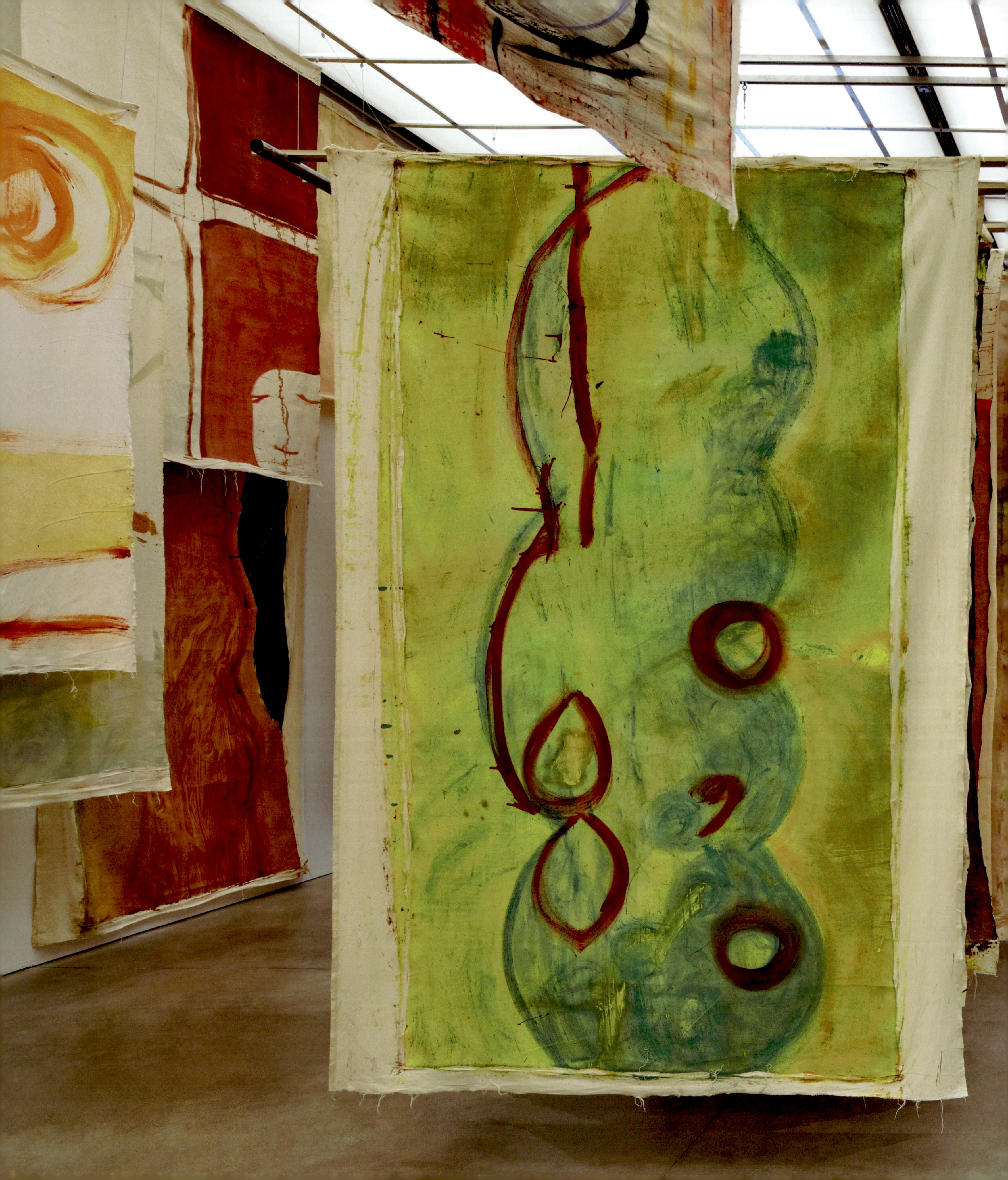

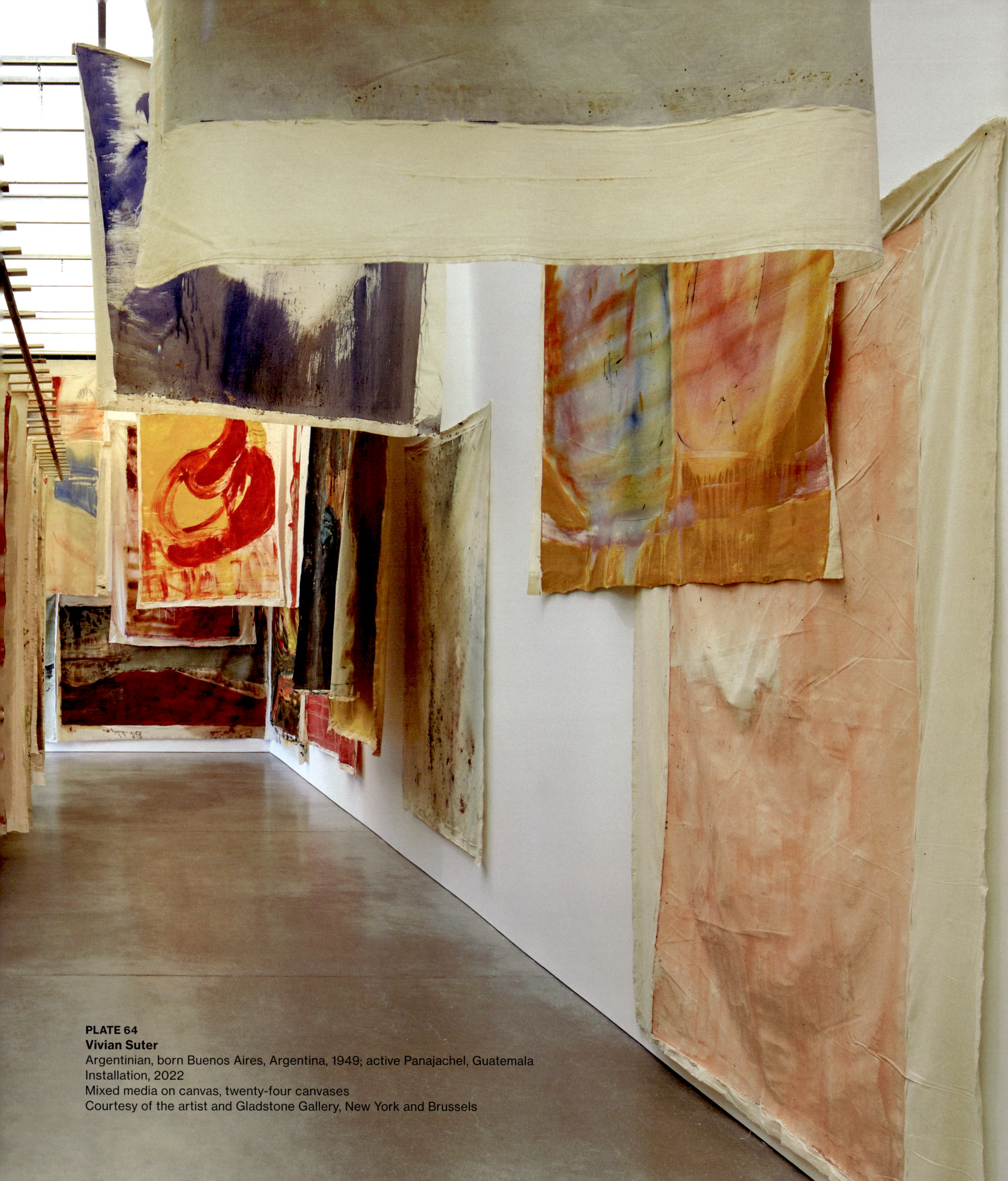

PLATE 64
Vivian Suter
Argentinian, born Buenos Aires, Argentina, 1949; active Panajachel, Guatemala
Installation, 2022
Mixed media on canvas, twenty-four canvases
Courtesy of the artist and Gladstone Gallery, New York and Brussels

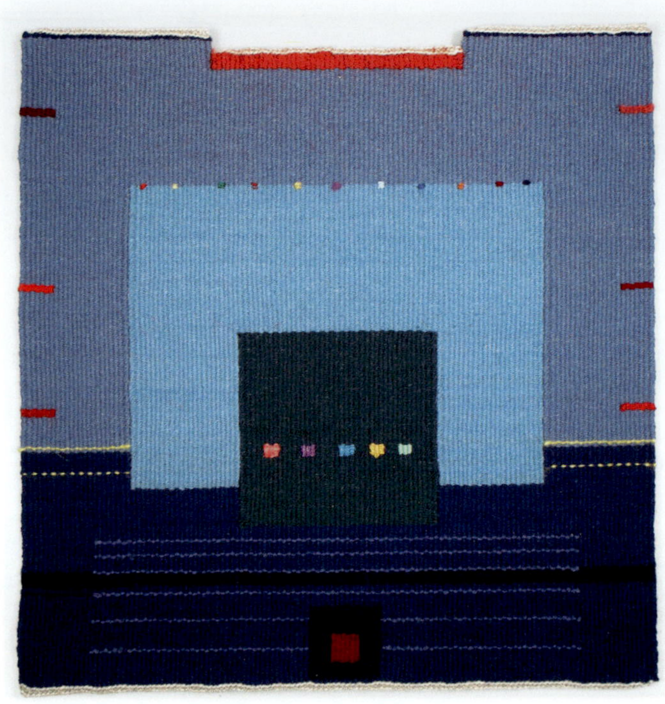

PLATES 65–67
Jana Vander-Lee
American, born Lansing, Illinois, 1945; active Chicago, Illinois

Truthfully, 2020
8/5 linen warp wool, rayon, acrylic, Lurex, and cotton linen

Night Passage, 2020
8/5 linen, wool, acrylic, cotton, viscose, silk, rayon, and mohair

Enlightened Ones, 2020
8/5 linen, wool, rayon, cotton, acrylic, and cotton linen

Courtesy of the artist and Inman Gallery, Houston, Texas

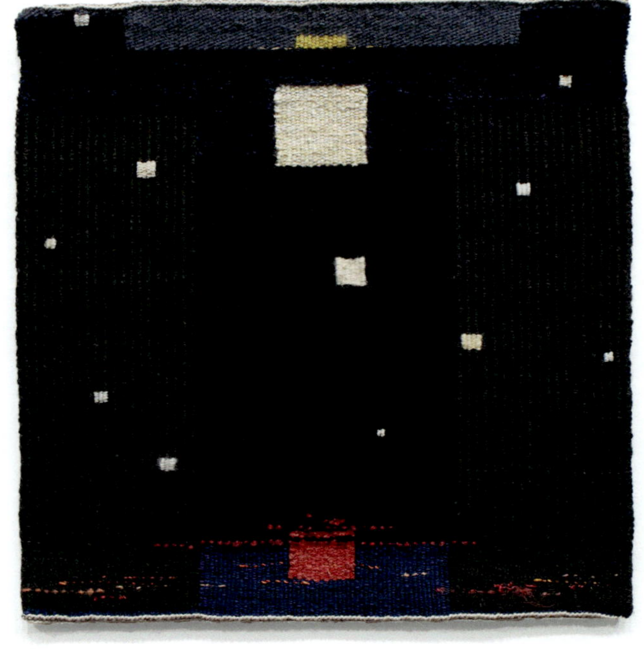

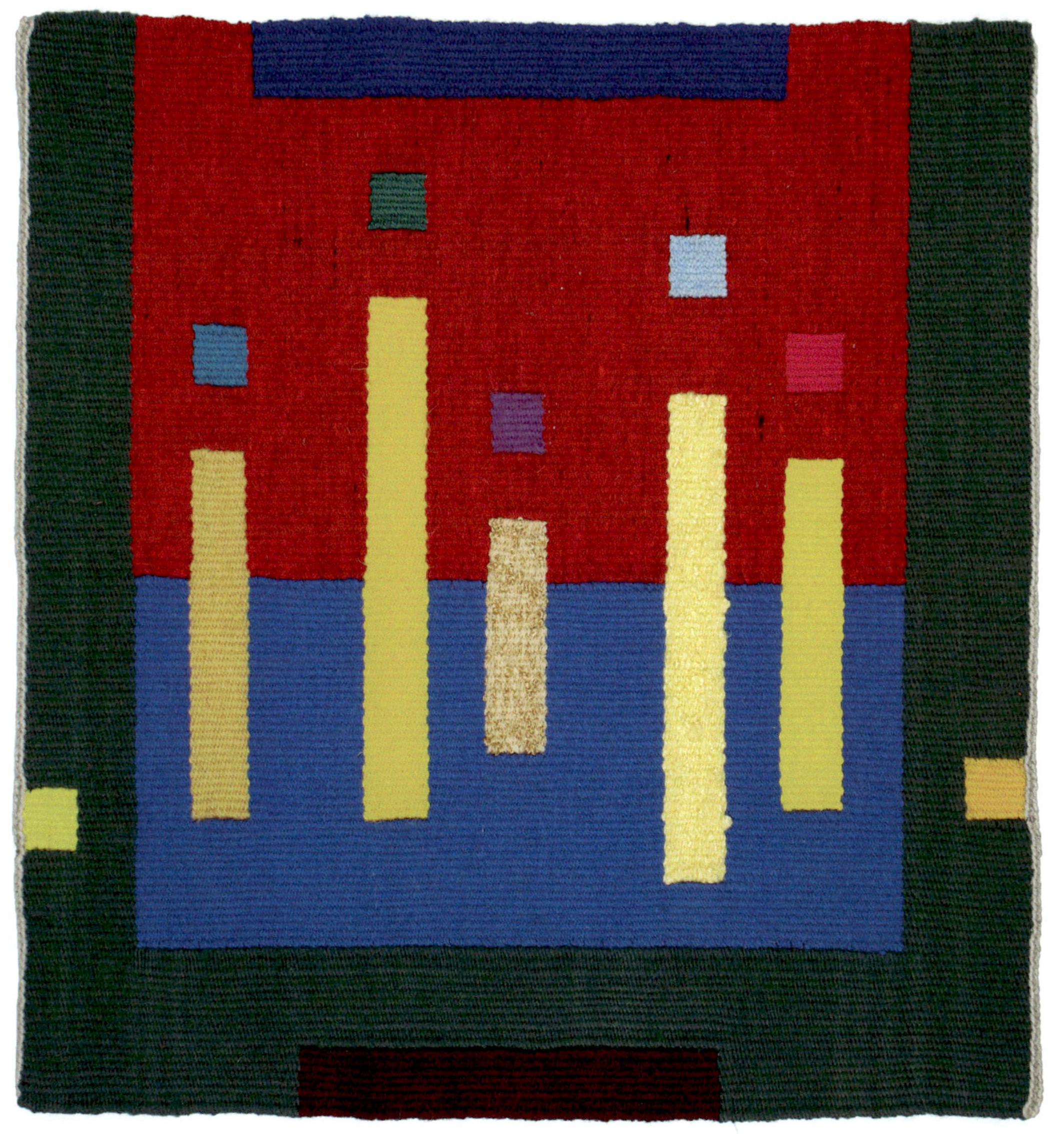

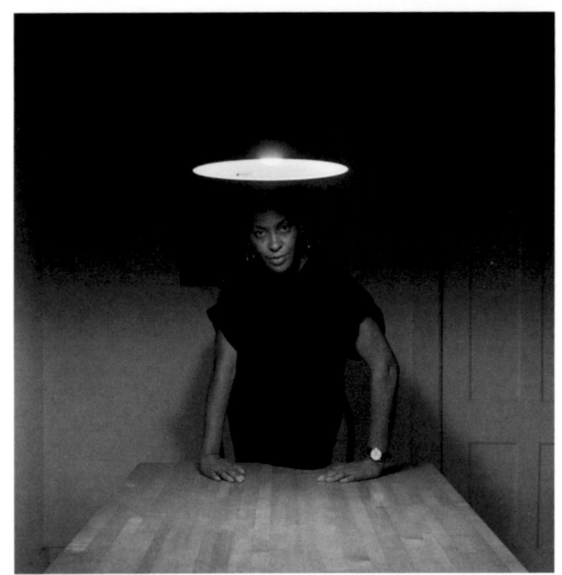 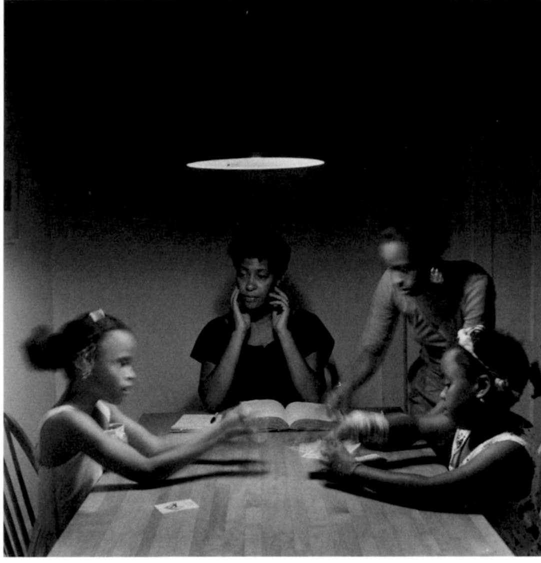 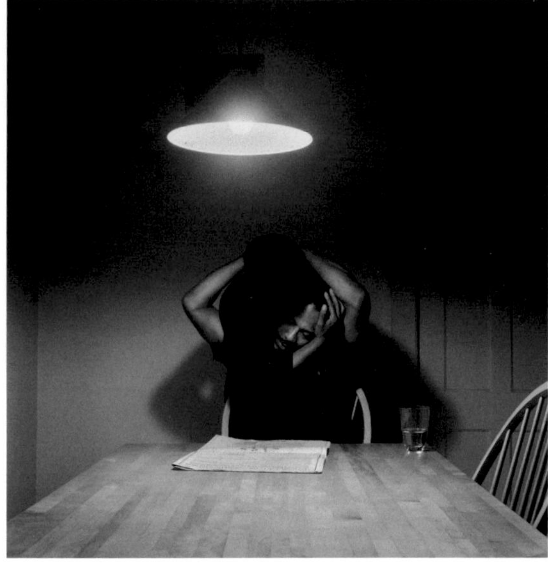

PLATE 68
Carrie Mae Weems
American, born Portland, Oregon, 1953; active New York, New York
The Kitchen Table Series (detail), 1990
Twenty platinum prints, fourteen letter-press texts
Private collection, Miami, Florida

PLATE 69
Akram Zaatari
Lebanese, born Sidon, Lebanon, 1966; active Beirut, Lebanon
Tomorrow Everything Will Be Alright, 2010
Single-channel video, color, and sound
Running time: 11 minutes, 48 seconds
Courtesy of the artist and kurimanzutto, Mexico City/New York

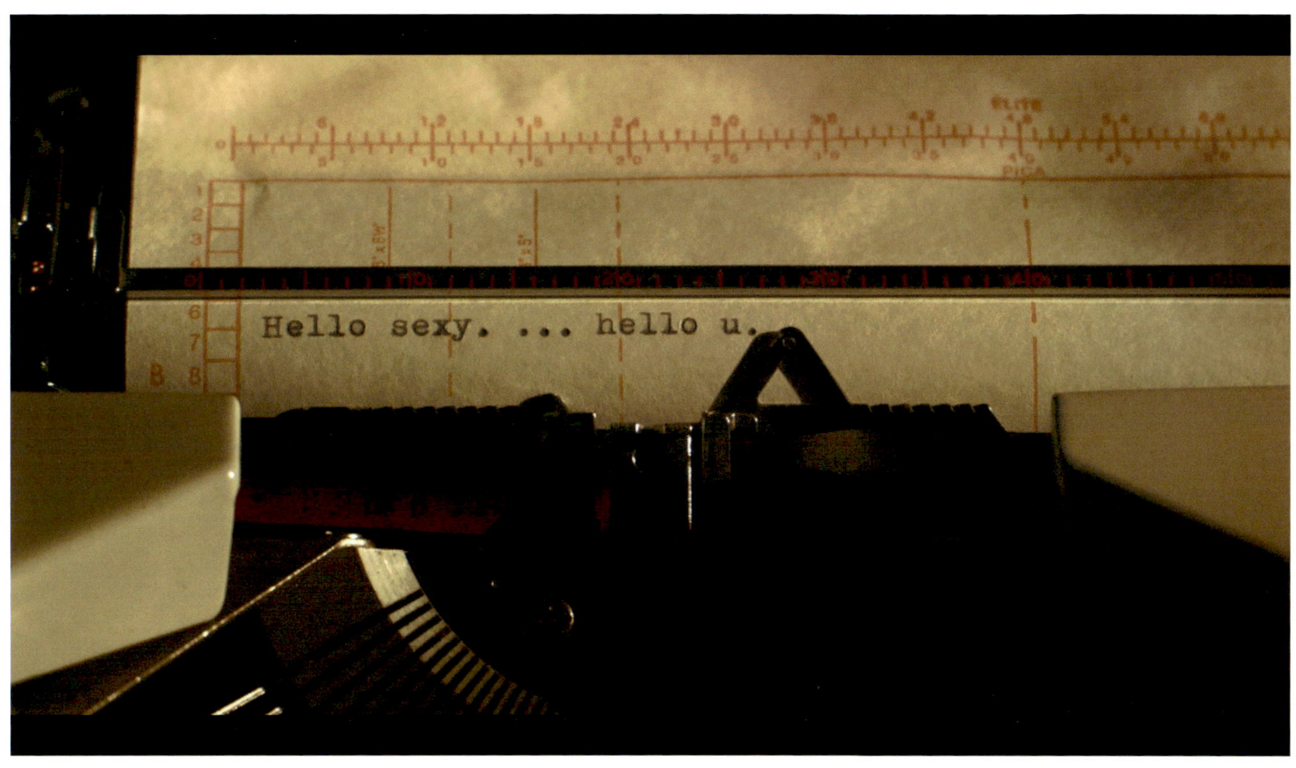

Hello sexy. ... hello u.

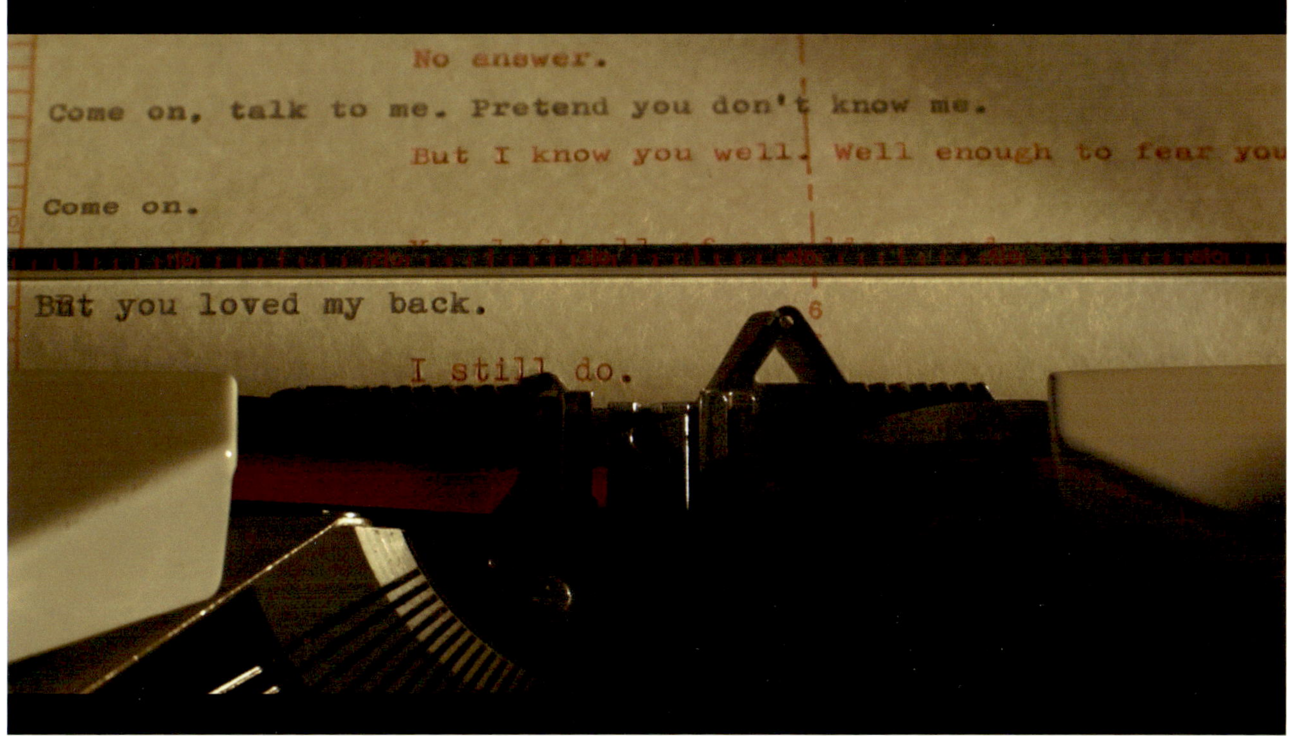

No answer.
Come on, talk to me. Pretend you don't know me.
But I know you well. Well enough to fear you
Come on.
But you loved my back.
I still do.

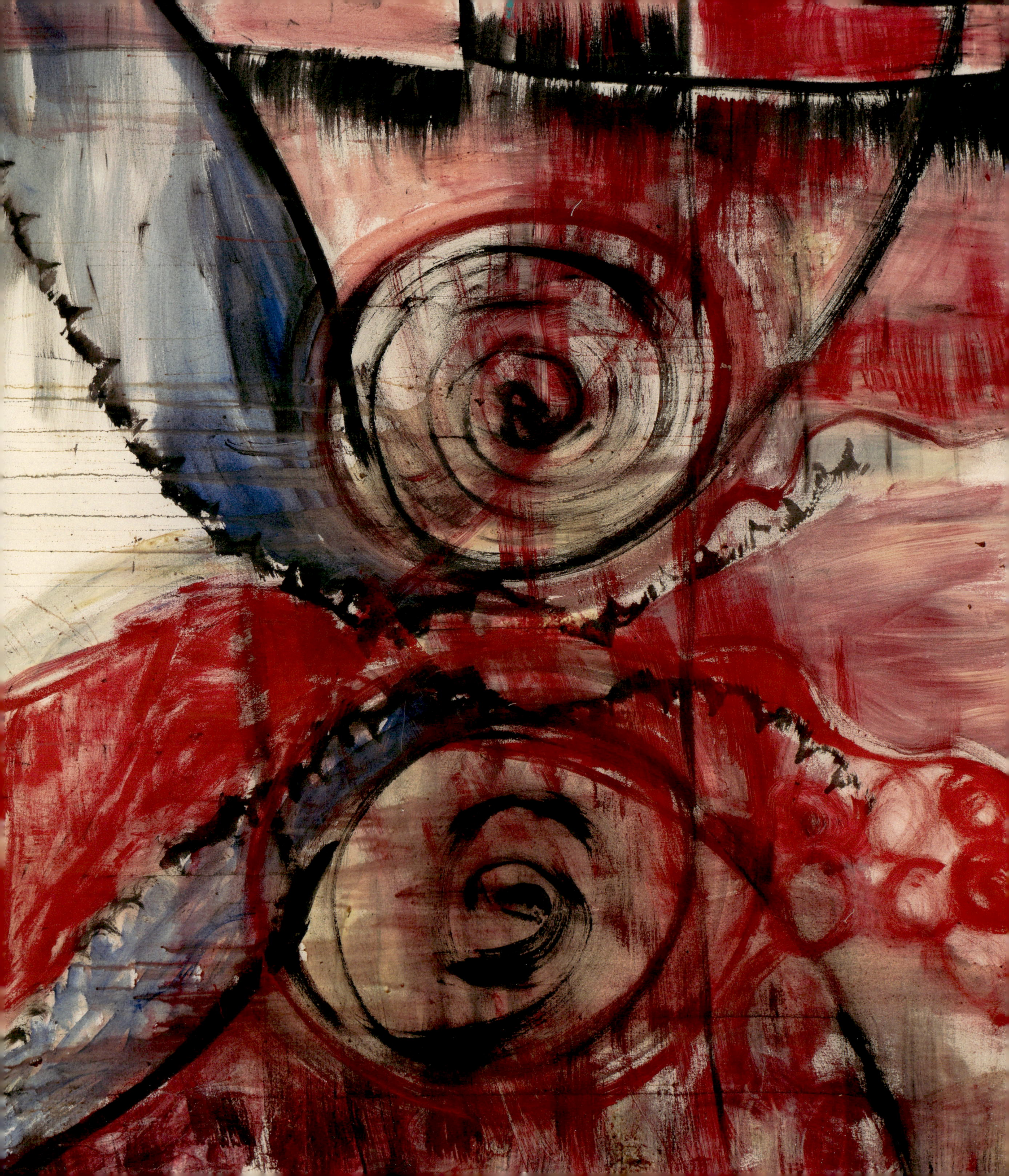

What Is Left Unspoken: The Appeal of Tenderness

"I was walking down a street in London. Paul Newman stepped out of a building. He was there, right in front of me, and I didn't get wet. Nothing. My vagina didn't bat an eyelid."

That's what she told me. To which I merely answered, "Paul Newman, for real?"

My mother and I were having a coffee on the terrace of a local café, which we ended up doing after never seeing each other had become too glaringly obvious. For a long time, maybe even forever, she had avoided intimacy; tenderness, confidences were out of the question. And for a long time, maybe even forever, I had been trying to coerce her and her motherhood. But on that day, while I was closing in on a fateful age—or so I believed—she was answering a question I had just asked her. I had said, "Can you tell me about your menopause?"

And she shot back, "Paul Newman."

Now, so many years later, my mother having died in the meantime, it is her reply that immediately springs to mind when I start looking into love in the time of menopause—this thing unspoken or, rather, so entirely shunned. The old age of sex, the creases of eroticism: all the things we don't reveal, don't talk about, or else broach only as if it were an illness—don't worry, we can treat it. Yes, I was thinking about all that, getting ready to research, take notes, take a closer look at my hot flashes, my mood swings, my vagina, when suddenly, *bing*: Paul Newman and my mother in London.

At the time, when this recollection resurfaced, I initially saw it as a welcome diversion, a way of postponing any introspection. Basically, it was an entertaining little story, a lighthearted memory that made me smile, recalling with amusement my reaction back then: I was vacillating between a burst of laughter and an outburst of anger, blown away by the vanity and pride of this woman. I also remembered my exasperation. It was always the same story: my mother so determined to never sound like a mother. I was so completely focused on being annoyed with her nymphomaniacal habits that I totally overlooked what she was telling me. And it probably took the full-on flourishing of my own difficult menopause, endured years ago, to realize, yes, good grief, of course: It was not about the story, even less about a distraction. If my mother's answers popped up like that, out of the blue, pushing aside every other thought, it was simply because it was undeniably relevant. A reasonable and healthy explanation, a reply that pretty much nailed it. What's menopause? Not getting wet when you see Paul Newman.

She wasn't talking to me from his point of view; she wasn't even thinking about the fact that, had he even noticed her, he probably wouldn't have considered her, past her prime. Not once did a moment of doubt, or even the certainty, that she'd no longer be able to seduce, as a woman who had become invisible and obscured by her withered skin, ever cross her mind. What others thought didn't concern her, no; she was talking about what she herself was feeling, her own lack of response. As if she were still the one making the decisions. As if it were all up to her. And her perfectly matter-of-fact tone suggested that this was just a simple observation. Without any regrets or nostalgia, she was stating that it was not abnormal, but also not insignificant, for a heterosexual woman of her generation not to desire Paul Newman, still undeniably handsome, with blue eyes to die for. She was just saying that she no longer desired him, after once having done so. Nothing more complicated than that. And no reason to get upset about it. Definitely not.

I know my mother. I know how much she always loved to be provocative, to boast about X-rated stories, her unfettered libido, her way of asserting her femininity at least as much as her feminism. As easy as can be, she liked to speak about what others don't (and even less so to one's daughter). Whether it was about Paul Newman or someone else, whether something actually happened or not, she would detour her conversations to add an aside about her relationships with married men, nights of lovemaking, quickies on the sly—and with graphic details, a full plate, without a shred of inhibition. In other words, she loved to rock the boat, which often shocked me due to the obvious satisfaction she derived from speaking the unspoken. So, I refused to listen to her. Now, I say, more power to her and to her mindset, that of a woman who didn't see herself as defeated nor as a victim nor, especially, as guilty.

Love in the time of menopause, the old age of sex, the creases of eroticism. She didn't pretend, which, at this point, is enough to fuel my admiration. Because in my case, at the first signs, I instinctively took a radically different stance. As soon as I noticed what I couldn't control—my vagina becoming insensitive and, even worse, painfully dry—as soon as, despite all my efforts and concentration, nothing seemed to work, this tiny part of my body that I believed I had so perfectly mastered up to that point, true or not, I started to get spooked. About not being able to handle it. About the other, the man. Steeped as I was in the idea that giving pleasure is part of the courtesy of love and of sex, the possibility of suddenly becoming a bad partner stressed me out. What happens when he can no longer find his way in?

What happens when he discovers my door closed, stubbornly shriveled up? Yes, I swear, that's exactly what I thought about in the very early days of my "after." I hadn't even stopped to worry about the loss of my own enjoyment before already worrying about no longer being able to fake it, if necessary, no longer being able to pretend—in other words, no longer able to fulfill my duty. I sized up my situation entirely through the eyes of the other, the man, realizing that I was programmed for the most hidebound romanticism, however much of a fantasy that was. One way and one way only: my female body, necessarily on offer.

As an unworthy daughter to my mother, my first concern would have been not to offend Paul Newman, in the event he'd have come on to me. What a joke, I know. Apparently, it wasn't just my body I no longer controlled but also my judgment. On top of hot flashes, let's add a bout of delirium. I suddenly wondered what combination of collective unconscious and individual neurosis went into my makeup for me to immediately and so fully take myself out of the race. Maybe it was just the collective unconscious? Or maybe just individual neurosis? And what race? Had literature and modernity taught me nothing about liberation? What was the use of everything I had read, the imprint of my mother, my life as an independent woman, and so much traveling and so many encounters? I had always been convinced that I would not get taken in; no way I'd get trapped by all those images of femininity—woman as an object of admiration, woman as a social issue, a young woman, forever. I obviously never fell for those relentless stereotypes—what do you take me for?

I kept telling myself that these knee-jerk simplifications would impact neither my reflexes nor my complexes. I knew that while diversity had finally become visibly acceptable, youth, however, had clearly remained an imperative. It's easier to display color, culture, morphology, gender, but still, there are lines you can't cross: you have to stay within the norms, stay presentable—as fresh as a rose, with "antiaging" and "firming" among the most ubiquitous sales arguments. But is awareness enough to avoid being splattered by all the marketing hype?

When I looked in the mirror, it wasn't my old age that started to catch my attention—the wizened skin on my neck, age spots here and there from the wear and tear of time, more and more blemishes. No, I had been expecting that, along with the compounding of these irreversible effects from wine and cigarettes. I accept all that; I like to face reality. That's not what first caught my attention but rather what this progression entailed: an absence, a deficiency, a shrinkage, and with no word to describe it. Here I was, severed from my "before," a time when, totally carefree, I just went for it. You want me, I want you; you move forward, I move forward. Flirtation was a foundation, an irrefutable proof of my existence, of my vitality, of my sociability. In this "before," all that mattered was mutual consent. Where there's a will, there's a way; the fun could start, with the tacit understanding: "you take me, and I give to you," the roles clearly delineated. The normal scheme of things: everyone in their place, and all's well with the world. But what if one side no longer holds up their part of the deal?

I could already imagine the scene: Paul Newman enters. His eyes undress me. His hands take over. We hug each other closer. The room is oozing sensuality, eros everywhere. It's shaping up to be hot and heavy, and then suddenly—nothing. Absolutely nothing. Maman was right. Sorry, a thousand times sorry, Paul. It's not your fault; it's mine. I'm so ashamed.

Orcas and pilot whales are apparently the only other females in the animal kingdom to suffer through the throes of menopause. I'd love to have met up with one of them, just to discuss the issue. Splashing around in the water maybe could have cleansed me of all this. Go figure. But the good part is that you no longer have to deal with periods; you're definitively free of this hassle. No chance that you'll ever have to explain to Paul Newman that it's not a good day. But that opportune blood wasn't a problem for me, anyway, not even awkward—just look at the countless slang words and gentle euphemisms we use: *code red, moon time, crimson tide, Aunt Flo, strawberry week, Lady Business*. No one would dream of blaming us for that. There's no possible comparison between periods and this dryness, this barrenness locked into the unspeakable, this *menopause*—such an ugly word, so gloomy that no one even utters it, or maybe only half-heartedly, just like another word, *incontinence*. But there's even indulgence with incontinence, what the elderly suffer—those poor little old people.

Ok, on the scale of planetary crises, vaginal stiffness can certainly wait; it's not a priority. Nevertheless, we can assume that although we're in the minority, a certain number of us are feeling guilty—not victims but definitely guilty. Isn't that enough to talk about this rough patch we're going through? And what if, for "menopausal," we found some equally lovely nicknames, not about having, but about being: *radiant, truant, blooming, vacationing, free, transformed*? Especially because as our life spans now stretch out like an endless rubber band, this "after" is going to last a long time—or rather, this "new," because yes, words matter; you don't need a writer to tell you that.

The fact is, at the time, when it happened, the word *symptom* spontaneously came to mind—that one word and no other, which led to a pressing urgency: make an appointment with my gynecologist; go tell her about my distress. To whom else could I legitimately discuss this lack of desire, of pleasure, the dried-up well, the used-up woman? I should have listened to my mother. All this had taken me totally by surprise.

"Please, tell me it will come back, please."

My gynecologist nodded. She wrote up a prescription—creams, lubricants, tubes—so that everything would go back to normal. As if she had been expecting this. Is it serious? No, it's not serious; it can be treated. Men take Viagra, don't they? Ah, yes, it's true. I went out and bought everything.

So, let's start over: Paul Newman enters. His eyes undress me. His hands take over. We hug each other closer. The room is oozing sensuality, eros everywhere. It's shaping up to be hot and heavy. The beauty of this guy has set my imagination on fire, and then suddenly: "Hold on a sec, I have to spread cream all over myself; otherwise, it's not going to work." The first person to tell me that lubricant could be a turn on, even licentious, is definitely a man. Because, truth be told, in a society where menopause is unspoken and where it's important to "keep those ruined goods out of sight," this gesture is flat-out creepy and, I repeat, degrading. Men undeniably hold an advantage: Viagra. Gulp it down, out of sight, out of mind. The perfect crime. They can fess up, or not. They can lie, dissemble, bluff. I'll never know if Paul Newman swallowed a little blue pill.

My gynecologist asked me if I had a friend, a partner, a lover. "Yes," I replied.

"And?" she asked.

"And what?"

"Is intercourse painful?"

"Is that any of your business?" I would have liked to retort; instead, I heard myself say, "yes."

"Creams will save you," she concluded.

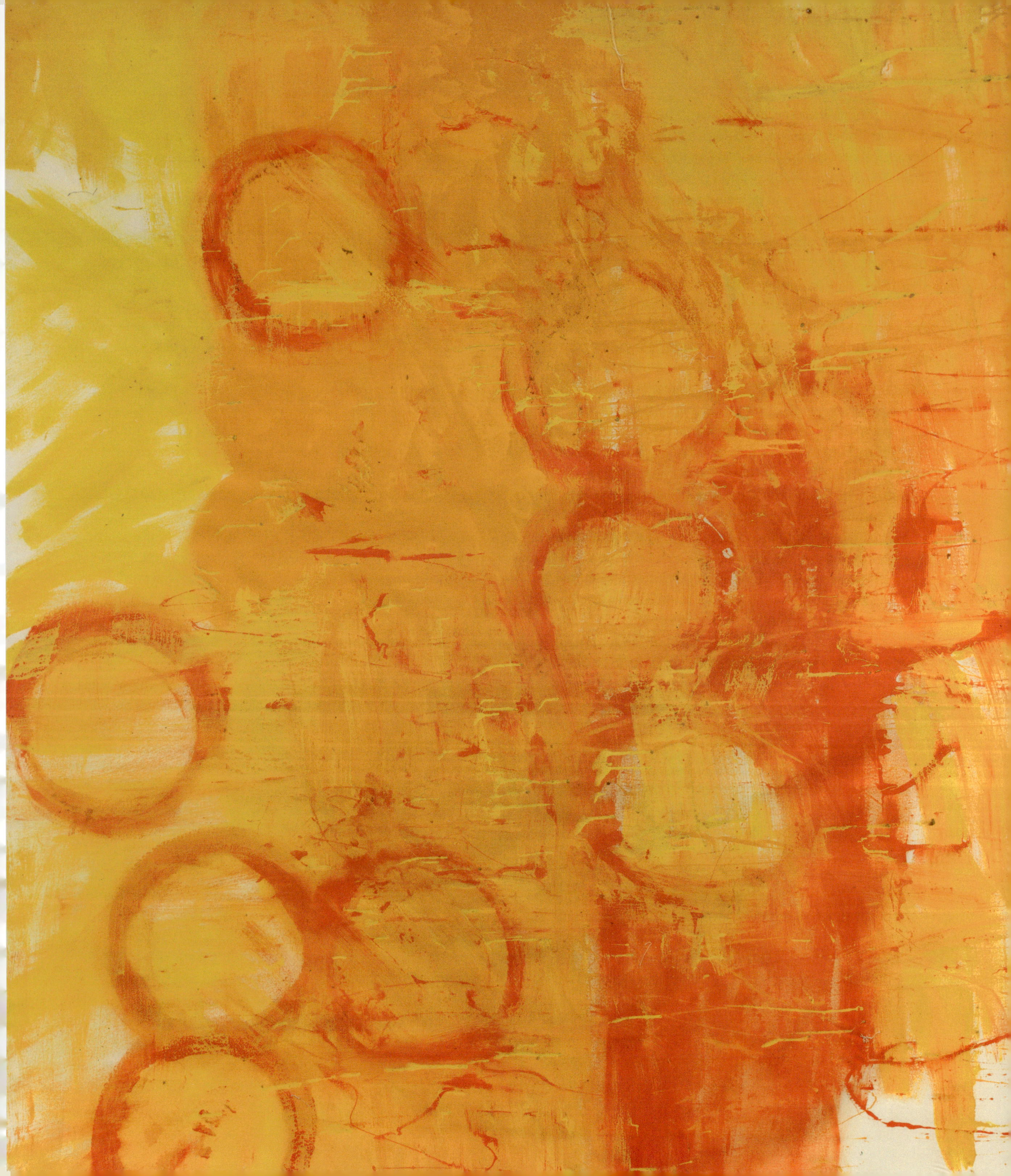

Orange Boy

The first stab of love is like a sunset, a blaze of color—oranges . . .[1]
—Anna Godbersen

I am two years old, dwarfed by a giant, papier-mâché triceratops painted neon orange. This self-proclaimed "Dinosaur Park" sits in the back forests of Connecticut, the first homage to my mother's skill of finding me out-of-the-box children's attractions. My father releases her hand to swing me onto the neck of this holy beast. From this height, I see all the painted dinosaurs, their colors flooding into one another. I will never forget this day: the only happy memory I have of my parents together. The meteor of divorce is coming, yet I cling to this moment in spite of all of my parents' papier-mâché failings. I grasp for this molten love.

•

I cannot tell you how or when I fell in love with the color orange, only that in my twenty-eight years, this devotion has saturated me. When I talk about my favorite color, I am often met with unease, confusion, and disgust; one person even dubbed orange "the color that shall not be named." Orange is misunderstood, both fiercely remembered and confidently ignored. From its disgusting neon on construction site signs to its soft palette sweeping an autumn landscape to its boisterous and crumbling heart within a meteor, orange takes on many names, many forms.

•

In their book *The Secret Language of Color*, color tourists Joann and Arielle Eckstut write, "For millennia, orange was a color without an identity. In many languages, it's one of the very last, if not the last, color named in the rainbow."[2] Cultural historian Kassia St. Clair expresses a similar difficulty with orange. Since it wasn't considered its own distinct color until relatively recently, it is "forever in danger of sliding into another color: red and yellow on either side, brown below."[3] Scientifically speaking, no two people on the planet see the same shade of any color. Therefore, colors are always at risk of being subsumed or diluted, constantly and quickly falling into society's social constructs: blue is sadness, red is rage, orange is . . . . As the possibilities of orange seep in, the construct falls apart.

•

"AYO! Did you fuck Nickelodeon?" My seventh-grade classmates turn their eyes toward me and are blinded. Dressed completely in orange, I am an unusual sunrise making its way across the North Bronx. In the cafeteria, I hear them: *sun fucker, freak,*

OPPOSITE PAGE
Vivian Suter (Argentinian, born Buenos Aires, Argentina, 1949; active Panajachel, Guatemala), *Untitled* (detail), n.d., mixed media on canvas, courtesy of the artist and Gladstone Gallery, New York and Brussels.

faggot. I sign everything I write that year with the signature Orange Boy. I absorb their insults and, in doing so, internalize them. Orange becomes another word for gay, for different, for wrong.

•

In English, there was no name for the color orange until the sixteenth century. Rather, orange was referred to as *giolureade*, or yellow-red. The first recorded use of the word orange to describe a particular color was in 1502 when Margaret Tudor, Queen of Scots, described a pair of sarcenet sleeves on a dress.

When I close my eyes, I see an orange dress—not the Queen's but the one from my childhood. At the Cross County Mall in Westchester, New York, my mother is fumbling in the fitting room of Macy's while I walk the aisles of women's dresses. I let the fabrics swim through my fingers, and there it is: an orange spring dress with frills around the shoulders, flowers dancing across its long, flowing bottom. In my memory, some days they are sunflowers; other days they are dahlias. Suddenly, my mother yanks my ear. "Didn't you hear me calling you!" I didn't; I heard something else. Did I want to wear the dress? Did I want to be a woman wearing the dress? Did I simply want to be held by orange? The bright honesty of orange blinds me. I bury the memory.

•

One of the few organic gemstones on the planet, amber's orange color has danced with gold and brown throughout history. Mythically thought to be a liquid produced by sunrays, amber is fossilized tree resin that hardens over time, preserving everything that falls into it with striking vitality. When my father tells me to "leave the past in the past," I think of amber.

My parents divorced when I was two years old, and for the next decade, I was told their separation was my mother's fault. This lie worked hand in hand with the woman divorce made of her. A striking contradiction, her many faces often left me awestruck. A loving, dedicated family woman and a superb schoolteacher, she was a sturdy exterior ransacked by grief. Throughout my childhood, I grew to understand that my face was my father's face, so when she hit me, she saw him, amber preserving her misery. While I trained myself in her omens—a searing glance, a shifting palm—I could not avoid the reds growing across my face, my

arms, my ass, my back. Our amber bodies held every hit, every argument, every trauma, but also every tenderness, every milestone, every smile. We preserved these ten years with striking vitality, love and abuse hardening over time.

•

In his book *Concerning the Spiritual in Art*, Russian abstract artist Wassily Kandinsky writes, "Orange is like a man, convinced of his own powers."[4] After the divorce, my father bloomed in a way that wouldn't be made clear to me for years. Naively, I saw a man liberated from the oppression of women, patriarchal freedom at its height. He was a single bachelor with a studio apartment who had the hard-earned resources to buy me whatever I wanted. He was stylish, assertive, stubborn, intellectual, walled off, yet kind. Most confusing of all, he was kind toward my mother. When I criticized her, he would say, "Be patient. Listen to her. There is a bigger picture you're not aware of." My parents' contradictions infuriated me, and I grew into a pith of silence and rage.

I was a pendulum—constantly sure I was escaping one extreme emotion only to arrive at another. My mother's abuse became reciprocal; her pain became my pain. My father *did* leave us, and in this shared feeling of abandonment, my mother used me as a weapon against him. Many nights after she hit me, she would return crying, whispering, "Never forget that your father left us. It's just you and me." In the muddled grays of this lie, my mother and I became different shades of the same pain. She taught me how to paint with the same hands she painted me with.

•

Before pigments were readily available for sale, artists employed colormen—individuals who produced, traded, and obtained rare pigments from around the world. Orange, or orpiment, was one of the most dangerous pigments to gather, found in the sulphureous fumaroles surrounding volcanoes. Highly toxic and rich in lethal arsenic, orpiment was considered one of the key ingredients in creating a philosopher's stone.

As art critic Kelly Grovier writes, "to dabble in the occult of orange was to flirt with mortality and immortality in equal measure."[5] My parents were inextricably linked. As my father gained life, my mother lost sight of hers, and I was only audience to her. As divorce rotted my mother, it, in turn, rotted me. Yet nothing prepared me for the truth of their divorce: my father had left my mother because he came out as a gay man.

When I reflect on my father coming out to me, I remember his body language. I see his assured smile, the casual motion of his palms through the air. The only words I hear are, "this shouldn't change anything between us" and "do you have any questions?" He takes my thirteen-year-old silence to mean acceptance and leaves the room. In hearing the truth, my world was inverted. I had been lied to, but even worse, I was coerced to act upon that lie. In those ten years, I learned to hate my mother, fueled by both her abuse and my father's "good parent" complex. In that same decade, my mother refused to sign the divorce papers, clinging savagely to the man she loved. She took him to pray-the-gay-away retreats, harassed him when he began dating men, and begged him to consider using her as a beard. My father was her immortality, her doorway toward that amber happily ever after, her dream of the white-picket fence, the suburban house, and the two kids. In her eyes, she had done everything right, and without warning, everything went horribly wrong.

My father endured her actions because he loved her, and she acted in this way because she loved him. My father says he will always love her, and as the possibilities of queer love flood in, the construct falls apart.

·

The Spanish city of Sevilla boasts 40,000 orange trees. They line almost every city block and drop like the heaviest blessings, marking their territory with the origin of their Dravidian name, meaning "fragrant." Alameda de Hércules, the city's gay-friendly district, reverberates with the sounds of discotèques, bottles dipped and shattered, bodies teetering like pendulums. Within this fragrance, I teach Kyle how to dance salsa. We spin under the deep-orange strobe lights as he tells me he is a singer-songwriter from Jamaica. His beard brushes against mine, and our bodies twirl beneath plastic palmetto palms as only Caribbean boys can. Suddenly he walks away, leaving me drunk and stepping alone. I find him outside smoking a cigarette I wish to be. He says he was embarrassed and ran away because he forgot my name. We kiss goodnight. I never see him again. I play his songs on repeat.

·

While it is possible to grow an orange from a seed, most are infertile. They are grown through grafting, where a bud is taken from an existing orange tree and attached to a seedling rootstock. Every orange tree in California, the birthplace of America's citrus industry, comes from two parent trees planted in Riverside by Eliza Tibbets in 1873. These trees, originally from Bahía, Brazil, gave birth to the genus we call the Washington Navel Orange.

When my father came out, he had no one. As many gay men before and after him, he created his own family through friendship. Paul, Peter, Juan, Johnny, Ruben, and Ralph: these men were my father's rootstock, the nourishment that allowed him to grow and blossom. In this same way, my mother turned to her circle of friends for support, strong and caring women from the hood who held her through the dark. In them, I learned the importance of community, of creating and maintaining friendships and, more specifically, queer relationships.

The rootstock of my father's freedom grew into a grove of queer community. For over a decade, I thought he had escaped my mother, but he had escaped heterosexism. His liberation was a queer liberation: what I witnessed was my father's ability to finally live the life he wanted. At the same time, he had lied, first about his identity and then about the fallout, and in doing so, my mother fell into a decade-long spiral of grief. I was born between lies and love, between a doorway and a vow. I am entrenched in their amber, holding my parents' complexities alongside my own, unable to turn away.

Every night I begged God for my parents to be together, to return us to the Dinosaur Park, to see them holding hands again. As a child, I did not know that this was the antithesis of love. In my selfish naivety, I would deny my father his self-love and my mother a partner who would love her how she deserved to be loved. The divorce was inevitable, my mother's devastation and my father's liberation intertwined in the pith of me, but what will I grow from their rootstock?

·

Over dinner, my father demands, "Explain to me how it makes any sense that my own son wouldn't come to his gay father about kissing his first man." In my early twenties, my father is a man of absolutes, of binaries. Bisexuality does not exist, trans people are a complexity beyond the gay scene he lived through, and I needed to stop overthinking my identity. My father asks me to choose: gay or straight, woman or man, child of him or child of the new millennia. I dig my hands into the thick pulp of memory. I search my lovers' genitals. I stare at myself in the mirror, hoping to name my body without referring to another's craving. All I find is orange. The construct falls apart, and I am flooded with questions.

•

My best friend Lauren tells me that in an interview about *The Sixth Sense*, M. Night Shyamalan said that every scene where the natural and supernatural worlds collide, there is the color red. You may not notice it at first, but once you see it, you can never unsee it. This is how Lauren thinks about queerness: it was always there, a color that follows but one we must choose to see.

•

In 2019, I moved from New York City to Oxford, Mississippi, in part so that my mother would not find me celebrating what is forbidden, and in part so that I could avoid my father's questioning. I flee any conversation that may spin the past back into them. My father is slowly learning to accept me and offers his advice: "If you don't know what you are yet, then it is better to leave your mother in the dark."

In Mississippi, I have learned to shine. In this transition, I have found a destination where I reach closer and closer toward my body. I paint it with orange eyeshadow, nail polish, and lipstick. I lay my torso bare. I strut in high heels. I move my fingers through the dress.

•

The Washington Navel Orange gets its name from the growth of a second fruit at its apex, which protrudes slightly to appear like a human navel. This fruit, this color, this queer love has lived within me for years, beneath my mother's grief and above my father's freedom. It has been my companion and compass, unearthed by confronting both the pain and love at my apex. My parents and I wounded each other and were wounded; yet we also embodied the many faces of love: love for your child, love for your partner, love for your community, love for yourself.

Yet, when my father told me to leave my mother in the dark, I misunderstood him. I believed he wanted me to lie to her, to silence myself as he had done decades before. But he was trying to protect me from the acrimony of love, its vicious intricacies. "You are not special, Noel," he says sternly, "and I am afraid you think your mother will treat you differently than me."

Orange teaches us to tell the hard truths, in all their unnamable abundance, to confront the vast amber of ourselves, to grow through grafting, each stem supporting the next. Groves and groves of orange trees—I want the vast grove of my mother's love as much as I wanted the Dinosaur Park. I want to tell my mother the truth, but I am not prepared for the rancor of her love, for the distinct possibility that she will not change, even for me. At this delicate site of both utter devastation and indescribable joy, oranges can bloom. I choose the precarious gamble of grafting our lives together, of nurturing what may die, but also, what may grow to love again.

Notes

1   Anna Godbersen, *The Luxe* (New York: HarperCollins, 2007), 108.

2   Joann Eckstut and Arielle Eckstut, *The Secret Language of Color* (New York: Black Dog and Leventhal, 2013), 71.

3   Kassia St. Clair, *The Secret Lives of Color* (New York: Penguin, 2017), 94.

4   Wassily Kandinsky, *Über das Geistige in der Kunst (Concerning the Spiritual in Art)*, trans. M.T.H. Sadler (New York: Dover, 1977), 38.

5   Kelly Grovier, "The Toxic Colour that Comes from Rainbows," *BBC*, February 27, 2018, https://www.bbc.com/culture/article/20180227-the-toxic-colour-that-comes-from-volcanoes.

Selected Bibliography

Ackerman, Diane. *A Natural History of Love*. New York: Random House, 1995.

Adnan, Etel. "The Cost for Love We Are Not Willing to Pay." In *100 Notes, 100 Thoughts: Documenta Series No. 006*. Stuttgart, Germany: Hatje Cantz, 2012.

Agamben, Giorgio. *The Adventure*. Translated by Lorenzo Chiesa. Cambridge, MA: The MIT Press, 2018.

Agamben, Giorgio. *Creation and Anarchy: The Work of Art and the Religion of Capitalism*. Translated by Adam Kotsko. Stanford, CA: Stanford University Press, 2019.

Agamben, Giorgio. *Nymphs*. Translated by Kevin McLaughlin and Amanda Minervini. New York: Seagull Books, 2013.

Agamben, Giorgio. *Stanzas: Word and Phantasm in Western Culture*. Minneapolis: University of Minnesota Press, 1993.

Agamben, Giorgio. *What Is an Apparatus?* Translated by David Kishik and Stefan Pedatella. Stanford, CA: Stanford University Press, 2009.

Alteveer, Ian, Helen Molesworth, Dieter Roelstraete, and Abigail Winograd. *Kerry James Marshall: Mastry*. New York: Rizzoli, 2016.

Badiou, Alain. *In Praise of Love*. Translated by Peter Bush. New York: The New Press, 2012.

Badiou, Alain. *Philosophy and the Event*. With Fabien Tarby and translated by Louise Burchill. Cambridge: Polity Press, 2013.

Barthes, Roland. *A Lover's Discourse: Fragments*. Translated by Richard Howard. New York: Hill and Wang, 1993.

Belcove, Julie. "Artist Rashid Johnson Took a Hike in Aspen, Then Shot a New Film about the Black Experience." *Robb Report*, June 29, 2019. https://robbreport.com/shelter/art-collectibles/artist-rashid-johnson-the-hikers-2855719/.

Birt, Robert. "King's Radical Vision of Community." In *The Liberatory Thought of Martin Luther King Jr.: Critical Essays on the Philosopher King*, edited by Robert Birt, 157–175. Lanham, MD: Lexington Books, 2012.

Black Lives Matter Global Network Foundation. "Black Lives Matter 2020 Impact Report." https://blacklivesmatter.com/wp-content/uploads/2021/02/blm-2020-impact-report.pdf.

Bonnet, Frédéric, ed. *General Idea: Haute Culture; A Retrospective, 1969–1994*. Zürich: JRP Ringier, 2011.

Bordowitz, Gregg, ed. *AIDS Riot: Collectifs d'artistes face au Sida/Artist Collectives Against AIDS; New York, 1987–1994*. Grenoble, France: Magasin, 2003.

Bordowitz, Gregg, and James Meyer, ed. *The AIDS Crisis Is Ridiculous and Other Writings (1986–2003)*. Cambridge, MA: The MIT Press, 2004.

Browning, Elizabeth Barrett. "Sonnet 43: How Do I Love Thee? Let Me Count the Ways." In *Sonnets from the Portuguese*. London: Caradoc Press, 1906; Project Gutenberg, 2015. https://www.gutenberg.org/cache/epub/2002/pg2002-images.html.

Cleage, Pearl. *Things I Should Have Told My Daughter: Lies, Lessons, and Love Affairs*. New York: Atria Books, 2014.

Comer, Stuart, Juan Vicente Aliaga, and Mark Westmoreland. *Akram Zaatari: The Uneasy Subject*. Mexico City: Museo Universitario de Arte Contemporáneo, 2011.

Cooper, Laurence D. "Human Nature and the Love of Wisdom: Rousseau's Hidden (and Modified) Platonism." *Journal of Politics* 64, no. 1 (February 2002): 108–125.

Cunningham, Laurence S., ed. *Thomas Merton: Spiritual Master; The Essential Writings*. New York: Paulist Press, 1992.

Debord, Guy. *The Society of the Spectacle*. Translated by Fredy Perlman. Detroit: Black and Red, 1970.

Dempster, Heike. "Ebony G. Patterson '…while the dew is still on the roses…'" *ArtPulse*. Accessed June 26, 2021. http://artpulsemagazine.com/ebony-g-patterson-"…while-the-dew-is-still-on-the-roses…".

Farred, Grant. "Love Is Asymmetrical: James Baldwin's *The Fire Next Time*." *Critical Philosophy of Race* 3, no. 2 (2015): 284–304.

Gessen, Masha. "A Powerful Statement of Resistance from a College Student on Trial in Moscow." *The New Yorker*, December 7, 2019. https://www.newyorker.com/news/our-columnists/a-powerful-statement-of-resistance-from-a-college-student-on-trial-in-moscow.

Gobsch, Wolfram. "The Idea of an Ethical Community: Kant and Hegel on the Necessity of Human Evil and the Love to Overcome It." *Philosophical Topics* 42, no. 1 (Spring 2014): 177–200.

Gonzalez, Jennifer. "Paul Pfeiffer." *Bomb Magazine*, April 1, 2003. https://bombmagazine.org/articles/paul-pfeiffer/.

Grayston, Donald. "*Consonantia* in Thomas Merton: Harmony Personal, Social, and Cosmic." *The Merton Annual* 28 (2015): 97–111.

Green, Kai M. "In the Life: On Black Queer Kinship." *Women, Gender, and Families of Color* 7, no. 1 (Spring 2019): 98–101.

Hong, Cathy Park. *Minor Feelings: An Asian American Reckoning*. New York: One World, 2020.

hooks, bell. *all about love: new visions*. New York: William Morrow and Company, 2000.

Hung, Wu. *Beyond: Recent Photographs by RongRong&inri*. Chicago: Walsh Gallery, 2005.

Irving, Kahlil Robert. "Black Matter." MFA thesis, Sam Fox School of Design and Visual Arts of Washington University, 2017.

Kierkegaard, Søren. *Works of Love: Some Christian Reflections in the Form of Discourses*. Edited and translated by Howard and Edna Hong. New York: Harper and Row, 1962.

King, Martin Luther, Jr. "Letter from Birmingham Jail," June 12, 1963.

King, Martin Luther, Jr. *Strength to Love*. Minneapolis: Fortress Press, 1981.

Konstan, David, trans. *Aspasius, Anonymous, Michael of Ephesus: On Aristotle's Nicomachean Ethics 8 and 9*. Ithaca, NY: Cornell University Press, 2001.

Lewis, Sarah, and Adrienne Edwards, eds. *Carrie Mae Weems: Kitchen Table Series*. Bologna, Italy: Damiani, 2016.

Lippard, Lucy, and Michelle Stuart. *Michelle Stuart: Sculptural Objects; Journeys In and Out of the Studio*. Milan: Edizione Charta, 2011.

Lippitt, John. *Kierkegaard and the Problem of Self-Love*. New York: Cambridge University Press, 2013.

London, Barbara, Cuauhtémoc Medina, José Luis Barrios, Manuel DeLanda, Príamo Lozada, Victor Stoichita, and Bárbara Perea. *Rafael Lozano-*

Hemmer: Some Things Happen More Often Than All of the Time. Mexico City: Turner/A&R Press, 2007.

Marzona, Daniel. "1914: Magnus Plessen." Unpublished manuscript. Microsoft Word file. https://www.danielmarzona.com/wp-content/uploads/magnus_plessen-1914_essay.pdf.

McKeon, Richard. "Love and Wisdom: The Teaching of Philosophy." *Journal of General Education* 15, no. 4 (January 1964): 239–249.

Merton, Thomas. "As Man to Man." *Cistercian Studies* IV (1969): 90–94.

Merton, Thomas. *Conjectures of a Guilty Bystander*. New York: Doubleday, 1966.

Merton, Thomas. *No Man Is an Island*. New York: Harcourt, Brace and Company, 1955.

Molon, Dominic, and Jane Farver. *Paul Pfeiffer*. Chicago: Museum of Contemporary Art, 2003.

Ngai, Sianne. *Ugly Feelings*. Cambridge, MA: Harvard University Press, 2005.

Nhat Hanh, Thich. "Remove the Dressing." *Thich Nhat Hanh Dharma Talks* (blog), April 10, 2018. https://tnhaudio.org/2018/04/10/remove-the-dressing/.

Nhat Hanh, Thich. *Silence: The Power of Quiet in a World Full of Noise*. New York: Harper One, 2015.

Nygren, Anders. *Agape and Eros*. Chicago: University of Chicago Press, 1982.

Ostrander, Tobias, Maria Eugenia Hidalgo, and Olive Senior. *Ebony G. Patterson: ...while the dew is still on the roses....* Miami: Pérez Art Museum, 2019.

Pakaluk, Michael, ed. *Other Selves: Philosophers on Friendship*. Indianapolis: Hackett, 1991.

Pakaluk, Michael, trans. *Aristotle: Nicomachean Ethics, Books VIII and IX*. Oxford: Clarendon Press, 1998.

Pangle, Lorraine Smith. *Aristotle and the Philosophy of Friendship*. New York: Cambridge University Press, 2003.

Peck, M. Scott. *The Road Less Traveled: A New Psychology of Love, Traditional Values, and Spiritual Growth*. New York: Simon and Schuster, 1978.

Plato. *The Symposium*. Edited by M. C. Howatson and Frisbee C. C. Sheffield. Translated by M. C. Howatson. New York: Cambridge University Press, 2008.

Ravetto-Biagioli, Kriss. "Shadowed by Images: Rafael Lozano-Hemmer and the Art of Surveillance." *Representations* 111, no. 1 (Summer 2010): 121–143.

Rich, Adrienne. *On Lies, Secrets, and Silence: Selected Prose, 1966–1978*. New York: W. W. Norton and Company, 1979.

Roberts, Jennifer L. *Dario Robleto: Unknown and Solitary Seas; Dreams and Emotions of the 19th Century*. Cambridge, MA: Radcliffe Institute for Advanced Studies, Harvard University, 2019.

Robleto, Dario. "The Heart: The Heart's Knowledge Will Never Decay." In *Designing for Empathy: Perspectives on the Museum Experience*, edited by Elif M. Gökçiğdem, 19–30. Arlington, VA: American Alliance of Museums; Lanham, MD: Rowman and Littlefield, 2019.

Rooks, Michael, and Eileen Myles. *Susanna Coffey: Paintings*. Hanover, NH: Dartmouth College, 1998.

Rounthwaite, Adair. "Split Witness: Metaphorical Extensions of Life in the Art of Felix Gonzalez-Torres." *Representations* 109, no. 1 (Winter 2010): 35–56.

Sans, Jérôme. "AA Bronson." *Purple Magazine*, The Love Issue #34. Accessed June 8, 2021. https://purple.fr/magazine/the-love-issue-34/aa-bronson-3/.

Storr, Robert, ed. *Think with the Senses, Feel with the Mind: Art in the Present Tense*; *La Biennale di Venezia 52*. New York: Rizzoli, 2007.

Swearingen, James E. *Reflexivity in "Tristram Shandy": An Essay in Phenomenological Criticism*. New Haven, CT: Yale University Press, 1977.

Szymczyk, Adam, R. H. Quaytman, and Moyra Davey. *Vivian Suter*. Ostfildern, Germany: Hatje Cantz Verlag, 2019.

Throckmorton, Jodi, Lauren Schell Dickens, Rachel Kent, and Allie Biswas. *Rina Banerjee: Make Me a Summary of the World*. Philadelphia: Pennsylvania Academy of the Fine Arts, 2019.

Viorst, Judith. *Necessary Losses*. New York: Simon and Schuster, 1986.

Ware, Owen. "Love Speech." *Critical Inquiry* 34, no. 3 (Spring 2008): 491–508.

Yerebakan, Osman Can. "'Humor Makes People Aware and Uncomfortable': Veteran Performance Artist Patty Chang Is Back with Her Most Anxiety-Provoking Work Yet." *Artnet News*, March 25, 2021. https://news.artnet.com/art-world/patty-chang-milk-debt-1953685.

Zara, Janelle. "Patty Chang's Affecting Videos and Photographs Find Emotion in Breast Milk, Death, and More." *ARTnews*, October 23, 2020. https://www.artnews.com/art-news/artists/patty-chang-milk-debt-profile-1234574889.

Zelevansky, Lynn, ed. *Keith Edmier and Farrah Fawcett: Recasting Pygmalion*. New York: Rizzoli, 2002.

Zuckerman, Heidi, and Manuela Moscoso. *Rashid Johnson: The Hikers*. New York: Hauser & Wirth; Aspen, CO: Aspen Art Press, 2021.

Checklist of the Exhibition

PLATE 1
Ghada Amer
American, born Cairo, Egypt, 1963;
active New York, New York
The Words I Love the Most, 2012
Bronze with black patina
57 × 58 inches
Courtesy of the artist and Tina Kim Gallery,
New York
© 2022 Ghada Amer/Artists Rights Society (ARS), New York/
ADAGP, Paris. Photo by Christopher Burke Studios.

PLATE 2
Rina Banerjee
Indian, born Kolkata, India, 1963;
active New York, New York
*Take me, take me, take me . . .
to the Palace of love*, 2005
Plastic, antique Anglo-Indian Bombay black
wood chair, steel and copper framework, floral
picks, foam balls, cowrie shells, quilting pins,
red-colored moss, antique stone globe, glass,
synthetic fabric, shells, and fake birds
161⅜ × 161⅜ × 226⅜ inches
Courtesy of the artist
© Rina Banerjee. Photo by We Document Art.

PLATE 3
Rina Banerjee
Indian, born Kolkata, India, 1963;
active New York, New York
*Garish and Golden while tied up pretty and never
perfect she woke to walk to do this and that. She
never frittered or felt frozen. She broke all spells
of sluggishness, dressed brightly into sunny
movement without his paternal patronizing
folded.*, 2021
Copper tape, gold leaf, cotton velvet, cotton eyelet fabric, acrylic, ink, pencil, and dye on paper
35 × 24 inches
Courtesy of the artist and Hosfelt Gallery,
San Francisco
© Rina Banerjee. Photo by We Document Art.

PLATE 4
Rina Banerjee
Indian, born Kolkata, India, 1963;
active New York, New York
*Her hair was there while lost in one place. Not to
stare if her sunny dome could be roped to be
opened. Buttered in benevolence, seated dead
center her a balding beacon, her mind a temple,
crossing all paths, all forsaken, never stolen and
always bolder.*, 2021
Ink and acrylic on paper
35 × 24 inches
Courtesy of the artist and Hosfelt Gallery, San
Francisco
© Rina Banerjee. Photo by We Document Art.

PLATE 5
Rina Banerjee
Indian, born Kolkata, India, 1963;
active New York, New York
*Muscle and music made her cupid shy while he
was quiet and stylist, whisked her body, captured
she traversed to guard false against masculinities
fated to be very stupid.*, 2020
Ink and acrylic on paper
35 × 24 inches
Courtesy of the artist and Hosfelt Gallery, San
Francisco
© Rina Banerjee. Photo courtesy by We Document Art.

PLATE 6
Thomas Barger
American, born Mattoon, Illinois, 1992;
active Brooklyn, New York
Love Me, Protect Me Chair, 2018
Paper pulp, plywood, two wooden chairs,
polyurethane, and paint
44 × 60 × 38 inches
Courtesy of the artist and Salon 94 Design
© Thomas Barger. Photo courtesy of the artist.

PLATE 7
Patty Chang
American, born San Leandro, California, 1972;
active Los Angeles, California
Que Sera Sera/Invocations, 2013
Two-channel video
Running time: 3 minutes, 45 seconds
Courtesy of the artist and BANK Gallery, Shanghai,
China
© Patty Chang. Photo courtesy of the artist.

PLATE 8
Susanna Coffey
American, born New London, Connecticut, 1949;
active New York, New York
Self Portrait (for Roy Snow), 1993
Oil on linen
20 × 16 inches
The Art Institute of Chicago, gift of the American
Academy of Arts and Letters, New York, from the
Hassam, Speicher, Betts and Symons Funds, 1996
© Susanna Coffey. Photo courtesy of The Art Institute of Chicago/
Art Resource, New York.

PLATE 9
Susanna Coffey
American, born New London, Connecticut, 1949;
active New York, New York
Self Portrait (Madonna's Lipstick), 1993
Oil on canvas
20 × 18 inches
Courtesy of Marianne and Goran Strokirk
© Susanna Coffey. Photo by Nathan Kirkman.

PLATE 10
Susanna Coffey
American, born New London, Connecticut, 1949;
active New York, New York
Self Portrait (Bay), 2001
Oil on linen
12 × 11 inches
Courtesy of Linda Garrison
© Susanna Coffey. Photo courtesy of the artist.

PLATE 11
Susanna Coffey
American, born New London, Connecticut, 1949;
active New York, New York
Self Portrait (Ice), 2001
Oil on linen
12 × 11 inches
Courtesy of Linda Garrison
© Susanna Coffey. Photo courtesy of the artist.

PLATE 12
Susanna Coffey
American, born New London, Connecticut, 1949;
active New York, New York
Self Portrait (Queen Helene), 2001
Oil on linen
12 × 11 inches
Private collection, courtesy of Tibor de Nagy
Gallery, New York
© Susanna Coffey. Photo courtesy of the artist.

PLATE 13
Susanna Coffey
American, born New London, Connecticut, 1949;
active New York, New York
Telling, 2018
Oil on panel
12 × 11 inches
Courtesy of the artist
© Susanna Coffey. Photo courtesy of the artist.

PLATE 14
Susanna Coffey
American, born New London, Connecticut, 1949;
active New York, New York
Video et Tacio, 2018
Oil on panel
12 × 11 inches
Courtesy of the artist
© Susanna Coffey. Photo courtesy of the artist.

PLATE 15
Susanna Coffey
American, born New London, Connecticut, 1949;
active New York, New York
James' Woman's Skull One, 2015
Oil on panel
12 × 11 inches
Courtesy of the artist
© Susanna Coffey. Photo courtesy of the artist.

PLATE 16
James Drake
American, born Lubbock, Texas, 1946; active
Santa Fe, New Mexico
Tongue-Cut Sparrows (Inside and Out),
2006–2007
Three-channel video
Running time: 30 minutes, 36 seconds
Courtesy of the artist
© 2022 James Drake/Artists Rights Society (ARS), New York.

PLATE 17
James Drake
American, born Lubbock, Texas, 1946; active
Santa Fe, New Mexico
Tongue-Cut Sparrows (Gabriella), 1996
Graphite on paper
52 × 72 inches
Denver Art Museum, gift of Polly and Mark
Addison, 2011.302A–I
© 2022 James Drake/Artists Rights Society (ARS), New York.
Photo courtesy of the Denver Art Museum.

PLATE 18
Keith Edmier and Farrah Fawcett
Keith Edmier, American, born Chicago, Illinois,
1967; active New York, New York
Farrah Fawcett, American, born Corpus Christi,
Texas, 1947; died Santa Monica, California, 2009
Keith Edmier and Farrah Fawcett, 2000,
2000–2002
Diptych; bronze, white marble, silver, and diamond
a) 70 × 50 × 45 inches b) 84 × 48 × 24 inches
Courtesy of Keith Edmier and Petzel Gallery,
New York
© Keith Edmier. Photo by Larry Lamay.

PLATE 19
Alanna Fields
American, born Marlboro, Maryland, 1990; active
New York, New York
Our Love Was Deeply Purple, 2021
Pigment prints mounted on museum board;
encaustic on panel
Dimensions variable
Courtesy of the artist
© Alanna Fields. Photo courtesy of the artist.

PLATE 20
Dara Friedman
German, born Bad Kreuznach, Germany, 1968;
active Miami, Florida
Romance, 2001
Single-channel video
Courtesy of Pérez Art Museum Miami,
gift of Mimi Floback
© Dara Friedman. Photo courtesy of the artist.

PLATE 21
Andrea Galvani
Italian, born Verona, Italy, 1973;
active New York, New York,
and Mexico City, Mexico
The End (Action #5), 2015
16mm film transferred to video, displayed on
MacBook Air on concrete pedestal
Dimensions variable
High Museum of Art, Atlanta,
promised gift of the artist
© Andrea Galvani. Photo by Andrea Galvani Studio.

PLATE 22
General Idea (AA Bronson, born Michael Tims,
Vancouver, British Columbia, Canada, 1946;
Felix Partz, born Ronald Gabe, Winnipeg,
Manitoba, Canada, 1945–1994;
Jorge Zontal, born Slobodan Saia-Levy, Parma,
Italy, 1944–1994), active 1967–1994
Great AIDS (Cadmium Orange Light), 1990/2019
Acrylic on linen
59 × 59 inches
Courtesy of the Estate of General Idea and Mitchell-
Innes & Nash, New York. © General Idea, Inc.
© General Idea/courtesy of General Idea, Toronto, and
Mitchell-Innes & Nash, New York. Photo by Adam Reich.

PLATE 23
General Idea (AA Bronson, born Michael Tims,
Vancouver, British Columbia, Canada, 1946;
Felix Partz, born Ronald Gabe, Winnipeg,
Manitoba, Canada, 1945–1994;
Jorge Zontal, born Slobodan Saia-Levy, Parma,
Italy, 1944–1994), active 1967–1994
Great AIDS (Pyrrole Orange), 1990/2019
Acrylic on linen
59 × 59 inches
Courtesy of the Estate of General Idea and Mitchell-
Innes & Nash, New York. © General Idea, Inc.
© General Idea/courtesy of General Idea, Toronto, and
Mitchell-Innes & Nash, New York. Photo by Adam Reich.

PLATE 24
Jeffrey Gibson
American, Mississippi Choctaw-Cherokee,
born Colorado Springs, Colorado, 1972; active
Hudson, New York
The Love You Give Is the Love You Get, 2020
Punching bag, glass beads, artificial sinew,
and acrylic felt
50½ × 14½ × 14½ inches
High Museum of Art, Atlanta, promised gift of
John Auerbach
© Jeffrey Gibson. Photo by Robert Wedemeyer.

PLATE 25
Felix Gonzalez-Torres
American, born Guáimaro, Cuba, 1957; died
Miami, Florida, 1996
"Untitled" (Perfect Lovers), 1987–1990
Wall clocks
13½ × 27 × 2 inches
Dallas Museum of Art, fractional gift of The
Rachofsky Collection
© Felix Gonzalez-Torres, courtesy of The Felix Gonzalez-Torres
Foundation.

PLATE 26
Kahlil Robert Irving
American, born San Diego, California, 1992;
active St. Louis, Missouri
My Grandmother's Cupboard (Artifact), 2020
Glazed ceramics and wooden cabinet
70 feet × 240 feet × 35½ inches
Courtesy of the artist
© Kahlil Robert Irving. Photo by Kalaija Mallery.

PLATE 27
Tomashi Jackson
American, born Houston, Texas, 1980; active
Cambridge, Massachusetts
*Love Rollercoaster (2016 Butler County Line)
(1965 John Lewis Accepts Voting Rights Act
Signing Pen from LBJ)*, 2020
Acrylic, Pentelic marble, Ohio Underground
Railroad site soil, American electoral ephemera,
and paper bags on canvas and fabric
88⅛ × 81 × 8 inches
Collection of Suzanne McFayden
© Tomashi Jackson. Photo courtesy of the artist and Tilton Gallery,
New York.

PLATE 28
Tomashi Jackson
American, born Houston, Texas, 1980; active
Cambridge, Massachusetts
*Is Anybody Gonna Be Saved? (1948 Middle of
Voter Registration Line) (1965 Abernathy and
King Watch the Signing of the Act)*, 2020
Acrylic, Pentelic marble, Ohio Underground
Railroad site soil, American electoral ephemera,
and paper bags on canvas and fabric
92 × 80 × 8 inches
Courtesy of the artist and Tilton Gallery, New
York
© Tomashi Jackson. Photo courtesy of the artist and Tilton Gallery,
New York. Commissioned by the Wexner Center for the Arts at The
Ohio State University.

PLATE 29
Tomashi Jackson
American, born Houston, Texas, 1980; active
Cambridge, Massachusetts
*Ecology of Fear (Abrams for Governor of
Georgia) (Negro Women Wait to Congratulate
LBJ)*, 2020
Archival prints on PVC marine vinyl, Pentelic marble
dust, acrylic paint, American election flyers, Greek
ballot papers, paper bags, and muslin
84 × 60 inches
Collection of Arthur Lewis and Hau Nguyen
© Tomashi Jackson. Photo courtesy of the artist and Night Gallery,
Los Angeles.

PLATE 30
Tomashi Jackson
American, born Houston, Texas, 1980; active
Cambridge, Massachusetts
*Contradiction (1948 Head of Voter Registration Line)
(1965 Clarence Mitchell, Patricia Roberts Harris, and
Others Watch the Signing of the Act)*, 2020
Acrylic, Pentelic marble, Ohio Underground
Railroad site soil, American electoral ephemera,
and paper bags on canvas and fabric
89½ × 80 × 8 inches
Pizzuti Collection
© Tomashi Jackson. Photo courtesy of the artist and Tilton Gallery,
New York. Commissioned by the Wexner Center for the Arts at The
Ohio State University.

PLATE 31
María de los Angeles Rodríguez Jiménez
Cuban, born Holguín, Cuba, 1992;
active Miami, Florida
Caridad, 2019
Oil, rubber, and glass on satin over fence post
structure, hung with wire on wall; acrylic paint
and glass on floor
96 × 48 inches
Courtesy of the artist and David Castillo
© María de los Angeles Rodríguez Jiménez.
Photo by Zachary Balber.

PLATE 32
María de los Angeles Rodríguez Jiménez
Cuban, born Holguín, Cuba, 1992;
active Miami, Florida
Glass, Yale University, December 14, 2018, 2018
Single-channel video
Running time: 3 minutes, 34 seconds
Courtesy of the artist and David Castillo
© María de los Angeles Rodríguez Jiménez.
Photo by Zachary Balber.

PLATE 33
Rashid Johnson
American, born Chicago, Illinois, 1977; active New
York, New York
The Hikers, 2019
16mm film transferred to digital video with sound
Running time: 7 minutes, 14 seconds
High Museum of Art, Atlanta,
anonymous gift, 2021.171
© Rashid Johnson. Photo courtesy of the artist.

PLATE 34
Gerald Lovell
American, born Chicago, Illinois, 1992;
active Atlanta, Georgia, and New York, New York
Friendship Tower, 2021
Oil on panel
96 × 48 inches
High Museum of Art, Atlanta, promised gift of
John Auerbach
© Gerald Lovell. Photo by Mike Jensen/courtesy of the
High Museum of Art, Atlanta.

PLATE 35
Gerald Lovell
American, born Chicago, Illinois, 1992;
active Atlanta, Georgia, and New York, New York
Searcy at Grant Park, 2021
Oil on panel
72 × 60 inches
Courtesy of the artist and P•P•O•W, New York
© Gerald Lovell. Photo by Mike Jensen/courtesy of the
High Museum of Art, Atlanta.

PLATE 36
Rafael Lozano-Hemmer
Mexican, born Mexico City, Mexico, 1967;
active Montréal, Canada
Pulse Room, 2006
Incandescent light bulbs, voltage controllers,
heart rate sensors, computer, metal, and sound
Dimensions variable
Museum of Modern Art, New York, gift of Karin
Srb, 213.2014
© 2022 Artists Rights Society (ARS), New York/VEGAP, Madrid.

PLATE 37
Kerry James Marshall
American, born Birmingham, Alabama, 1955;
active Chicago, Illinois
Souvenir I, 1997
Acrylic, collage, and glitter on canvas
108 × 157 inches
Museum of Contemporary Art Chicago,
Bernice and Kenneth Newberger Fund, 1997.73
© Kerry James Marshall. Photo courtesy of the artist
and Jack Shainman Gallery, New York.

PLATE 38
Felicita Felli Maynard
American, born Brooklyn, New York, 1989;
active New Orleans, Louisiana
Angelo Lwazi Owenzayo from the series
Ole Dandy, the Tribute, 2018
Gelatin silver print
16 × 20 inches
Courtesy of the artist
© Felicita Felli Maynard. Photo courtesy of the artist.

PLATE 39
Felicita Felli Maynard
American, born Brooklyn, New York, 1989;
active New Orleans, Louisiana
Vueltiao from the series *Ole Dandy,
the Tribute*, 2017
Tintype and ambrotype
7 × 5 inches
Courtesy of the artist
© Felicita Felli Maynard. Photo courtesy of the artist.

PLATE 40
Felicita Felli Maynard
American, born Brooklyn, New York, 1989;
active New Orleans, Louisiana
Jean Loren Feliz in the Studio from the series
Ole Dandy, the Tribute, 2019
Ambrotype
7 × 5 inches
Courtesy of the artist
© Felicita Felli Maynard. Photo courtesy of the artist.

PLATE 41
Felicita Felli Maynard
American, born Brooklyn, New York, 1989;
active New Orleans, Louisiana
Angelo's Shoes from the series
Ole Dandy, the Tribute, 2019
Ambrotype
7 × 5 inches
Courtesy of the artist
© Felicita Felli Maynard. Photo courtesy of the artist.

PLATE 42
Felicita Felli Maynard
American, born Brooklyn, New York, 1989;
active New Orleans, Louisiana
Pre-Jean from the series
Ole Dandy, the Tribute, 2018
Ambrotype
7 × 5 inches
Courtesy of the artist
© Felicita Felli Maynard. Photo courtesy of the artist.

PLATES 43
Felicita Felli Maynard
American, born Brooklyn, New York, 1989;
active New Orleans, Louisiana
Jean with Hands Up from the series
Ole Dandy, the Tribute, 2019
Ambrotype
3½ × 4½ inches
Courtesy of the artist
© Felicita Felli Maynard. Photo courtesy of the artist.

PLATE 44
Felicita Felli Maynard
American, born Brooklyn, New York, 1989;
active New Orleans, Louisiana
Jean Loren Feliz from the series
Ole Dandy, the Tribute, 2019
Ambrotype
3½ × 4½ inches
Courtesy of the artist
© Felicita Felli Maynard. Photo courtesy of the artist.

PLATE 45
Felicita Felli Maynard
American, born Brooklyn, New York, 1989;
active New Orleans, Louisiana
Pre Angelo, Zulu XY from the series
Ole Dandy, the Tribute, 2018
Tintype
4½ × 3½ inches
Courtesy of the artist
© Felicita Felli Maynard. Photo courtesy of the artist.

PLATE 46
Felicita Felli Maynard
American, born Brooklyn, New York, 1989;
active New Orleans, Louisiana
Pre Angelo, Zulu XX from the series
Ole Dandy, the Tribute, 2018
Tintype
3½ × 4½ inches
Courtesy of the artist
© Felicita Felli Maynard. Photo courtesy of the artist.

PLATE 47
Felicita Felli Maynard
American, born Brooklyn, New York, 1989;
active New Orleans, Louisiana
Untitled V, Angelo Lwazi Owenzayo from the
series *Ole Dandy, the Tribute*, 2020
Ambrotype
4½ × 3½ inches
Courtesy of the artist
© Felicita Felli Maynard. Photo courtesy of the artist.

PLATE 48
Felicita Felli Maynard
American, born Brooklyn, New York, 1989;
active New Orleans, Louisiana
Untitled IV, Angelo Lwazi Owenzayo
from the series *Ole Dandy, the Tribute*, 2020
Ambrotype
3½ × 4½ inches
Courtesy of the artist
© Felicita Felli Maynard. Photo courtesy of the artist.

PLATE 49
Felicita Felli Maynard
American, born Brooklyn, New York, 1989;
active New Orleans, Louisiana
Untitled, Angelo Lwazi Owenzayo from the series
Ole Dandy, the Tribute, 2020
Ambrotype
3½ × 4½ inches
Courtesy of the artist
© Felicita Felli Maynard. Photo courtesy of the artist.

PLATE 50
Wangechi Mutu
Kenyan, born Nairobi, Kenya, 1972; active
Brooklyn, New York
Sisters, 2019
Bronze
10½ × 15 × 12 inches
Courtesy of the artist
© Wangechi Mutu. Photo courtesy of the artist.

PLATE 51
Wangechi Mutu
Kenyan, born Nairobi, Kenya, 1972; active
Brooklyn, New York
Water Woman, 2017
Bronze
36 × 65 × 70 inches
Courtesy of the artist
© Wangechi Mutu. Photo courtesy of the artist.

PLATE 52
Ebony G. Patterson
Jamaican, born Kingston, Jamaica, 1981;
active Chicago, Illinois
. . . they stood in a time of unknowing . . .
for those who bear/bare witness, 2018
Hand-cut jacquard woven photo tapestry with
glitter, appliques, pins, embellishments, fabric,
tassels, brooches, acrylic, glass pearls, beads,
and hand-cast heliconias
152½ × 200½ inches
Courtesy of the artist and Monique Meloche
Gallery, Chicago
© Ebony G. Patterson. Photo courtesy of the artist.

PLATE 53
Paul Pfeiffer
American, born Honolulu, Hawaii, 1966;
active New York, New York
John 3:16, 2000
Digital video loop, metal armature,
and LCD monitor
Running time: 2 minutes, 7 seconds
7 × 7 × 36 inches
Courtesy of the artist and Paula Cooper Gallery,
New York
© Paul Pfeiffer/courtesy of Paula Cooper Gallery, New York.
Photo by Steven Probert.

PLATES 54
Magnus Plessen
German, born Hamburg, Germany, 1967; active
Berlin, Germany
Untitled (Fig. 6), 2019
Oil and charcoal on canvas
65 × 50 inches
Courtesy of the artist and White Cube
© Magnus Plessen. Photo by Jochen Littkemann/courtesy of White Cube.

PLATES 55
Magnus Plessen
German, born Hamburg, Germany, 1967; active
Berlin, Germany
Untitled (Fig. 11), 2020
Oil and charcoal on canvas
90½ × 74½ inches
Courtesy of the artist and White Cube
© Magnus Plessen. Photo by Jochen Littkemann/courtesy of White Cube.

PLATES 56
Magnus Plessen
German, born Hamburg, Germany, 1967; active
Berlin, Germany
Untitled (Fig. 13), 2020
Oil and charcoal on canvas
78 × 55⅛ inches
Courtesy of the artist and White Cube
© Magnus Plessen. Photo by Jochen Littkemann/courtesy of White Cube.

PLATES 57
Magnus Plessen
German, born Hamburg, Germany, 1967; active
Berlin, Germany
Untitled (Fig. 16), 2020
Oil and charcoal on canvas
53½ × 45⅝ inches
Courtesy of the artist and White Cube
© Magnus Plessen. Photo by Jochen Littkemann/courtesy of White Cube.

PLATES 58
Magnus Plessen
German, born Hamburg, Germany, 1967; active
Berlin, Germany
Untitled (Fig. 20), 2021
Oil and charcoal on canvas
62³⁄₁₆ × 46⁷⁄₁₆ inches
Courtesy of the artist and White Cube
© Magnus Plessen. Photo by Jochen Littkemann/courtesy of White Cube.

PLATE 59
Gabriel Rico
Mexican, born Lagos de Moreno, Mexico, 1980;
active Guadalajara, Mexico
VI Mural from the series Reducción objetiva
orquestada, 2021
Mixed media, acrylic paint, and neon
135⅞ × 167⅛ × 35½ inches
Courtesy of the artist and Perrotin
© Gabriel Rico. Photo courtesy of the artist.

PLATE 60
Dario Robleto
American, born San Antonio, Texas, 1972;
active Houston, Texas
Love, Before There Was Love, 2018
Earliest waveform recordings of blood flowing
from the heart both before and during an
emotional state (1870), rendered and
3D printed in brass-plated stainless
steel, brushed steel, and glass
Diptych, 58 × 17 × 17 inches each
Courtesy of the artist and Inman Gallery,
Houston, Texas
© Dario Robleto. Photo by Michael O'Brien.

PLATE 61
Dario Robleto
American, born San Antonio, Texas, 1972;
active Houston, Texas
Time Measures Nothing But This Love, 2008
Handblown glass beakers, stretched audiotape
of field recordings of the world's oldest married
couple (80 years), stretched and pulled
audiotape of the earliest recording of time
(experimental clock, 1878), ground resurrection
plant, ground rosebuds and rosehips, silk, satin,
leather, brass, iron, fir, typeset
35½ × 130½ × 52½ inches
Courtesy of the artist and Inman Gallery,
Houston, Texas
© Dario Robleto. Photo by Michael O'Brien.

PLATE 62
RongRong&inri, active Beijing, China
RongRong, born Zhangzhou, Fujian Province,
China, 1968
inri, born Kanagawa Prefecture, Japan, 1973
In Fujisan, Japan, 2001
Silver gelatin and color photograph,
set of sixteen prints
15⅜ × 17¾ inches each
Collection of Charles Jing
© RongRong&inri. Photo courtesy of the artist.

PLATE 63
Michelle Stuart
American, born Los Angeles, California, 1933;
active New York, New York
In the Beginning: Time and Dark Matter,
2016–2020
Archival pigment prints, metal and wood table,
shells, and beeswax plates
Wall: 72 × 126½ inches;
table with objects: 25 × 48 × 24 inches
Courtesy of the artist and Galerie Lelong & Co.,
New York
© Michelle Stuart. Photo courtesy of the artist.

PLATE 64
Vivian Suter
Argentinian, born Buenos Aires, Argentina, 1949;
active Panajachel, Guatemala
Installation, 2022
Mixed media on canvas, twenty-four canvases
Dimensions variable
Courtesy of the artist and Gladstone Gallery,
New York and Brussels
© Vivan Suter. Photo courtesy of the artist.

PLATE 65
Jana Vander-Lee
American, born Lansing, Illinois, 1945;
active Chicago, Illinois
Truthfully, 2020
8/5 linen warp wool, rayon, acrylic, Lurex, and
cotton linen
17⅛ × 17⅝ inches
Courtesy of the artist and Inman Gallery,
Houston, Texas
© Jana Vander-Lee. Photo courtesy of the artist.

PLATE 66
Jana Vander-Lee
American, born Lansing, Illinois, 1945;
active Chicago, Illinois
Night Passage, 2020
8/5 linen, wool, acrylic, cotton, viscose, silk,
rayon, and mohair
17¼ × 17½ inches
Courtesy of the artist and Inman Gallery,
Houston, Texas
© Jana Vander-Lee. Photo courtesy of the artist.

PLATE 67
Jana Vander-Lee
American, born Lansing, Illinois, 1945;
active Chicago, Illinois
Enlightened Ones, 2020
8/5 linen, wool, rayon, cotton, acrylic,
and cotton linen
17¾ × 17¼ inches
Courtesy of the artist and Inman Gallery,
Houston, Texas
© Jana Vander-Lee. Photo courtesy of the artist.

PLATE 68
Carrie Mae Weems
American, born Portland, Oregon, 1953;
active New York, New York
The Kitchen Table Series, 1990
Twenty platinum prints, fourteen letter-press
texts
Images: 20 × 20 inches each;
text: 15 × 15 inches each
Private collection, Miami, Florida
© Carrie Mae Weems. Photo courtesy of the artist and Jack
Shainman Gallery, New York.

PLATE 69
Akram Zaatari
Lebanese, born Sidon, Lebanon, 1966; active Beirut, Lebanon
Tomorrow Everything Will Be Alright, 2010
Single-channel video, color, and sound
Running time: 11 minutes, 48 seconds
Courtesy of the artist and kurimanzutto,
Mexico City/New York
© Akram Zaatari. Photo courtesy of the artist.

Published in conjunction with the exhibition
What Is Left Unspoken, Love organized by
the High Museum of Art, Atlanta.

What Is Left Unspoken, Love
March 25–August 14, 2022

This exhibition is made possible by

**Major funding for this exhibition
is provided by**

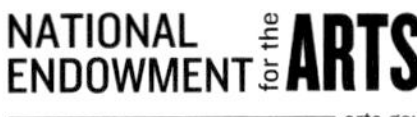

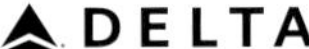

Funding provided by
Taylor Family Fund

Premier Exhibition Series Sponsor

▲ DELTA

Premier Exhibition Series Supporters
ACT Foundation, Inc.
Sarah and Jim Kennedy
Louise Sams and Jerome Grilhot
Dr. Joan H. Weens Estate

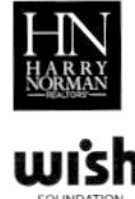

wish.

Benefactor Exhibition Series Supporters
Robin and Hilton Howell

Ambassador Exhibition Series Supporters
The Antinori Foundation
Corporate Environments
The Arthur R. and Ruth D. Lautz
    Charitable Foundation
Elizabeth and Chris Willett

Contributing Exhibition Series Supporters
Farideh and Al Azadi
Sandra and Dan Baldwin
Lucinda W. Bunnen
Marcia and John Donnell
Mrs. Peggy Foreman
Helen C. Griffith
Mrs. Fay S. Howell/The Howell Fund
Mr. and Mrs. Baxter Jones
Joel Knox and Joan Marmo
Dr. Joe B. Massey
Margot and Danny McCaul
The Ron and Lisa Brill Family Charitable Trust
Wade Rakes and Nicholas Miller
The Fred and Rita Richman Fund
In Memory of Elizabeth B. Stephens by
    Powell Stephens, Preston Stephens,
    and Sally Stephens Westmoreland
USI Insurance Services
Mrs. Harriet H. Warren

Generous support is also provided by
Alfred and Adele Davis Exhibition
    Endowment Fund
Anne Cox Chambers Exhibition Fund
Barbara Stewart Exhibition Fund
Dorothy Smith Hopkins Exhibition
    Endowment Fund
Eleanor McDonald Storza
    Exhibition Endowment Fund
The Fay and Barrett Howell Exhibition
    Fund
Forward Arts Foundation
    Exhibition Endowment Fund
Helen S. Lanier Endowment Fund
Isobel Anne Fraser–Nancy Fraser Parker
    Exhibition Endowment Fund
John H. and Wilhelmina D. Harland
    Exhibition Endowment Fund
Katherine Murphy Riley Special Exhibition
    Endowment Fund
Margaretta Taylor Exhibition Fund
RJR Nabisco Exhibition Endowment Fund

Published in 2022 by the
High Museum of Art, Atlanta,
and DelMonico Books • D.A.P.

High Museum of Art, Atlanta,
1280 Peachtree Street, N.E.
Atlanta, Georgia 30309

DelMonico Books
available through ARTBOOK | D.A.P.
75 Broad Street, Suite 630
New York, New York 10004
artbook.com
delmonicobooks.com

Designed by Angela Jaeger
Edited by Emma Simmons
Production coordination by Laura Malone
Color separations by iocolor, Seattle
Printed and bound in China by
    Artron Art Group

ISBN: 978-1-63681-073-7

A catalogue record is on file with the
Library of Congress.

Cover:
Rina Banerjee
Indian, born Kolkata, India, 1963;
active New York, New York
*Take me, take me, take me . . .
to the Palace of love* (detail), 2005
Plastic, antique Anglo-Indian Bombay
black wood chair, steel and copper
framework, floral picks, foam balls, cowrie
shells, quilting pins, red-colored moss,
antique stone globe, glass, synthetic
fabric, shells, and fake birds
Courtesy of the artist
© Rina Banerjee. Photo by We Document Art.

Backcover:
Rashid Johnson
American, born Chicago, Illinois, 1977;
active New York, New York
The Hikers (detail), 2019
16mm film transferred to digital video
with sound
Running time: 7 minutes, 14 seconds
High Museum of Art, Atlanta,
anonymous gift, 2021.171
© Rashid Johnson. Photo courtesy of the artist.

Page 1:
Felicita Felli Maynard
American, born Brooklyn, New York, 1989;
active New Orleans, Louisiana
Vueltiao from the series
Ole Dandy, the Tribute (detail), 2017
Tintype and ambrotype
Courtesy of the artist
© Felicita Felli Maynard. Photo courtesy of the artist.

Frontispiece:
Rafael Lozano-Hemmer
Mexican, born Mexico City, Mexico, 1967;
active Montréal, Canada
Pulse Room (detail), 2006
Incandescent light bulbs, voltage
controllers, heart rate sensors, computer,
metal, and sound
Museum of Modern Art, New York, gift of
Karin Srb, 213.2014
© 2022 Artists Rights Society (ARS), New York/VEGAP, Madrid.

Pages 4–5:
Wangechi Mutu
Kenyan, born Nairobi, Kenya, 1972;
active Brooklyn, New York
Sisters (detail), 2019
Bronze
Courtesy of the artist
© Wangechi Mutu. Photo courtesy of the artist.

Page 132:
RongRong&inri, active Beijing, China
RongRong, born Zhangzhou, Fujian
Province, China, 1968
inri, born Kanagawa Prefecture,
Japan, 1973
In Fujisan, Japan (detail), 2001
Silver gelatin and color photograph,
set of sixteen prints
Collection of Charles Jing
© RongRong&inri. Photo courtesy of the artist.